D1193868

! **BOX** to remove this checkout from your re~~rd.
:urn on or before date due.

┌ ⌐TE DU⌐   ⌐⌐

The
Mermaid
and The
Minotaur

The Mermaid and The Minotaur:

Sexual Arrangements and Human Malaise

Dorothy Dinnerstein

HARPER & ROW, PUBLISHERS

New York   Hagerstown   San Francisco   London

FIRST EDITION

Designed by Dorothy Schmiderer

Library of Congress Cataloging in Publication Data

Dinnerstein, Dorothy.
    The mermaid and the minotaur.

    1. Sex role. 2. Psychology. 3. Social structure.
I. Title.
BF692.D54 1976   301.41   72–23879
ISBN 0–06–011047–3

76 77 78 79 10 9 8 7 6 5 4 3 2 1

Contents

Preface

It must have been somewhere around 1970 that people began urging me to get this book out soon, while it was still timely. But I had in fact outlined the main themes of its first nine chapters, and started writing it, years before it was at all timely in the newspaper-TV sense these people meant. The argument offered here took shape in me not in response to the wave of feminist activism that has swept around it —and here and there into it— while it was being written, but as part of a larger project that started to preoccupy me in the late fifties. I originally thought of this project as a single book, entitled *The Mermaid and the Minotaur*, of which "Sexual Arrangements and Human Malaise" would be one chapter. In the early sixties I started trying out that book's ideas on Rutgers undergraduates in a series of courses: on the pull between individuality and the social milieu; on the split between work and play; on religion; on the love of death and the concept of evil; and —in 1966— on the present book's topic. It became clear that I was working on several books at once, and (by 1968 or so) that of these the one that should be pulled together first was this one, since so many people had suddenly started thinking so hard about the problems it goes into.

But I am a slow, slow writer. In 1976 a book on the gender arrangements can hardly be thought of as freshly topical. That much is just as well, since what I have to say would at no point recommend itself as topical anyway. (Keeping *au courant* is not my style: newspapers and magazines, and especially TV, are phenomena of which a very little goes a very long way with me; the same is true for meetings, conferences, and workshops.) This statement—except for Chapter 10, which I did not think out until 1970—touches only occasionally and lightly on the present crisis of feminist feeling, deep as my own sense of emotional continuity with it has been. And feminism itself (or, more precisely, the broad task of restructuring our male-female arrangements: one part of this task is to understand why, in practice, it has for so long been carried mainly by women) will be with us for a while, provided that we ourselves turn out to be around for a while.

What is not just as well is that in the years it has taken me to finish this statement it has become steadily less and less possible to feel sanguine about the question of whether we *will* be around for a while: less and less certain that anything anyone thinks or writes can make a difference for the deathly overall direction that human affairs are taking. Much of what I wrote even two years ago sounds idiotically sunny-minded to me now.

Right now, what I think is that the kind of work of which this is an example is centrally necessary work. Whether our understanding makes a difference or not, we must try to understand what is threatening to kill us off as fully and clearly as we can. Willy-nilly, it is a matter that we cannot help being interested in. And in addition, it is part of a struggle that we cannot help engaging in, part of our impulse to pit our energies against that threat as efficiently as possible. There is no way to feel confident that this struggle can really turn the lethal tide; but neither can we be certain that it will not. And in either case, to fight what seems about to destroy everything earthly that you love —to fight it not passively and autistically, with denial; and not unrealistically, with blind force; but intelligently, armed with your central resource, which is passionate curiosity— is for me the human way* to live until you die.

As for what kind of statement this is: It is a distillation from an inner reservoir in which personal experience has flowed together

---

* No one has the right, I suppose, to say what is *the* human way; but it is surely one essential human way. Another possible way is to withdraw your central love from what seems about to be destroyed —life on earth— and focus it on something smaller: the immediate moment. Or on something larger: the cosmic reality within which the earth itself is insignificant. The contemporary turn away from history into religious experience seems at least in part to be an expression of this possibility.

with varied streams of formal thought: social-philosophical, so-cial-scientific, literary, and psychoanalytic streams, and even some streams from the experimental study of perception and cognition, at which I have spent a good part of my working life.

What it is, then, is not a scholarly book: It makes no effort to survey the relevant literature. Not only would that task be (for me) unmanageably huge. It would also be against my principles. I *believe* in reading unsystematically and taking notes erratically. Any effort to form a rational policy about what to take in, out of the inhuman flood of printed human utterance that pours over us daily, feels to me like a self-deluded exercise in pseudomastery.

Neither is it a scientific book: There is no formal way —and cannot be, so far as I can see— to "test" the validity of the kind of formulation on which its central argument rests. (Some of the minor assertions it makes could be restated as hypotheses for empirical testing, but this is not the kind of scientific work I myself most enjoy doing.) Its method is to appeal to the reader's own experience: if the result feels in any way enlightening, the argument is validated insofar as it can be.

I mention these limitations in a spirit not of apology but of warning. To the extent that it succeeds in communicating its point at all, this book will necessarily enrage the reader. What it says is emotionally threatening. (Part of why it has taken me so long to finish it is that I am threatened by it myself.) And what the reader must be warned against, therefore, is a temptation: Since my argument is not armored with the wall of scholarly references and comprehensively acknowledged counter-consider-ations that a writer of different talents and temperament might have marshaled, it will be possible to fasten upon the gaps in my exposition —to welcome the presence of omissions and oversim-plifications— as a means of avoiding the acute discomfort that must be faced if the main point I am making is valid. The temp-tation will be to discharge this discomfort in annoyance at this book's limitations (as people do, for instance, with Melanie Klein's *Envy and Gratitude:* see Chapter 6, below) and thereby to side-step its central challenge. The alternative, of course, need not be to overlook those limitations; it should be, rather, to focus on that challenge (as I have tried in Chapters 7 and 9, for instance, to focus on the challenge of Norman O. Brown's threatening *Life Against Death*, a book whose impact one can easily avoid by quibbling over its flaws) and wrestle with it until it becomes part of one's own active stance.

This book is dedicated to the women and men, living and dead, who have been central for me: first of all to my daughter, my mother, my brother, my father, and my husband. Each of these five does or did deviate staunchly from the composite portraits of "normal" masculinity and femininity whose roots in our prevailing female-dominated child-rearing arrangement are analyzed here. Indeed, it is the ways in which they (and I) have deviated from these gender norms —together with the profound ways in which they (and I) were at the same time shaped by the childhood condition that underlies these norms— that form the body of private data on which the account offered here most intimately draws.

Among the other people whom I have known well enough to feel their femaleness and maleness in anything like its full personal depth, the majority have come closer than these central five to fitting the impressionistic gender sketches offered here. Needless to say, none have fitted perfectly. And a few have hardly fitted at all. (In particular, three of my four grandparents flamboyantly showed me, long before I could begin as a schoolgirl to think about such problems, what crude violence societal expectations organized around gender can do to human individuality.) But what taught me the most was the way in which something in all these people, including myself, *has* in fact genuinely and inwardly consented to the prevailing gender arrangements; also the way in which this consent has suffused *both* what was joyous, loving, and sensible in each of us *and* what was closed off and obtuse, mean and rejecting, crazy and sad.

Most immediately, I owe to my husband, Daniel Lehrman (1919–1972), the personal experience that moved me to attempt this task. In my time with him (middle-aged time: we met late) I found out how deep the prevailing form of emotional symbiosis between the sexes can go; how much of what we are right to cherish most passionately is woven into it; and how terrifying it is to outgrow it, as we must.

The intellectual background out of which this account grows includes the Gestalt research tradition in which the laboratory-experimental side of my identity as a psychologist is rooted. In that tradition —particularly as I met it in Max Wertheimer and Wolfgang Kohler— emphasis on human reason and intellectual creativity is basic. But it is in Solomon Asch's *Social Psychology* that the implications of this emphasis for the nature of our social life are really spelled out. To anyone who has read that book and reads this one it will be clear how much I learned from Asch when I was his student. What will also be clear is the extent to which my later thinking came to diverge from his.

The divergence has to do with the other main intellectual tradition —psychoanalytic thought— on which this account draws. Like Asch and other Gestaltists, I am disturbed by certain grave distortions in the Freudian perspective. I am disinclined, however, to use them as a basis for ignoring the disquieting questions to which Freud —and most impressively, following him, Norman Brown— draws our reluctant attention: these questions are too fundamental.

Similarly I am disturbed, like other radical critics of our gender arrangements, by the sexual bigotry that is built into the Freudian perspective. But I am disinclined to let the presence of that bigotry deflect my attention from the key to a way out of our gender predicament that Freud, in a sense absent-mindedly, provides. Feminist preoccupation with Freud's patriarchal bias, with his failure to jump with alacrity right out of his male Victorian skin, seems to me wildly ungrateful. The conceptual tool that he has put into our hands is a revolutionary one. If we are afraid to use it —and using it is frightening— we have only ourselves to blame.

The account I offer here attempts, then, to resolve the contradictions between the Freudian and the Gestalt vision of societal processes (it amends and extends both these visions, moreover, to embrace the implications of Darwinian reasoning, now supported by archaeological data, concerning human evolution). And it relates the outcome of this attempt to the broad project of restructuring our gender arrangements, a project which, as I see it, provides a solution in turn to some unresolved difficulties in the Freudian view of our species' predicament.

Freud's contribution has radically deepened our awareness of certain central structural defects in human life, one of which is the immense strain imposed both on male and on female personality by the fact (a fact whose effects stem from certain cognitive and emotional peculiarities of humans: they do not occur in other animals) that the main adult presence in infancy and early childhood is female. In this sense Freud is revolutionary. What is conservative is his assumption that this structural defect constitutes a fixed condition of our species' existence, and that all we can gain from understanding it better is the grace to accept the inevitable without wasteful fuss.

What the present account does is challenge this assumption, spell out the consequences for our male-female situation that follow when it is challenged, and show how these consequences bear, in turn, on the possibility of outgrowing other features of the communal neurosis to which Freud points.

In doing so, it points to a crucial gap in the outlook of social philosophers who have been trying to diagnose the runaway acceleration of life-antagonistic trends in human institutions: They ignore the importance of our traditional gender symbiosis in perpetuating what they warn us must be ended. Our sexual arrangements, I argue, are used to keep unresolved a core ambivalence that centers upon our species' most characteristic, vital, and dangerous gift: our gift for enterprise, for self-creation. In this argument, I compare Norman Brown's underemphasis on what is constructive in the positive side of that ambivalence with de Beauvoir's underemphasis on what is constructive in its negative side: each, in dialectic fashion, overcompensates for the one-sidedness of sensibility traditionally demanded of her/his sex.

Readers concerned with practical action toward equity between the sexes may feel on first reading that this is a discouraging book: If it is true, as I say, that certain present abuses are inevitable so long as early child care is female-dominated, how can we now work to abolish them? How can we counteract what is built into "normal" —i.e., mother-reared— personality? There are two answers to this question. First, normal personality has in fact never really accepted those abuses. Fight against them, on every level, rises out of tensions inherent in that kind of personality and will inevitably go on. I want this fight —which is intensified now for the reasons explored in Chapter 10— to be strengthened by insight into the depth of the necessity for shared early parenthood. And second, people are moving toward shared early parenthood anyway, without thinking about the considerations I explore here, for other reasons. I want their effort to be fortified by full awareness of these considerations. This effort of theirs, moreover, is supported by all the forms of action now being taken toward equity in the economic, political, legal, etc., spheres.

I am grateful to many people for their contributions to this book: more people than I can list here.

To begin with, I owe to conversations with Annette Overby, much more than to any reading, my understanding of: the way in which adult feeling resonates with the emotional atmosphere of infancy; the overwhelming power, attractiveness, and hatefulness of the person or persons who tend the body, and support the emerging personality, of the pre-verbal child; and the ways in which men and women differ emotionally, and evoke different emotions from others, as a consequence of the fact that the persons who provided this crucial early care for all of us were female.

I am grateful to my friend Robert Hinde, and to my editor's consultant, Signe Hammer, for extremely detailed and thoughtful comments (his in the spring, hers in the fall, of 1974) on major portions of this manuscript. Insofar as I could accommodate these comments, the effort strengthened my argument. But there were many I could do nothing about. Each of these two people made vivid for me how a reader feels who finds large sketches of her/his own intellectual landscape (comparative studies of animal social behavior in his case, certain aspects of psychoanalytic thought in hers) inadequately represented in a discussion of this kind. Each of them also made vivid for me one of the many kinds of dismay that the simplified, impressionistic method I found it necessary to use here can evoke: the shock, in his case, of a disciplined scientist who probably thought of me till now as a reasonably sane fellow scientist (what on earth can a nice laboratory psychologist like Dorothy be doing in the middle of a mess of indefensible statements like this?); and the impatience, in her case, of a person in whose own milieu active experimentation with new male-female forms has for some time been fashionable (where has Dinnerstein been for the last ten years? doesn't she know that people —a minority, maybe, but an important minority — are busy outgrowing the patterns she describes? what makes her so sure these patterns are as hard to shake off as she says?).

I owe thanks also to the successive waves of Rutgers-Newark students on whom I tested the ideas in this book between 1966 and 1974, and whose reactions became part of it. It is impossible to mention, or even remember, all of them. But they include Joe Cannarelli, Lois Goorwitz, Steve Koncsol, Ken Mazey, Pat Mills, Gwen Reyes, Ellen Souberman, and Sheila White.

My colleagues Howard Gruber and Kay Schick read an early draft of Part I. Erwin Glikes, Evelyn Raskin, Ann Salomon, Jay Rosenblatt, Annette Overby, Nina Lehrman, Susan Lowes, and Albert Dinnerstein read a number of chapters. Some of these people gave me extremely useful comments, and all gave me important encouragement.

There are two friends to whom I am especially indebted. One is Thelma Chesney, with whom I have had many discussions of my central argument and who has given the whole manuscript two careful readings at different stages. Her incomparably balanced, lucid, subtle intellectual perspectives have been more helpful than I can say: She goes right to the heart of a question while staying tuned in to its nuances. Her literary acumen has helped clarify my prose at a number of points (I often wished she were writing the book). And what has been equally helpful is her moral support, on which I have heavily depended.

The other is Joan Herrmann, who came and stayed with me during two periods when I would otherwise have been unable to work at all, and who during one of those periods (the summer of 1973) gave all her time to working with me on the manuscript. Her reactions to Chapters 1–6 (reactions in which science and poetry are fused in the way that is peculiarly hers) have been helpful at a number of points. And for the first part of Chapter 8 (pages 160–176) she acted as a collaborator: Working from conversations in which I outlined for her what I wanted that part of the chapter to say, she wrote a first draft of it. Much of the language in the present version is hers; so is much of the way that its bones are fleshed out. As for the book as a whole, if she had not offered me the intensely nurturant involvement in it that she did, I doubt that it could have been completed.

Among the people who helped in the preparation of the manuscript, I owe special thanks for intelligently empathetic typing to Lorraine Schor, to Lillian North, and to my daughter, Naomi Miller. To the latter, what I am lovingly grateful for in addition is a reading, sometimes in successive versions, of every chapter in the book; detailed and trenchant intellectual comment and literary advice; and steady, vital emotional support.

Finally, I owe to Fran McCullough all the things that one owes to an extraordinarily gifted editor.

Spring, 1976

PART ONE

The Mermaid and The Minotaur

1

Terms and Aims

Myth-images of half-human beasts like the mermaid and the minotaur express an old, fundamental, very slowly clarifying communal insight: that our species' nature is internally inconsistent; that our continuities with, and our differences from, the earth's other animals are mysterious and profound; and that in these continuities, and these differences, lie both our sense of strangeness on earth and the possible key to a way of feeling at home here.[1]*

As this cryptically stated dream-insight gradually translates itself into active waking language, a body of central human projects emerges. One of these (and I shall be pointing throughout this book to its place among the others) is *the project of loosening and restructuring the rigid forms of symbiosis, of fixed psychological complementarity, which have so far dominated relations between women and men.*

It is not my intent here to urge this project upon the reader. To arrive at for oneself and communicate to others a sense of pressing necessity, a feeling of "must," is of course an essential part of the mental work that moves such a project forward. But another essential part of that work is to examine the nature of communal resistance to this feeling of "must": to analyze the conservatism — in oneself as well as in others— that blocks the project's achievement. This is the task with which the present inquiry is con-

* Numbered notes appear in the Notes section beginning on page 278.

2

cerned. It is an inquiry intended not to exhort but to subvert. Its aim is not to condemn male-female conservatism,* but rather, by uncovering certain of its emotional sources, to undermine it.

The most potent sources of sexual conservatism are buried in the dark, silent layers of our mental life: it is this burial that keeps them potent. To articulate them openly, to see them in the light of full awareness, is a necessary condition for growth toward liberty —away, in other words, from tightly, coercively predefined modes of feeling and action— between women and men.

It is not a *sufficient* condition —clearly, social change depends on many processes at once— but it is a *necessary* one. Without it we cannot know how to unravel with life-respecting hands, and reweave into life-respecting new patterns, the network of overlapping intimacies among persons upon which the massive, uneasy societal stasis that is organized around gender† has so far rested.

This network has constructed itself over long time. It is deep and dense — wearing out now, but still awesomely tough and supple. In its present form, it embodies our collective neurosis, which we both want and want not to outgrow. Yet it is a network from which we draw essential sustenance. Indeed, its continued

---

* Indeed, some readers will surely feel that I am somehow *excusing* this conservatism. I am not excusing it, I am confronting it with itself. Still, forgiveness of a kind *is*, as the proverb says, an inevitable by-product of understanding. This is why fighters against social evil often fear "too much" understanding. They feel —mistakenly, I think— that the special rage which understanding dispels is the right and necessary fuel for energizing constructive struggle.

† Most readers of a book like this one, of course, are apt to live in sectors of our society in which social forms organized around gender now look anything but static. Such readers may doubt the relevance of understanding a stasis which they themselves do not experience. But in fact it is vitally important for the few people who do live in this atmosphere of acute change to recognize what it is that they have in common, so far as underlying sexual attitudes are concerned, with the many people who do not. The change so far achieved in this special atmosphere is still tentative, still equivocal. Its outcome will depend on whether the movement toward dissolution of old forms is steered by clear enough insight into what has held these forms together until now.

existence in some form —the existence of *some* web of durable, generation-spanning primary-group bonds— is a matter on which our humanness itself depends.

Terms

By "sexual arrangements," I mean the division of responsibility, opportunity, and privilege that prevails between male and female humans, and the patterns of psychological interdependence that are implicit in this division. The specific nature of such arrangements varies, often dramatically, under varying societal conditions. Their general nature, however, stems from a core fact that has so far been universal: the fact of primary female responsibility for the care of infants and young children.

By "human malaise," I mean our species' normal psychopathology, which has pervaded our cultural —and perhaps even the more recent stages of our physical— evolution: the maladaptive stance, chronically uncomfortable and at this point critically life-threatening, that humanity maintains toward itself and toward nature.

What I shall try to show here is that our sexual arrangements provide a way of handling some aspects of this basic human malaise, a way that maintains and deepens the underlying sickness while superficially allaying its pain. They are part of a larger disease. Changing them and outgrowing the disease are inseparable processes.

What I shall *not* try to show here is (a) that the prevailing mode of psychological interdependence between the sexes does in fact need to be changed, or (b) that there is in fact some basic pathology shaping our species' stance toward itself and nature, a pathology whose chances of killing us off quite soon, if we cannot manage to outgrow it first, are very good indeed. *This book starts with the assumption that the reader is already wholly convinced on both these points.* My argument takes them as axiomatic, and is addressed *only* to people who are prepared to do the same. The reader who is not thus prepared will have trouble following the argument, and I am in no way undertaking to be helpful with that kind of trouble.

The images of the mermaid and the minotaur have bearing not only on human malaise in general (this they have in common with all the creatures of their ilk —harpies and centaurs, were-wolves and sphinxes, winged nymphs, goat-eared fauns, and so on— who have haunted our species' imagination) but also on our sexual arrangements in particular. The treacherous mermaid, seductive and impenetrable female representative of the dark and magic underwater world from which our life comes and in which we cannot live, lures voyagers to their doom. The fearsome mino-taur, gigantic and eternally infantile offspring of a mother's un-natural lust, male representative of mindless, greedy power, in-satiably devours live human flesh.

What this book's title as a whole is meant to connote, then, is both (a) our longstanding general awareness of our uneasy, am-biguous position in the animal kingdom, and (b) a more specific awareness: that until we grow strong enough to renounce the pernicious prevailing forms of collaboration between the sexes, both man and woman will remain semi-human, monstrous.

Aims

Our male-female arrangements have developed out of central pressures —bodily, technological, emotional— inherent in our species' past. They are ramifications of a core fact —predomi-nantly female responsibility for the early care and education of neonatally immature, slow-growing, intelligent young— which seems to have been built into our history since forms of life now identifiable as incipiently human first emerged. While much of our pleasure in living has been woven into these arrangements, they have apparently never felt wholly comfortable or beneficial to either of the sexes. Indeed, they have always been a major source of human pain, fear, and hate: a sense of deep strain between women and men has been permeating our species' life as far back into time as the study of myth and ritual permits us to trace human feeling.* Still, we have had no reason, before now, to think of them as part of a massive immediate threat to the future of life on earth; nor have we ever until now been in a position —bodily, technologically, or emotionally— to consider tampering with them.

Now, quite suddenly, such tampering is not only feasible but urgent. What we have always experienced as a static, built-in dilemma ("You can't live with them and you can't live without them" is the way I heard wisecracking adults put it, long before I could begin to feel what they meant) has lost its aura of inevitability. Explosively accelerating technological changes have made our ancient sexual symbiosis —in fact for those sectors of the world population whose life has been revolutionized by these changes and in principle for all of us— more and more clearly obsolete. The concomitant growth of our collective sensibility has made it more and more sharply intolerable. An ancient, inchoate, chronic sense of strain has abruptly turned acute.

The old symbiosis is breaking down — openly where its technological obsoleteness is clearest, and, more subtly, in people's minds, wherever the news that it can in principle become obsolete is grasped. It is breaking down, however, against strong resistance. We have been living with it under proverbial duress; and yet, confronted with the practical possibility of living without it, we tend to lose our nerve. A time-honored bluff has been called — what we have always seen as a set of necessary evils, to be complained about and endured, must now be ended or defended — and we respond with a kind of terror. This terror could be overcome more rapidly if it were more thoroughly understood. In the present study, I address myself to this task of understanding.

To reiterate, then: *it is not my aim here to help spell out what is intolerable in our gender arrangements.* Other writers have for some time been handling that task very well indeed. I shall assume that the reader has assimilated the gist of what they have been saying; I have nothing to add to it. *My aim is to help clarify the reasons why people go on consenting to such arrangements.*

---

* See H. R. Hays' *The Dangerous Sex* for a harrowingly detailed documentation of this point.

The most central of these reasons, I think, are on the whole unrecognized, both by contemporary opponents and by contemporary advocates of change in our sexual status quo. The former are understandably attracted by the notion that these reasons are too tightly built into the human condition to be budged at all, the latter by the notion that all that is needed to dislodge them is sufficiently vigorous and determined action. Sexual conservatives are accordingly apt to think of people's consent as inborn, as somehow "natural." Their tendency (now that describing it as "God-ordained" has become intellectually unfashionable) is to overestimate the rigidity of its roots in our species' biology: they see it as less genuinely reversible than it actually is. Champions of change, on the other hand, are apt to think of people's consent as enforced and/or "learned." Their tendency is to underestimate the intricacy of its roots in our species' psychopathology: they see it as more directly, externally, mechanically reversible than it actually is.

What at this point most basically enforces our consent, I shall be saying, is something much more deeply mutable than the defenders of the present arrangements, lay and scholarly, would have us think: It is not, most basically, our anatomy, or our hormones. It is not some mysterious genetically determined remnant of the mechanisms that guide the ecologically adaptive relations of male and female gorillas, chimps, and baboons. Neither does it bear any magic and sacred relation to the needs of infants and young children: indeed, it violates some of the most vital of these needs.

At the same time, our consent is far less simple to withdraw than many feminists would like to believe: The law, custom, economic pressure, educational practice, and so on that stand in the way of change —essential as it is to identify and fight each of these on its own level— are the symptoms, not the causes, of the disorder that we must cure. The prevailing symbiosis between men and women is something more than a product of societal coercion. It is part of the neurotic overall posture by means of which humans, male and female, try to cope with massive psychological problems that lie at the heart of our species' situation. At the present stage of technological development, it is primarily because they help us to maintain this doomed posture that the specific societal mechanisms supporting the sexual status quo continue to feel necessary.

To understand the most basic reasons for our consent we must examine the roots of a peculiarly human pleasure —the pleasure of enterprise, of mastery— through which (as Freud points out) each member of our species tries, while at the same time harboring deep misgivings about the value of the effort, to console itself for a peculiarly human loss —the loss of infant oneness with the world— and to assert itself against a peculiarly human discovery — that the most important features of existence elude control. We must also grasp the importance of the fact that conscious human concern extends peculiarly far into the past and the future, an extension that is made possible (as Solomon Asch points out in his *Social Psychology*) not only by our species' special neural capacities for memory and foresight, but also by its special abilities to pool knowledge and to build social structures based on the interpenetration of subjectivities. It is these cognitive abilities that make possible our singular feelings of vulnerability and loneliness, our singular awareness of mortality, and the singular emotional techniques that we have worked out to make these feelings and this awareness bearable.*

Thinking about these matters means surveying certain distinctive properties of human infancy and early childhood; it means taking a real look at the ominous significance of these properties for the development of "normal" human personality; and it means beginning to see the full implications of a so far taken-for-granted condition of our existence: that the auspices under which human infancy and early childhood are lived out are predominantly female auspices.

It is senseless, I shall argue, to describe our prevailing male-

* This is a point whose real weight Freud did not appreciate. And Asch, who is eloquent about the relevance of our cognitive abilities to the unique character of our social life, takes no real account of the aspects of our condition to which Freud drew attention.

female arrangements as "natural." They are of course a part of nature, but if they should contribute to the extinction of our species, that fact would be part of nature too. ⎡*Our impulse to change these arrangements is as natural as they are, and more compatible with our survival on earth⎦ To change them, however, we need to understand* not only the societal mechanisms by which they are supported, but also *the central psychological "adjustment" of which they are an expression.* What makes it essential for us to understand this "adjustment" is that its existence rests on our failure to understand it: It is a massive communal self-deception, designed to allay immediate discomfort and in the long run —a run whose end we are now approaching — suicidal.

2

The Human Project of Sexual Liberty

The gathering impulse to break loose from our existing gender arrangements, to free ourselves from the fixed symbiotic patterns that have so far prevailed between women and men, is part of the central thrust of our species' life toward more viable forms. It is of the same order as, and inseparable from, our long effort to identify and surmount the forces that make us each other's murderers, tyrants, prey: the effort toward what in a male-dominated world is still called brotherhood. Both are members of that constellation of projects in which the creative-integrative, constructive-reparative human urge —the urge that Freud labeled "eternal Eros" and called upon to assert itself now against its "equally immortal adversary"— is most broadly expressed: They affirm, in other words, our will to come to some terms with the hateful fact of death that do not involve marching to meet death halfway. Another member of this constellation is the project of making friends with our bodies, and healing the life-sapping split which in our case alone divides the basic activity impulse that we share with other beasts into work on the one hand and play on the other. Another is the project of achieving perspective on the role that we have carved out for ourselves, half blindly, in nature, and accepting the responsibility to protect nature that is now, whether we like it or not, in our hands. Another is the project of reconciliation between the rational and the pre-rational layers of our sentience: our effort to learn, as verbal and logical beings, how to heed and cherish and honor that wordless alogical being who lives inside each of us — how to draw easily and gratefully on the vitality of that other, less civilized self whom we now largely deny and bury and who therefore now exerts a dark, rebellious, chaotic power over the shape of our lives.

Together, such projects embody our struggle to outgrow what this book's title calls human malaise. They interpenetrate; to explore some of the ways in which they do so is to examine the most basic reasons underlying people's continued consent, under advanced technological conditions, to our prevailing sexual arrangements; and at the same time it is to examine the most basic sources of their longing to withdraw this consent. Another way to state the theme of this book, then, is to say that it starts to look, from the vantage point of the project of sexual liberty, at the larger body of central human projects of which this one is part.

Liberty is a word that has been badly misused in connection with sex; it is nevertheless too good a word to be abandoned for that reason. It is used here not in the narrow sense of freedom of body-erotic expression (although this project does embrace our yearning toward true spontaneity and ease in that sphere) but in the wider sense of liberty to reject what is oppressive and maiming in our prevailing male-female arrangements; liberty to restructure them to fit our conception of full humanity, and to restructure them again as that conception continues to develop. In moving toward this kind of liberty, we are forced to deal with certain general features that all projects of such an order have in common.

Some Features of Central Human Projects

The development of a central human project takes the following course:

First, as our experience is cumulatively pooled in the course of history and our collective awareness deepens, those in whom this awareness is most vividly embodied come to feel more and more clearly that the project is urgent.

At the same time, it also becomes clearer and clearer that what blocks the project's achievement is something more than the difficulty (formidable as that is) of concrete social reorganization. There are also less tangible difficulties, rooted in deep-lying features of what we think of as human nature.

Finally, as the presence of this contradiction comes into steady focus, it in turn becomes clearer and clearer that an obstacle rooted in what we think of as human nature cannot for that reason be regarded as immutable. In this way we come step by step to face a fearful truth: that the quintessential feature of human life, along with its pervasive inner instability and stress, is its self-creating nature: its control —for better or for worse— over the direction in which it develops.* Until we are ready to look hard at this truth, we cannot go on with the project.

What this means for the project of sexual liberty is that the stone walls that activism runs into have buried foundations. Any reader who has pushed in a practical way against the legal or economic or other institutional barriers blocking change in some specific part of our overall male-female situation —even quite modest, limited change— knows how sturdy these concrete societal barriers are, and how fiercely defended. But what must be recognized is that these external problems are insoluble unless we grapple at the same time with internal problems, of feeling and understanding, that are at least equally formidable. It is important to be aware that part of the trouble we experience in

---

* It would of course be plain silly in our present predicament to feel confident that enough of us will now face this truth fast enough to head off the snowballing consequences of our failure to face it sooner. The process of self-creation that got us where we are now has been so largely blind and chaotic that we have quite likely managed, like stupider species before us, to work our way into a lethal trap. Still, even if so, our steady growth toward a more open-eyed, foresightful awareness of this self-creative process will have been the essence of our species' life while it lasted, the core of its impulse to know itself and live itself out.

getting on with a project of this kind —no matter how urgent we know it to be— is that in the face of it our hearts *must* to some degree fail us, and as a result our minds *must* to some degree go fuzzy. For it confronts us not only with the terrifying communal truth referred to just above (i.e., that there are major contradictions at the heart of our species' situation, and that our common fate, which rests upon their resolution, is in our own frail and crazy hands), but also with a personal truth that carries a lonelier, more intimate kind of terror. Contributing to the project's achievement, we come to see, means starting to renounce certain familiar emotional patterns, certain familiar ways of surviving mentally from one day to the next, on which our private sense of connectedness with the world now rests.

The rest of this chapter is concerned with issues that evoke both these varieties of terror. Eventually such issues are digested, emotionally and intellectually, on the level of shared sensibility at which central human projects ripen. Until then —and it helps a little to know that this is the case— they are bound to stupefy and enrage us. Even if I could formulate them with perfect clarity and calm, as of course I cannot, my formulation would be bound nevertheless to confuse and anger many a level-headed, well-intentioned reader.

What I shall be outlining is, first, some peculiarities of human sexuality; then some evolutionary considerations that bear on the project of sexual liberty; and then the nature of the contemporary question that this project faces.

Some Peculiarities of Human Sexuality

Animal species whose continuation requires copulation and parental care need ways to induce fertile adults to do their unwitting work for posterity. The bribes that have evolved to fill this need are simple: physical pleasure, and relief from physical tension.

Humans have an anomalous relation to such bribes.

First, the work that the human animal does for posterity is by no means unwitting: our species has a unique awareness of its own continuity, a uniquely conscious interest in perpetuating itself.

Second, our reaction to physical urges is very far from simple: Bodily pleasure and tension offer opportunities and ordeals against which we take a peculiarly human pride* in asserting ourselves; we are capable of resisting them as a matter of principle. At the same time, the body's urges have for us a peculiarly human intensity, suffused as they are with the uniquely wide, deep, and temporally extended content of human consciousness.

This means, first, that the simple carnal bribes by which we, like other beasts, are pushed to reproduce our kind are in one sense superfluous: Other, more complex, motives push us toward this same end. Second, it means that these bribes elicit from us an unpredictable response: on the one hand, they can fail to move us; on the other hand, they can move us much more powerfully than mere reproduction requires.

For us, sensual experience is embedded in a highly developed mental life, a mental life the physiological basis for which is as concrete a part of our biological equipment as our organs of touch, vision, smell: Our most fleeting and local sensations are shot through with thoughts and feelings in which a long past and future, and a deep wide now, are represented. And when another sentient being is present for us, even in fantasy, our thought and feeling are in turn shot through with impressions of that being's state of awareness. This state of awareness, moreover, we perceive as including —actually or potentially— some knowledge of our own sentient presence. Sexual feeling in our case thus radically transcends momentary and solitary sensory pleasure or relief. It is experienced as extending backward and forward into time, and it interpenetrates with the subjectivity —accurately or erroneously apprehended— of the creature who attracts us.

---

* This pride not only complicates our obedience to physical urges. As Chapter 7 will show, it also permeates our more general attitudes toward woman as compared with man, and deeply colors the overall status of each sex.

These facts in themselves would under any conditions give sex a place in human life decisively unlike its place in the lives of other animals; if this difference is not grasped, certain readily observable resemblances between our own male-female patterns and those of our non-human relatives are open to serious mis-interpretation. But our sexuality is also characterized by another major peculiarity, one that is central for the project of changing our arrangements: *It resonates, more literally than any other part of our experience, with the massive orienting passions that first take shape in pre-verbal, pre-rational human infancy.*

The bodily complementarity of males and females, then, is for us something much more than a source of agreeable sensation. It can be (and is, under favorable conditions, which have so far, to be sure, remained proverbially elusive*) a central manifestation of the human delight in existence, a focal part, symbolizing and providing expressive release for the whole, of our erotic connect-edness to the world.

The trouble is that this same bodily complementarity also works to maim us. Traditionally, it has carried with it a social and psychological complementarity, a division of responsibility for basic human concerns, a compartmentalization of sensibility, that makes each sex in its own way sub-human. The sub-human-ity of women is proverbially obvious. What is now surfacing is a venerable underground intuition: that the sub-humanity of men may in fact be more ominous.

The effort to outgrow this maiming psychological comple-mentarity without forfeiting the broader erotic function of sex, to let men and women be equally and wholly human while keep-ing hold of the peculiarly human emotional intensity of bodily

---

* Why they remain elusive is a question that many writers, naturally enough, have explored. One part of the answer surely is that the feelings I have called "massive orienting passions," which take shape in infancy, include not only our basic feelings of attraction and attachment to life but also some basic counter-feelings of loss, loathing, and distrust. In Chapters 4 and 7 I indicate how such counter-feelings, jelled into certain aspects of our male-female arrangements, help mute the broader erotic ecstasy that human sex can carry.

intercourse, is a core feature of the self-conscious growth of our species' life.

Like other such central efforts, it embodies paradox. Our sexuality under the present arrangements lends itself to pathological uses; we sense that our fear of disrupting these uses by changing the arrangements is cowardly, lazy, neurotic. But we sense also that our sexuality, quite apart from its reproductive outcome, can —and sometimes, even under present conditions, does— fulfill for us precious, biologically profound, in a sense religious, life functions; and we are stubbornly, inarticulately convinced that our fear of disrupting these functions by changing the arrangements in which we have so far mainly seen them fulfilled is legitimate, valid.

Surmounting this paradox is a matter, I think, of mustering courage and beginning to outgrow the pathology; for it is only in the process of melting down the neurotic patterns in which our deepest energies are now contained, expressed, released, that we can start to feel out the new forms of expression, of release, that are possible. Part of this melting-down process —the part to which this book is addressed— is coming to understand what the pathology is.

The matters with which the following section is concerned also take courage. In thinking about them people find themselves befogged. What they feel is existential vertigo, for to look at the evolutionary background of our male-female arrangement is to be confronted in a peculiarly sharp way with our species' dismaying built-in fragility, with its lonely, responsible place in the natural order. But to refuse this dizzying confrontation is to remain ignorant of the essence of our sexual situation.

Some Evolutionary Considerations

The old intuition that the human is a self-creating animal is now supported by archaeological findings which link the use of fashioned tools by pre-human primates with the emergence of *Homo sapiens* as a species. *These findings cast light on the biological factors historically responsible for our traditional sexual arrangements; they cast light also on other, closely related, biological factors which have worked steadily to subvert these traditional arrangements.*

"The fossil record" —to quote a well-known account, by anthropologist Washburn, of the kind of educated speculation to which this kind of evidence gives rise— "substantiates the suggestion, first made by Charles Darwin, that tool use is both the cause and the effect of bipedal locomotion. Some very limited bipedalism left the hands sufficiently free from locomotor functions so that stones or sticks could be carried, played with and used. The advantage that these objects gave to their users led both to more bipedalism and to more efficient tool use. . . ."

Homo sapiens seems, then, to have evolved physically in an environment already modified by the inventions, the expanding enterprises, the growing socially pooled know-how of incipiently human ("hominid") ancestors. "The success of the new way of life based on the use of tools changed the selection pressures on many parts of the body, notably the teeth, hands and brain, as well as on the pelvis. But it must be remembered that selection was for the whole way of life . . ."

Cumulative intellectual and technical achievements, the evidence suggests, grew and were passed on by teaching and learning from generation to generation. Simultaneously, biological changes made possible by these achievements developed; and these in turn made possible further achievements. "The skull of the man-ape is that of an ape that has lost the structure for effective fighting with its teeth. Moreover, the man-ape has transferred to its hands the function of seizing and pulling, and this has been attended by reduction of its incisors. Small canines and incisors are biological symbols of a changed way of life; their primitive functions are replaced by hand and tool. . . ."

Our bodies, then —our large brains, versatile hands, upright skeletons— seem to have taken shape across the ages in response to changes in our environment which were themselves the product of our own pooled intelligence and effort. And at the same time this cumulative product became more elaborate, more massive, as our evolving bodies made us capable, in turn, of still more intelligent, more intentionally and efficiently pooled, effort: ". . . the way of life made possible by tools changed the pressures of natural selection and so changed the structure of man . . ." In this changed structure, the most remarkable feature is the brain. "The reason that the human brain makes the human way of life possible is that it is the result of that way of life. Great masses of the tissue in the human brain are devoted to memory, planning, language and skills, because these are the abilities favored by the human way of life."

These bodily results of, and capacities for, enterprise, inventiveness, and abstract reasoning developed, of course, in female as well as male humans. Pre-history has thus equipped woman, like man, with a physique, and most important a higher central nervous system (see Box A), built by and for purposeful and socially communicated reaching out into a lifespace of ever increasing temporal and spatial extent, complexity, and inner depth.

Pre-history has also imposed upon her, however, a responsibility that has limited the use of this nervous system, a responsibility until now biologically enforced (and now, under conditions that reduce the biological pressure, still enforced by society, largely for the psychological reasons that are examined below). As Washburn puts it:

> The emergence of man's large brain occasioned a profound change in the plan of human reproduction. The human mother-child relationship is as unique among the primates as is the use of tools.* In all the apes and monkeys the baby clings to the mother; to be able to do so, the baby must be born with its central nervous system in an advanced state of development. But the brain of the fetus must be small

---

* Actually, we are not the only primates who use tools. What distinguishes human tools (and of course the term "tool" includes intangible inventions: language, for example) is that they have been cumulatively elaborated over countless generations: they represent a pooling of creativity across time, a process of preservation, transmission, reworking, and expansion, that immeasurably exceeds the inventive capacity of any single individual or group of contemporaries.

enough so that birth may take place. In man adaptation to bipedal locomotion decreased the size of the bony birth-canal at the same time that the exigencies of tool use selected for larger brains. This obstetrical dilemma was solved by delivery of the fetus at a much earlier stage of development. But this was possible only because the mother, already bipedal and with hands free of locomotor necessities, could hold the helpless, immature infant. . . . Bipedalism, tool use, and selection for large brains thus slowed human development and invoked far greater maternal responsibility. The slow-moving mother, carrying the baby, could not hunt, and the combination of the woman's obligation to care for slow-developing babies and the man's occupation of hunting* imposed a fundamental pattern on the social organization of the human species. ["Tools and Human Evolution"]

Box A

As common sense has long told us, and as experimental psychology has recently made overwhelmingly clear, nervous systems demand to be used. Deprived of exercise, they rot, produce pathological aberrations, or at best drive their owners into fixed patterns of sterile activity: The visual system of the chimpanzee reared in darkness deteriorates. The human subject in a sensory-deprivation experiment hallucinates. The captive squirrel runs monotonously in his circular treadmill. The laboratory rat rigidly alternates between left and right pathways, both leading to the same reward, in a too familiar maze. My neighbor imprisoned in underdemanding housewifery waxes and rewaxes her intrinsically shiny vinyl floor.

---

* Washburn's account is quoted here for its lucid formulation of the bodily self-creation of our species. Evidence that has accumulated since he wrote it changes the picture he draws in certain of its details: hominids, for example, seem to have existed very much earlier than archaeologists guessed in 1960; also, it seems likely that at least some of them were not hunters, but food gatherers. But the large outlines of his picture, as they bear on my central point about the evolutionary background of our gender arrangements, still stand. (See also note 2.)

Thus if what we mean by "human nature" is the *Homo sapiens* physique, and the "fundamental pattern . . . [of] social organization" which apparently prevailed when that physique first took shape, then human nature involves the female in a strange bind*: Like the male, she is equipped with a large brain, competent hands, and upright posture. She belongs to an intelligent, playful, exploratory species, inhabiting an expanding environment which it makes for itself and then adapts to. She is the only female, so far as we know, capable of thinking up and bringing about a world wider than the one she sees around her (and her subversive tendency to keep trying to use this capacity is recorded, resentfully, in Eve and Pandora myths). She thus seems, of all females, the one least fitted to live in a world narrower than the one she sees around her. And yet, for reasons inherent in her evolutionary history, she has been, of all females, the one most fated to do so. Her young are born less mature than those of related mammals; they require more physical care for a relatively longer time; they have much more to learn before they can function without adult supervision. Without contraception, she must spend most of her vigorous adult life pregnant or lactating. Given these handicaps to wide-ranging mobility, she has been the logical keeper of the hearth and doer of domestic tasks, and also (usually in collaboration with other females) the logical guardian and educator of the slow-maturing toddler.[1]

As a result, until quite recent technological developments opened new possibilities (so far largely unused), most of the world's women have been obliged to invest major energy in the biological task of perpetuating the species. This reproductive task has tended to make them specialists in the exercise of certain essential human capacities, capacities crucial for empathic care of the very young and for maintenance of the social-emotional arrangements that sustain everyday primary-group life. At the same

---

* It also involves her mate in a complementary bind. Her predicament is clearer to the naked eye, since it involves restriction of overt activity and overt social power. His will be explored more fully as we probe more deeply the nature of their mutual dependence.

time, it has tended to prevent them from exercising certain other essential human capacities, capacities for demanding, sustained enterprise that extends beyond (and can violate) close interpersonal concerns. It has limited their opportunity, in other words, to contribute to those aspects of the growth of our species' cumulatively pooled achievement that change the gross, overt shape of our shared reality: to make history.

Female exclusion from history (like male exclusion from "female" realms) has never, of course, been total. Women proverbially have, through their influence on children and men, made incalculable contributions of an indirect, informal, anonymous kind to the growth of collective sensibility and the shape of large new events.[2] They have also made calculable contributions of a direct and overt kind. Throughout recorded history exceptional women, or ordinary women under exceptional circumstances, have done so here and there. And during unrecorded (that is, pre-historic) history, it is surmised that women did so steadily, and on a very substantial scale indeed. During this period, when basic technological advances could be achieved at or near home, the human female seems to have managed, despite her unusually heavy reproductive responsibility, to make major material changes in the environment in which our life developed. (See Box B.)[3]

It has been in a biological sense "natural," then, for the overt activity of women to remain relatively restricted, and equally "natural" for them to use their human nervous systems (which are as organic as their reproductive organs) to transcend this restriction. But what is most "natural" of all, humanly, is precisely this internal stress and inconsistency.

The point is, humans are by nature unnatural. We do not yet walk "naturally" on our hind legs, for example: such ills as fallen arches, lower back pain, and hernias testify that the body has not adapted itself completely to the upright posture. Yet this unnatural posture, forced on the unwilling body by the project of tool-using, is precisely what has made possible the development of important aspects of our "nature": the hand and the

Box B

It is speculated that women probably invented fishing nets, and also basketry, weaving, and pottery. Receptacles in which to store food are by no means a trivial cultural achievement. They extend the time scale on which life can be lived, changing food gathering from a hand-to-mouth activity to one that refers to the future and whose results can be experienced with reference to the past. Also, as Hays suggests, weaving and basketry probably required the grasp of more complex arithmetic and geometric relations than were needed by the male hunter.

Women may also have invented the techniques for mixing clay with other materials for heat-tempered pottery, and discovered the process of leavening bread. They may well have been the first tailors and shoemakers, and also the first domesticators of grain, i.e., the originators of agriculture.

What should be added to these speculations is a more central point about which there is probably less room for argument: There seems no reason to doubt that the baby-tending sex contributed at least equally with the history-making one to the most fundamental of all human inventions: language.

brain, and the complex system of skills, language, and social arrangements which were both effects and causes of hand and brain. Man-made and physiological structures have thus come to interpenetrate so thoroughly that to call a human project contrary to human biology is naïve: we are what we have made ourselves, and we must continue to make ourselves as long as we exist at all.

"Anatomy is destiny" is a timid half-truth (Freud, indeed, advocated such timidity not for himself but for his wife). The other, bolder, half of the truth is that quasi-consciously chosen destiny has shaped anatomy. Now that we know this truth, we can if we wish go on consciously to evolve further anatomical changes. But of course we have another alternative as well: we can do our best to keep the bodies we have and feel fond of, and invent new ways to use them.*

For a thinker who wants to feel stymied, to be sure, the paradox that the evolutionary background of the project of sexual liberty embodies can seem conveniently insoluble: Our prevailing male-female arrangement is rooted in our biological history; it is part of what we have always been. Yet the feelings that make us restless with it —an intolerance of constriction, a resentment of bondage, an urge to grow— are also part of what we have always been. Which is more valid, then, more central to "human nature" —the arrangement, or the restlessness it engenders?

As a purely intellectual problem, this paradox is hardly overwhelming. But its presence can be used to nurse a static sense of confusion. And that confusion not only makes it possible, as I pointed out above, to avoid confronting the position in nature that our flawed, self-created, self-responsible species has somehow gotten itself into. It also makes it possible to avoid a more specific question: What is it that now keeps the old arrangement going?

This is an emotionally risky question. For what at this point mainly keeps the arrangement going is not its longstanding bio-technological function, which it has largely outlived, but the defensive psychological function (perhaps nearly as longstanding, since our hominid ancestors were mentally complex beings) that it still serves. When enough of us are clearly enough aware of this function, it will disintegrate; and its disintegration, in turn, will undermine certain time-honored modes of interaction —deadly, but cozily familiar— which now govern our intimate everyday relations with each other and with the natural environment.

What must be seen from the outset is that the trouble people have in thinking about our male-female symbiosis is not pri-

_____

* I am among those who opt for the latter choice. It follows that I am also for controlling our numbers and cherishing the earth, instead of evolving into creatures who could comfortably colonize other planets. That alternative is attractive, I think, mainly to people who reject what I have described as the central human projects.

marily intellectual trouble. Thought in this region (even for thinkers who are committed to the project of sexual liberty) is inevitably slowed down by fear: we are thinking about a question whose answer is bound to melt the ground under our feet. It is dangerous, uncomfortable ground, and it is high time we stepped off it; still, it is the ground we stand on now, the only ground we know.

The Contemporary Question

What, then, does keep the old arrangement going? How are we to understand the fact that the relative restrictions on woman's lifespace, the curbs on her capacity for the kind of enterprise that would take her, mentally or physically, far from home, have outlasted the situation originally responsible for them? Present technological conditions make it possible to provide reliable contraception; at the same time they cut down infant mortality, and prolong the mature years. The time really needed for uterine child-bearing and lactation (the only parts of the long human parental task that men cannot directly and fully share) now amounts, therefore, to only a tiny portion of the female adult life span. (See Box C.) These same technological conditions, moreover, have made physical size and strength largely irrelevant for economic prowess and social power. They have also made male "aggressiveness" —if the existence of a temperamental propensity inflexible enough to deserve this label is indeed an unambiguous fact at the human level*— into a clearly maladaptive trait. These things being so, what now keeps woman out of history? Why is her access to the public domain, even in the technologically advanced sectors of present-day society, still so restricted, her formally recognized creative contribution still so much slimmer than man's?

The most basic reasons, I believe, lie in two large and closely interrelated conditions of our existence. One of these will not be

* See note 3.

Box C

Contemporary technology has not only provided means of birth control; it has made a large number of births per female urgently inadvisable: with the death rate among infants, children, and young people so drastically reduced that nearly everyone who is born grows into a fertile adult, the human population, far from demanding woman's utmost uterine efforts to keep it from shrinking, is growing like a cancer in our ecosphere.

A generous estimate of the average number of children a maternally inclined woman would produce, if maternity were genuinely optional, is perhaps three. This is a speculative approximate figure, which might serve to keep the number of humans within bounds, assuming that under such conditions many women would choose not to bear young at all.

Another generous average estimate is that each birth might remove a woman from her normal sphere of activity for at most six months. This assumes, of course, that except for lactation —which is also optional— the responsibility for child care is shared equally by men, and that working hours are short and flexible enough to make this possible. Both of these conditions are so well within our technical means that the problem is to explain why they do not now exist (that is, to understand the societal and psychological patterns that block their overdue development).

Six months times three is a year and a half. Thus to be physically a mother should in principle, for a woman who chooses this option, require *at most* about 3 percent of the fifty-year period of adult vigor between the ages of fifteen and sixty-five.

discussed until Chapter 9, since it cannot be fully appreciated until the other is examined. It is that *our species' painful misgivings about enterprise —about free rein for the spirit of mastery and inventiveness that led us to create ourselves in the first place— have not yet been felt through.* To maintain this central and precariously quiescent problem in its present unresolved state, woman must continue to be excluded from formal history, and the rest of our present sexual arrangement must therefore also be kept intact.

The other large condition is discussed in Chapters 3–8. It is that *women remain almost universally in charge of infant and early child care.* At the present stage of technological development, what makes this condition crucial is not the drain on adult female energy that it involves. Even without male help this drain could now be reduced to manageable proportions by more efficient societal arrangements.* *What is important is the effect of predominantly female care on the later emotional predilections of the child:* The point of crucial consequences is that *for virtually every living person it is a woman* —usually the mother— *who has provided the main initial contact with humanity and with nature.*

---

* By "more efficient societal arrangements," I do not mean round-the-clock public nurseries. I see these as an emergency measure to help disastrously isolated mothers and children. What I mean is reorganizing our primary group life into larger units, so that child care can be shared within stable close-knit communities, of village or extended-family size and coherence.

PART TWO

The Rocking
of the Cradle
and the Ruling
of the World

3

The Rocking of the Cradle

"The hand that rocks the cradle rules the world."
—FOLK SAYING

The deepest root of our acquiescence to the maiming and mutual imprisonment of men and women lies in a monolithic fact of human childhood: Under the arrangements that now prevail, a woman* is the parental person who is every infant's first love, first witness, and first boss, the person who presides over the infant's first encounters with the natural surround and who exists for the infant as the first representative of the flesh.

For the girl as well as the boy, a woman is the first human center of bodily comfort and pleasure, and the first being to provide the vital delight of social intercourse. The initial experience of dependence on a largely uncontrollable outside source of good is focused on a woman, and so is the earliest experience of vulnerability to disappointment and pain. A woman is the witness in whose awareness the child's existence is first mirrored and confirmed, the audience who celebrates its earliest acts of achievement. This woman, moreover, is the overwhelming external will

* Often, especially outside our own culture, it is not just one woman who provides the earliest care, but a number of women: grandmothers, aunts, big sisters, nurses, and so on typically act as auxiliary mothers. The differences that this makes are important in other connections, but they have no bearing on the main point I want to make here.

28

in the face of which the child first learns the necessity for submission, the first being to whose wishes the child may be forced by punishment to subordinate its own, the first powerful and loved creature whom the child tries voluntarily to please. She is, in addition, the person around whom the peculiarly ambiguous human attitude toward the flesh begins to be formed. It is in the relation with her that the child experiences the earliest version of what will be a lifelong internal conflict: the conflict between our rootedness in the body's acute, narrow joys and vicissitudes and our commitment to larger-scale human concerns.

To appreciate the implications of this feature of childhood, to understand what grows out of the fact that this fatefully powerful first parental person is a woman, it is necessary to recognize first, in more general terms, how profoundly the very existence of the human parent-infant tie —quite apart from the question of the parent's gender— shapes and colors the human condition.

Let me start with just one aspect of this tie's complex, pervasive influence: the effect it exerts on the nature of sexual feeling in our species.

The Infant-Parent Tie and Adult Sex

The peculiarly long dependence of the human infant underlies many of the ambiguities, complexities, and internal contradictions in the human situation. In the preceding chapter, I pointed to one such contradiction, the one that lies at the heart of the biological history of our sexual arrangement: On the one hand the immaturity of our young at birth, and their prolonged subsequent helplessness, is a characteristic phylogenetically inseparable from the uniquely enterprising, knowledge-pooling, cumulatively self-creating capacities of our species. And on the other hand it is this same species characteristic that has until now held half of us back —because of the heavy maternal responsibility that it has imposed— from full use of these enterprising, knowledge-pooling, cumulatively self-creating capacities.

In this chapter I shall be starting to discuss another such contradiction, one that has to do not with the practical burden the child's dependence imposes on the mother but rather with the emotional consequences of this dependence for the child itself: Human neonatal immaturity exerts —as one of its far-reaching effects on the character of our life— a paradoxical effect on human sexual feeling. On the one hand it vastly increases the potential depth of that feeling. On the other hand (and how this happens is explored in later chapters) it seriously cripples that feeling's direct expression.

As an exercise in understanding how our early dependence affects our later erotic sensibility, try picturing an adult who has had no helpless infancy. Suspend your logical objections to this venture, and imagine a human creature who is in all respects like those we know except that it was born mobile, verbal, rational, and competent. Think, in other words, of a human able from the very beginning to seek out food and interesting stimulation, to move away from unpleasant temperatures and noises, to flee from assault; a human magically ready at birth, moreover, to speak its group's language and very quickly to grasp all relevant knowledge and lore.

Image this person as able to form emotional ties to others; such ties —given its human cerebral capacities for empathy, memory, and planning— would, like ours, deepen with long association. And if these ties developed in a stable close-knit group, as most of ours do, they would in certain ways resemble what we think of as familial attachments. They would also, as with us, inevitably permeate sexual sensation, and endow it with some aspects of the peculiarly human emotional depth that it can have for us (see Chapter 2, pages 13–16). What would be missing, however, in the erotic experience of this imaginary human is a crucial quality of our own sexuality: the quality of resonance with the atmosphere of our very early emotional life.

In this pre-verbal, pre-logical life of ours, the feelings binding the infant to the adult who cares for it are dominated on the one hand by the infant's sense of vital need, the need of a helpless, immobile being for whom the swing between limitless anxiety and total bliss depends on outside succor; and on the other hand by the adult's passionate nurturing response to that need. This response, of which the infant becomes in some sense aware, includes intense attraction to the infant's growing body, and intense interest in the infant's mysterious, vivid, inarticulate, developing subjectivity.

The nature of these earliest ties colors all our later reactions to the environment, making them deeply different from those of our imaginary relative, human in every other way, who has had no infancy. It colors our stance toward nature, our response to the authority of social leaders and societal proscriptions, our relation to work and to play, our religious feelings.* And of course it colors our attitudes toward people: what attracts us to them, what we expect of them, what frightens or angers or delights us in them; and this, as we shall see later, has profound consequences for our male-female arrangements. Here, however, what we are considering is how it colors the quality of human sex pleasure.

For this question, the crucial fact is that the feeling, the vital emotional intercourse, between infant and parent is carried by touch, by taste and smell, by facial expression and gesture, and by mutual accommodation of body position. Until the sexual impulse that emerges at puberty throws us once more into acute, physiologically urgent need for contact with the body of another person, life offers us no comparable† avenue for direct expression of those feelings which are continuous with the feelings of infancy, feelings for which we then had no words, no language-dominated thoughts, and which cannot be rediscovered in their original fullness except in touch, in taste and smell, in facial expression and gesture, and in mutual accommodation of body position.

---

* Norman O. Brown's *Life Against Death* (despite the crucial omissions that cramp his thinking) is the most passionate and fertile recent analysis of these matters that I know of. Melanie Klein's *Envy and Gratitude* (for the reader who is willing to take as metaphoric her account of the mental life of a nursing infant) offers an equally profound analysis, narrower but in many ways less distorted. Both stand, of course, on Freud's shoulders, limited by the limitations of his vision in some respects, transcending it in others.

† See note 1.

This, as I understand it, is what Freud was getting at when he spoke of infantile sexuality and the latency period: So long as the parent-child relation revolves primarily around the parent's care of the child's body, and the parent's empathic response to the child's unspoken emotional needs —so long, that is, as parent and child are bound together on the same primitive, animal-poetic level on which men and women find each other sexually attractive— during this phase (which wanes sharply in intensity when the child can talk, walk, and feed itself, and tapers off finally* between the child's sixth and ninth year) the parent-child relation foreshadows adult sexuality. Between then and puberty, the intensity of these early feelings, in which our basic connection to the world is originally rooted, can be kept largely out of direct reach, since in these years we are temporarily disengaged from the biologically acute attraction to other bodies that guarantees the continuation of the species.[1] With puberty, these feelings become more literally recapturable.

They are not, however, necessarily recaptured: This is the paradox at the core of the relation between neonatal immaturity and human sex feeling. The option opened by puberty is often refused, wholly or in part. The depths of erotic feeling made possible by our long infancy are in fact explored only by some people, and by many of these only now and then. And our tendency to renounce full use of the peculiarly human capacity for sexual passion has the same source as this capacity itself: it, too, springs from our long infancy.

This deep-rooted tendency to renounce the sensuous-emotional world of our early childhood, to seal off the layer of personality in which the primitive erotic flow between the self and the surround has its source, is a puzzle with which psychoanalytic social philosophers† keep trying to come to grips. It is a puzzle that will

---

* Except in memory, of course: The relations between human parents and children maintain forever, even if in perverse form, the emotional residue of this early intimacy.

† I am thinking of such writers as (after Freud, of course) Schachtel, Reich, Brown, Marcuse.

not be solved, however, while the prevailing male-female arrangement continues to be taken for granted. As I shall show in
Chapters 4 and 7, what we seal off in ourselves will not be un-
sealed until we have met a necessary and radical precondition:
we must break the female monopoly over early child care. ⟩

Female Monopoly of Early Child Care

Consider now what it means that for virtually every human, the
central infant-parent relationship, in which we form our earliest,
intense and wordless, feelings toward existence, is a relation with
a woman.

It is in a woman's arms and bosom that the delicate-skinned
infant —shocked at birth by sudden light, dry air, noises, drafts,
separateness, jostling— originally nestles. In contact with her
flesh it first feels the ecstasy of suckling, of release from the
anguish of hunger and the terror of isolation. Her hands clean,
soothe, and pat its sensitive bottom. Her face is the first whose
expression changes reciprocally with its own. Her voice intro-
duces it to speech: it is the first voice that responds to the voice of
the child, that signals the advent of succor, whose patterns of
rhythm or pitch correspond to events the child notices or body
sensations it feels. She is the one who rocks or bounces it when it
feels tense, who thumps it when it needs to burp. She comes
when it feels anxious or bored and provides the sense of being
cared for, the interesting things to look at, touch, smell, and hear,
the chance to use growing powers of back-and-forth communication, without which human personality and intellect —and indeed
the body itself— cannot develop.

The child is, moreover, physically dependent on her for all
these things far into a period in which it is mentally developed
enough to be, in important ways, aware of this dependence. The
human baby, because it is immobile longer and at the same time
very much brighter, has a capacity for *feeling* powerless unlike
that of any other baby animal: It feels the bind of wanting to do
more than it can do. It must wait consciously for the will of

another person to relieve its bodily discomfort; to provide it with the sensory experience that it needs (for it needs much more complicated sensory experience than it can get for itself); to keep it company (for it actively wants company long before it is able to go and look for company, when all it can do is lie still and hope —or holler— for someone to come).

The child's bodily tie to the mother, then, is the vehicle through which the most fundamental feelings of a highly complex creature are formed and expressed. At her breast, it is not just a small furnace being stoked: it is a human being discovering its first great joy, handling its first major social encounter, facing its first meeting with a separate creature enormously more powerful than itself, living out its first awareness of wanting something for which it must depend on someone else, someone who is imperfectly benevolent and imperfectly reliable because she is (although the infant, of course, has no way of knowing that she is) also a human being. This tie is the prototype of the tie to life. The pain in it, and the fear of being cut off from it, are prototypes of the pain of life and the fear of death.

Notes Toward Chapter 4

The central fact of human childhood to which Chapter 3 has pointed works in a number of ways to guarantee that most babies —or in any case enough babies to keep intact the overall form of our social life— will grow into adults emotionally predisposed to consent, at whatever cost, to the prevailing male-female arrangements. What follows is an effort to sketch out just a few of these ways.

(I do mean sketch out. They are so many, and so complex, that to attempt a comprehensive account of their nature and scope would be the kind of enterprise for which I have neither taste nor talent. The alert reader, then, is bound to notice radical omissions and oversimplifications in what I am saying; and it will be all too easy, unfortunately, to focus annoyance on these flaws, to welcome them as distractions, in order to evade the anxiety that is apt to be stirred up when the matters to which my sketch refers are faced head-on: These matters are painful and frightening to think about —I have found them so, and the students and friends whom I have persuaded to think about them seem to feel the same way— and one is sharply tempted to concentrate on the dandruff on the shoulder, the stutter or the limp or the tic, of the stranger who utters emotionally unwelcome words. I hope that some readers at least will be able to resist this temptation well enough to hear, and let themselves feel, the gist of my argument.*

* See also Box D, pages 55–57.

It seems possible, in fact, that for people who find themselves impatient with the survey offered in Chapters 4–8, or who feel in danger of bogging down in its details [especially the details of Chapter 4] the best way to get at my gist may be to skip or skim over this survey for the moment and go first to Chapter 9. That chapter starts with a summary of those aspects of the preceding exposition which must be grasped if the central statement it then adds —a statement of what I see as the broadest societal implications of our gender arrangement— is to be understood.

To most readers the content of Chapters 4–8, however distressing it may be, will probably seem relevant in an immediate personal sense, quite apart from its bearing on our chances of reversing history's present deadly direction. On the other hand, there may be some for whom impressionistic and unprovable psychoanalytically oriented generalizations make uncongenial reading, but who want nevertheless to know if this book has anything new to say about the relation between the prevailing male-female symbiosis and the possibility of a human future. Such readers should unhesitatingly turn now to Chapter 9. They can decide afterward whether they do or do not feel like going back to the analysis that leads up to it.)

Chapter 4 shows how female-dominated child care guarantees male insistence upon, and female compliance with, a double standard of sexual behavior. Chapter 5 shows how it guarantees that women and men will regard each other, respectively, as silly overgrown children. Chapters 6, 7, and 8 show how it guarantees certain forms of antagonism —rampant in men, and largely shared by women as well— against women. These antagonisms include fury at the sheer existence of her autonomous subjectivity; loathing of her fleshly mortality; a deeply ingrained conviction that she is intellectually and spiritually defective; fear that she is untrustworthy and malevolent. At the same time, they include an assumption that she exists as a natural resource, as an asset to be owned and harnessed, harvested and mined, with no fellow-feeling for her depletion and no responsibility for her conservation or replenishment. Finally, they include a sense of primitive outrage at meeting her in any position of worldly authority.

Much of what I will be saying in these chapters has been said before — in a context, however, that blurs its meaning. It was Freud (followed by disciples like Bonaparte and Deutsch) who introduced into contemporary thought a sense of how deeply the existing psychological sex differences have to do with the circumstance that the first important figure in every childhood is a woman — that is to say, a same-sex figure for the girl and an opposite-sex figure for the boy. But neither he nor these disciples were ready —how many people are ready now?— to take the next step: to consider the possibility that this crucial childhood circumstance is mutable, and needs revision.

As Wilhelm Reich surmised in his early work on character and social structure, and as writers like Norman Brown and Herbert Marcuse have more recently insisted, the psychoanalytic approach has opened the way to fundamental change in our conception of —and therefore in the nature of— our species situation. But there is one large and inconvenient fact that these male thinkers have for the most part failed to face: that the radical change they herald implies a correspondingly radical revision of existing gender arrangements.

This is an omission which of course gravely warps their thinking. But it by no means follows that feminists can afford to ignore what they have to say. On the contrary, it is up to us to assimilate what they, and Freud, have really seen and to make it part of a wider, more actively constructive, view. To do so seems to me a task immeasurably more pressing than the task of documenting their biases and cataloging their errors. We have no time to waste in polemic (polemic is in any case a traditionally masculine vice: it is time now for men to give it up, not for women to fall into it) against theorists who fail to see all the implications of their own explosive theories. So long as we postpone exploring these implications for ourselves, we are helping to postpone necessary experiments in human survival.

4

Higamous-Hogamous

"Higamous hogamous, woman's monogamous.
Hogamous higamous, man is polygamous."

— FOLK RHYME

A central rule under a strikingly widespread range of conditions is, first, that men act sexually more possessive than women, and second, that women act less free than men to seek "selfish" sexual pleasure.

The reason for this rule can seem deceptively simple. Wherever we look common sense offers us glaringly visible explanations.* And the presence of these common-sense explanations —the exis-

---

* Men, for example, can bully women because, like males of other polygamous mammalian species, they are on the average stronger and heavier, and because the reduced mobility of females during pregnancy and lactation make male protection advantageous —often essential— if young are to be born and suckled. (Indeed, the obstetrical complications induced by our shift to an upright posture —see Chapter 2— and the especially prolonged helplessness of our infants, have made this even truer for women than for their animal sisters.) The more powerful males in such a species are therefore in a position not only to monopolize the females by driving away competing males but also to enforce female consent to this arrangement: to ride herd, as for example stallions do, on their harems.

The relative scarcity of males is sometimes also seen as an explanation, though it is in fact not at all clear that scarcity itself is a major basis for one-sided erotic prerogative. (Even when the usual numerical asymmetry between the sexes is minor, the erotic one remains major, the important fact being that females are unevenly distributed among the available males. There are circumstances, moreover, in the human case at least, in which it is females who happen to be scarce: When this is so, we do not typically find them enjoying access to harems of jealously guarded males; on the contrary, they are shared —think of whorehouses in boom towns, or the Eskimo wife hospitably offered to the guest— at male initiative and under male guardianship. Still, shaky as

tence of obvious *external* supports for the double-standard rule—
makes it easy to overlook the presence of vital, but less obvious,
internal supports. The rule will not be understood, or centrally
changed, until people see that it rests not only on brute force,
practical pressure, societal coercion, but also on something subtler
and harder to defy: it is supported within each person on that
stubborn wordless level of adult feeling which is continuous with
infant feeling and with the emotional realm of early childhood.

The "practical" bases for asymmetric human sexual privilege
have clearly started to crumble, and if advanced industrial civilization survives they will clearly crumble further.* What remains
very much intact, however, is its deepest emotional basis: A central psychological asymmetry between the sexes, laid down in the
first months, and consolidated in the first years, of life, is built
into the primary-group arrangement that Washburn (see page
19) describes as the "fundamental pattern . . . [of human] social

---

it is, the scarcity explanation sounds simple enough to help lull common-sense
curiosity about the real underpinnings of the higamous-hogamous rule.)

Overlaid on the obvious conditions that they share with other male animals,
men have certain purely human reasons, and purely human means, for enforcing inequality of sexual privilege. These, too, are obvious: Only humans
are mentally capable of being pained by the uncertainty of biological paternity, and therefore of trying to reduce this uncertainty by restricting female
sex activity. Only humans embody traditions of sexual coercion in a network
of legal, educational, economic, and social practice. Only humans are purposeful enough to be plausibly suspected of having formed a deliberate conspiracy
of the (male) strong to keep the (female) weak under control. (In recent
feminist literature, Friedan's *The Feminine Mystique* and Millet's *Sexual
Politics*, for example, offer vigorous, popular expressions of this suspicion.)

* As current technology advances and spreads, size and muscle, for example, have less and less to do with power to bully, and the physical hazards
that have made males scarce become increasingly obsolescent. At the same
time, less and less female energy needs to be devoted to childbearing (see
Box C, page 25). Better birth control, moreover, and readier access to safe
abortion will make doubt about biological paternity easier and easier to avoid.
Meanwhile this kind of doubt is apt to become more bearable in any case as
ties of blood become less and less dominant in determining the structure of
enduring groups. In addition, our present legal, educational, and socio-
economic traditions, and our present means for enforcing them, will necessarily be melting down and reforming on a massive scale; one consequence
will be that sex coercion will be less and less rigidly embedded in the old
network of other societal arrangements that help make it feasible now.

organization." This central asymmetry, which drives men to insist on unilateral sexual prerogative and inclines women to consent to their insistence, will endure as a powerful force until the "fundamental pattern" is outgrown — until, that is, the female monopoly of child care is broken.

To see how this complex asymmetry develops and ramifies, one must examine it aspect by aspect. (And the necessity, I must warn the reader, makes a certain amount of repetition inevitable.) Let us look first at the special sexual possessiveness of men; then at the special muting of women's erotic impulsivity; and then at a third tendency which is —in our own culture at least— a close relative of these two: the tendency for sexual excitement to be more tightly tied to personal sentiment in women than in men.

My discussion here, and throughout the following chapters, is in one sense frankly ethnocentric; it is mainly couched, in its literal details, in terms of the nuclear family of contemporary white-middle-class America. *Its central points are meant, however, to be usefully translatable to any human situation in which women preside over life's first stages and men are at the same time present as emotionally significant figures for young children.*

Unilateral Sexual Possessiveness

The human male's tendency to claim one-sided access to a female, and the human female's tendency to consent to this claim, are rooted first of all in infancy, in the differing relationships of boy and girl to the parent* who has so far always dominated the beginning of life. On this initial set of differences another set is

---

* Or parental figure or figures. See footnote, page 28. Diffusion of the early maternal role among a number of women probably bears on the later intensity of the child's one-to-one emotional ties, and perhaps on the distinctness of personal individuation. What it does not bear on is our basic male-female arrangement. Review of ethnographic data re adult relations between the sexes in societies differing in *degree* of male contact with infants would clearly be helpful. But for the present discussion what matters is that women are in any case normally the *main* early parental figures.

overlaid in early childhood. These two layers of experience (along with later ones) fuse, to be sure, in the formation of adult emotional proclivities; they are considered separately here only in order to help clarify their nature.

Roots in infancy

At the outset, for the infant (see Chapter 3), it is in the relation with the mother that all joy is centered, and it is largely through body contact that this joy comes. Other people with a claim on the mother's intimate concern, and especially on her body, are resented competitors for a vital resource. Boy or girl, one wants her for oneself; on the most primitive level of feeling, one remains unreconciled to sharing her: To possess a woman (more precisely, to possess a creature of the kind who later, as our perceptions develop, turns out to belong to the category "woman") is under present conditions every child's early wish. What happens to this wish —which survives throughout life in what used to be called the heart— depends on whether its original object is later reincarnated partially inside, or primarily outside, one's own skin. And this later reincarnation, of course, is inevitably a different matter for the girl than for the boy.

As I pointed out above (see Chapter 3, pages 31–34), the pleasure that lures animals into procreative activity has an additional function on the human level: it allows us to relive some of the original life-giving delight of infancy. When the boy, as an adult, finds this delight in heterosexual lovemaking, he finds it outside himself, as before, in a female body. And if the inhabitant of this female body feels free to bestow its resources on a competitor, she is re-evoking for him the situation in which mother, unbearably, did not belong to baby.

The girl grows up into a heterosexual situation significantly more complex. She has —at least partially— *become* the mother. She now lives in the female body that was once the vital source of nourishment, entertainment, reassurance. It is true, to be sure, that a man —despite his male physique— can provide for her, as she provides for him, a direct opportunity for reliving the original embrace. There are momentous physical facts to support this emotional opportunity*: he is corporeally large, warm, and strong, as the mother was; and his penis, taken into a yearning orifice of the body as the nipple once was taken, can provide a comparably miraculous joy. To the extent that he has this meaning for her, she is vulnerable to something like the simple, direct distress that he feels in the face of sexual competition. And yet their distress is not wholly the same. Hers is apt to be modulated in several ways.

First, despite the man's size, and his penis, the physical differences that are likely to exist between a man and the early mother —in shape and skin texture, in voice quality, gesture, rhythm— are important ones. His bodily presence typically cannot in itself call up the atmosphere of infancy for her in these respects so literally as hers can call it up for him. In the sense and to the extent that this is the case, his physical infidelity cannot revive the grief of infancy for her so graphically as hers can for him: its shock value for her is apt to be less concrete, more purely symbolic.

What may be more important, however, is the fact that even the *symbolic* shock value of the other's physical infidelity is far less absolute for her than for him. The mother-raised woman is likely to feel, more deeply than the mother-raised man, that she carries within herself a source of the magic early parental richness.† In this sense —even if not in others— she is more self-sufficient than the mother-raised man: what is inside oneself cannot be directly taken away by a rival.

---

* There are also, of course, momentous symbolic facts to support it. These form a major part of what is summed up in Chapter 10 as the crux of our male-female arrangement.

† Boys, too, identify with the first parent to some degree: we all know a few men who are more "motherly" than most women. But on the whole girls can probably do so more readily at the outset, even before they are aware of their own gender, because the mother is aware of it and acts accordingly. And surely it is easier for girls than for boys to maintain this identification later, when gender has become a salient category.

The tranquillity that goes with this conviction typically rests, of course, on external confirmation of the woman's feeling of inner richness; she requires evidence that somebody else depends on access to what she has.* It is not unusual for her to accept a man's infidelities —even to enjoy them, for reasons discussed below— so long as she is sure he would be desolate to lose possession of her.† If this is how she feels, it is only by making him give her up altogether that a rival can shake the foundations of her confidence in herself as a being equipped with an internal supply of what is most basically needed. The fact that this attitude is far less usual in a man stems not just from the pressure of convention. More basically it stems from the mother-raised boy's sense that the original, most primitive source of life will always lie outside himself, that to be sure of reliable access to it he must have exclusive access to a woman.

Roots in early childhood

There is another way in which female-dominated childhood tends to make jealousy more complex for women than for men, less continuous with the infant's imperious, monolithic rage at maternal infidelity, less likely to arouse sharp impulses of self-assertion. To understand it, one must consider not only the relation between the pre-verbal infant and its mother, but also the shape of the small child's situation as it starts to enter a wider world. During this period, formal sex-role education —learning

* "As long as heee needs meee!" sings Nancy of her brutal lover in the musical version of *Oliver Twist*. Imagine a man singing this song!

† One of Isaac B. Singer's vivid stories depicts a long happy marriage in which the husband enjoys numerous affairs and the wife —secure in his affections, sure that she is central for him, pleased at his attractiveness to women and his adventurousness— accepts them. After many years, they become persuaded that the arrangement is unfair, and with his encouragement she takes a lover. At once and irrevocably, their deep-lying rapport is broken. Their home becomes a desert: she is devastated by his willingness to share her; he is devastated both by the coldness she now shows toward him and by the unexpectedly withering impact of the lover's presence on his own ardor toward her.

what is expected of a girl and of a boy— is of course going on.
The importance of this process is by now well understood; it is a
process that deserves, and is currently getting, detailed attention
from writers oriented to the project of reorganizing our sexual
arrangements. Here, however, we are concerned with a set of
emotional facts whose significance is much less widely recognized, facts which have so far been discussed mainly in the conservative psychoanalytic spirit of understanding why things must
be the way they are, not in the revolutionary psychoanalytic spirit
of thinking out how they can be changed.

Under prevailing conditions the little girl, if she is to develop
the early orientation to gender that will later allow her to feel
heterosexual passion, must overcome an initial handicap. What is
required of her is a central shift of erotic allegiance: It is to this
shift that Freud and his students point, more unanimously than to
the shaky theory of penis envy, as a basis for their working assumption that woman's sexual disadvantage is inevitable. (And in
fact this assumption would be a wholly reasonable one, if female-
dominated childhood were inevitable. There is nothing wrong
with the logic behind it. The error is in its tacit initial premise.)
The girl's original love, they remind us, was, like the boy's, a
woman. Upon this prototypic erotic image, the image of man
must be superimposed.

This emotional feat is typically in progress during the two- or
three- to five-year-old period that Freud —naming it from the
viewpoint of the boy— called Oedipal. During these years, the
child's worldly awareness expands dramatically. The father becomes a more distinct figure, and as he does so it becomes clear
that there are two sexes, with physical and social differences between them that are crucial for one's own present and future
privileges, obligations, and opportunities. It becomes clear also
that there exists a special and exclusive relation between the parents, the nature of which has sharp bearing on one's own place in
the affections of each.*

* Among us this tight childhood triangle —like the isolated, exclusive
mother-infant pair— is more starkly drawn, less modulated by additional re-

"Oedipal" jealousy. The little boy's concern about his own position in the relation with the two parents is apt to be focused mainly on the father's rival claim to the mother: She is the parent with whom the boy has been physically intimate from the outset, and to whom he is likely still to be much more attached, in this way, than to his newly vivid father; and now his growing awareness of bodily and social maleness tells him that she is a member of the sex for whose affections he is destined to compete with other males.

In the girl's case, this jealous concern about one's place with the parents is typically much more deeply two-edged. The father's animal allure is likely to be more powerful for her than it is for the boy. (This may be simply because he acts more seductive with her: he can treat her openly as an attractive little female; he is less free to flirt on an animal-poetic level with his son.* It may also be —we do not know— that even in the small child some central neural basis for a specific interest in the opposite sex is already operating.) At the same time, the mother is for the girl, as for the boy, the parent around whom bodily based tender passion was first organized. This means that for her, love of this

---

lations with other parental people, than is the case in the extended families in which most of the world's children grow up (see footnote, page 84). The emotional possibilities added by the presence of a number of adults, valuable as they are, have no basic bearing upon the species-wide erotic problems that underlie the double standard. Even in our own nuclear families, the stark triangle discussed here is usually complicated by the presence of siblings, again without changing the main lines of male-female stress engendered in female-dominated childhood. I simplify for the sake of brevity.

* He is less *free* because of the ban on overt expression of homoerotic attraction (an attraction whose self-evidently prominent place in the hierarchy of attractions that we can feel toward the world's creatures would quite probably, if it were not suppressed, make it a lively part of every human life). If such a ban did not exist, he might in any case feel less sharply *interested* in flirting with his son than with his daughter; but so long as it does exist we cannot tell how great or how universal this possible difference in intensity of spontaneous interest might be.

Why this ban exists, and what the prospect of lifting it has to do with the propect of change in male-female arrangements, is too large a question to be discussed in this book.

kind is more evenly directed toward both parents than it is for the boy, and rivalry with the mother for the father's love is more evenly balanced against rivalry with the father for the mother's. The growing insight that this balance is scheduled to tip mainly in the father's direction is on some level wounding. To realize that one is a female, destined to compete with females for the erotic resources of males, is to discover that one is doomed to renounce one's first love.*

In the jealous woman, the emotional atmosphere of this child-hood discovery is apt to be reactivated: She can feel at the same time pained by the other woman's access to the man and excited by the man's access to the other woman, through which she is offered vicarious re-access to a female erotic figure. The eruption of this more or less buried early erotic interest can distract or humiliate or baffle her, taking the sharp edge off jealous anger. She may find herself helpless in the throes not only of masochistic satisfaction† at being forced to accept the painful presence of a rival but also of bisexual pleasure in simultaneous contact with a man and —vicariously— a woman.‡ (There are, of course, many women in whom no such feelings erupt, and whose jealousy is as fierce as any man's.)[1]

In the jealous man, two-edged feeling of this kind (though it does in fact often occur) is less typical. A certain degree of straightforward animal-poetic attraction toward the same-sex parent is likely to have been part of his, like the girl's, childhood Oedipal dilemma. The likelihood that this factor will later work to take the edge off heterosexual jealousy is less in his case, how-

* More precisely, what the girl is expected to renounce —again because of the ban on overt homoerotic expression— is the passionate body-based component of her first love.

† Much of the qualitative difference between female and male masochism must stem not from physical sex differences, and not from the direct training of women to be submissive, but from female-dominated childhood. This (like the implications of what I am saying here for homosexuality) is too large a topic to be dealt with in the present volume. But one important aspect of it is touched upon in Chapter 8.

‡ An overt expression of this emotional possibility is active lovemaking between co-wives in a harem.

ever, because his attraction to his father is apt to have differed in two crucial ways from the girl's attraction to her mother. One difference —to which I have referred just above from the father's point of view— is that the boy's erotic pull toward his father is apt to have been more ego-alien, less compatible with his own self-image and the expectations of the people around him, than the girl's toward her mother (which had to be accepted as an expression of the young child's still lively physical dependence on parental —a word that under prevailing conditions means maternal— care). Another, related, difference between these two early homoerotic pulls is that the onset of his was later. The father under present conditions tends to be a far less distinct figure than the mother until the child is verbal and mobile, and relatively knowledgeable and rational. The attraction to him is thus inevitably less primitive, more modulated from the beginning by the abstract considerations that language carries. It is an attraction, moreover, far less deeply tied up with sheer survival: bodily contact with him can be exhilarating and playful (he typically carries the child, and tosses it in the air), or threatening (he may administer corporal punishment, or show terrifying anger, or figure in violent sexual fantasies), but it does not ordinarily have to do, as contact with the mother does, with the basic maintenance of life.

What has been said above about the difference between the boy's "Oedipal" jealousy and the girl's, as these bear on one-sided male possessiveness in adult sex life, can be summed up as follows:

First, the young child's ties to its mother are earlier born, more continuous with the passions of helpless pre-verbal infancy, than those to its father. This means that in the mother-father-child triangle the heteroerotic side of the child's feeling has more primitive weight for the boy than for the girl, while the homoerotic side has more primitive weight for the girl than for the boy. The adult consequence of this difference is that a woman's heterosexual jealousy is apt to be more deeply complicated than a man's by homoerotic excitement, her rage more blurred, her impulse to get rid of the intruder less pure.

Second, not only is the homoerotic side of the boy's feeling in this early triangle later born and less primitive than the girl's; it is also more disgraceful. The adult consequence is that even where homoerotic excitement *is* strong enough to complicate a man's heterosexual jealousy, this excitement is likelier to be suppressed, since it is too shameful to be admitted into awareness. Suppressed, erotic feeling toward a rival does not defuse jealous rage as it can when it comes closer to the surface of consciousness. Indeed, it is apt to have the opposite effect: suppressed, its energy can feed into the rage, making the latter even more primitive and self-righteous.

But the boy's relation to the parents contrasts with the girl's in a way that goes far beyond these intimate strains within the original threesome.

The "Oedipal" dilemma and the wider human realm. It is true that both son and daughter in these early years feel —and handle somewhat differently for the reasons discussed above— the pull between an old love and the possibility of adding a new one. A momentous additional difference between his case and hers, however, lies in the human-social nature of this new possibility, its implications for one's future place in the world beyond the parent-child triangle.

In the son's case, what is apt to be salient is that resentment of the father's claims upon the mother threatens to interfere with a crucial opportunity that is now opening before him: attachment to his newly interesting and powerful male parent represents solidarity with his own sex, a solidarity upon which much of his thrust toward worldly competence is starting to depend. His main task is to find a balance between two contrasting varieties of love, one that provides primitive emotional sustenance, and another that promises —if rivalry over the first can be handled— to offer membership in the wider community where prowess is displayed, enterprise planned, public event organized. His old tie to his mother starts at this point to be felt as an obstacle to new and more grown-up ties with his own sex. These are the ties upon which —in the world he is beginning to know, the world as it now is— the opportunity will rest to exercise some of his most important human capacities.

This new difficulty in the boy's relations with his mother is now likely to coalesce with certain longer-standing grievances, rooted in the inevitable frustrations of infancy, that had been part of his feeling for her from the beginning. (What these grievances are, and how they bear on the atmosphere between men and women, is one of the questions to which Chapters 6, 7, and 8 are devoted. At this point, let me assert merely that they exist, and that they are formidable.) Together, these older and newer difficulties help form the basis for the eventual adult feeling that love for women must be kept in its place, not allowed to interfere with the vital ties between men.[2]

Ideally, the little boy manages to find some provisional balance between the old, jealous, aggrieved erotic tug toward the mother and the new feeling of friendship with the father. Later on, he will have an opportunity to resolve this conflict more decisively. He will discover that authority over a woman or women is a mark of status, respected by men. This discovery will help him reconcile what were once competing wishes: the wish for secure access to certain essential emotional resources, which in his experience reside in females, and the wish to take part in certain essential human activities, which in the world he now enters are defined as male.*

What is reflected in man's unilateral possessiveness, then, is not only the original, monolithic infant wish for ownership of a woman but also a second, more equivocal feeling, rooted in early

* It will occur to some readers at this point that these essential activities need not in fact be defined as male, and that if the public domain were open to mothers as well as to fathers one part, at least, of the situation I outline here might be deeply modified even if women did continue to dominate early child care. This mitigation of our trouble could come about, however, only if it were emotionally possible for mother-raised women and mother-raised men to take part freely and equally together in what are now male affairs. And unhappily, as Chapters 6–8 show, this is just what mother-raised men and women cannot do.

boyhood: that attachment to a woman is emotionally bearable, consistent with the solidarity among men which is part of maleness, only if she, and one's feelings toward her, remain under safe control.

For the girl, this aspect of the "Oedipal" conflict takes a different form and its resolution is likely to have the opposite outcome. To her, too, the father is an interesting, powerful figure through whom one reaches out toward the wider world. But he does not normally invite her, as he invites the boy, to follow him out into this fascinating world, and take on its challenges in recompense for the impossibility of owning the mother. Instead he offers the more direct recompense of a second erotic tie, excitingly, but not so sharply as in the boy's case, different from the first one. This second love at its outset valuably supplements the first (for the daughter, like the son, needs another relation to help her achieve perspective on the relation with the mother). And in the girl's situation, the new love for man —unlike the boy's new love for man— is expected gradually to supplant the original love for woman. Her jealousy of the parents, as I said earlier, is more two-edged than the boy's; and at the same time, neither parent is likely to contest her erotic claim on the other as directly as the father contests the boy's claim on the mother.* All in all, then, she is under less urgent pressure than the boy is to find some clear-cut way of reconciling the second love with the first.

It will nevertheless turn out to be true in her case, as in the

---

* The father, of course, sees his daughter as a much less threatening rival than his son. And the mother, for all the reasons under discussion here, is apt to show less heterosexual possessiveness than her husband does.

Indeed, in the triangle with her husband and daughter, the mother may well resent the man for his attractiveness to the little girl —who was once hers in the way she originally wanted her mother to be hers— more than she resents the little girl for her attractiveness to the man.

Recall the scene, in Bergman's film *The Virgin Spring*, in which a father and a mother try to understand the converging forces of evil responsible for their daughter's death. The mother confesses the hatred she felt toward her husband when she saw her daughter's love withdrawn from herself and turned to him. When a son goes off with his father, his mother's regret is more bearable; the father cannot replace her in a son's feelings as he can in a daughter's.

boy's, that ties to the opposite sex and solidarity with one's own sex will pull in opposite directions. But the nature of this pull — as she feels it in childhood, and as she acts on it later— is different for her than for him. For her the deepest obstacles to solidarity with one's own sex first appear not in the mother-father-baby triangle, where the boy first meets them, but in the deep ambivalence of the earlier mother-baby pair. Once the triangle forms, both the "truly masculine" boy and the "truly feminine" girl use its existence to help handle the formidable tensions inherent in the original pair. But they do so in contrasting ways; and the outcome is that women are on the whole far less able than men to balance dependence on each other against dependence on the opposite sex.*

When the father first emerges to offer the girl a tie that can supplement (and in part substitute for) the tie to the mother, he makes available to her a new way of handling —a way, that is, of side-stepping the task of resolving— the ambivalence at the heart of the infant-mother tie. What he offers is a fatefully tempting (pseudo) solution† to this central dilemma: positive feelings toward the mother are normally split off from negative ones in early life in order to preserve the possibility of feeling, at least sometimes, a sense of unqualified oneness with this central source of all that is good. What the girl can now do is transfer to the father —who starts out with a clean slate, so to speak, innocent of

---

* The importance of achieving this kind of balance depends on how rigidly society is organized around gender distinctions. So far, these distinctions have been a structurally basic feature of social life. When they are not, the balance will cease to be a problem. But right now —when women need solidarity in groups that go beyond intimate family ties, to work on broad human projects that turn out to be mainly in their hands— it is a serious problem. To get beyond where we are right now we will have to surmount it. And to do so we will have to use the capacities for personal growth inherent in our traditionally mother-reared personalities. The liberation of those capacities depends, I think, on insight into *why* mother-reared people have the problems that they have.

† This "solution" is not available to the boy, unless he takes a predominantly homoerotic stance. If he does so, however, he encounters other special complications: "escape" from unresolved ambivalence toward woman into romantic passion for man is an even less auspicious step for him than for the girl.

association with the inevitable griefs of infancy— much of the weight of these positive feelings, while leaving the negative ones mainly attached to their original object. She thus gains a less equivocal focus for her feelings of pure love, and feels freer to experience her grievances against her mother without fear of being cut off altogether from the ideal of wholehearted harmony with a magic, animally loved, parental being.*

This opportunity comes at a particularly timely point in her development since a new grievance against the mother is just adding itself to those already stored up: just as the boy, during this period, is learning that outside the family an arena exists in which he can exercise some central human capacities, the girl (who possesses these same capacities, and is too young to have been persuaded that she does not) also learns of this arena and begins at about the same time to grasp the strange fact that she is unwelcome to enter it. This misfortune she is apt to blame on her omnipotent mother, who has so far been responsible for every misfortune —as well as every delight— in her young life.† The father, if she is to become a "truly feminine" woman who contents herself with motherhood and the maintenance of family life, is typically absolved of blame for her exclusion from this vital extrafamilial arena. Indeed, he is all the more glamorous and newly needed because he provides the only access to it —vicarious access‡ —that she can expect to have. He is glamorous also

---

* She does not, of course, always use this opportunity. Other "solutions" are available: she can, for example, over-idealize the mother, and/or project onto the father (with disruptive consequences for her later relations with men) most, or some, of the negative feelings. But I am focusing here on processes that lead to the traditional symbiotic emotional equilibrium that is thought of as heterosexual "adjustment."

† This is the core of truth in the Freudian statement that the girl blames her lack of a penis on the mother. All that is missing from the Freudian formulation is the insight that the value of the penis lies mainly not in its charm as a water toy, or in its magic erectile properties (of which the small girl, in our culture at least, is often ignorant), but rather in the social prerogatives it confers. (But this is a point that de Beauvoir has made so well that it surely needs no further belaboring.)

‡ It is in fact a peculiarly privileged and societally significant vicarious access that he offers, an access upon which the stability of our present arrangements heavily rests. See Chapter 9.

because the special compensation that she will be offered for keeping the home fires burning and forgoing the rewards of effort in the wide world —the compensation that lies in a certain kind of erotic attention, in exemption from certain risky challenges, in safety from certain possible humiliations*— is foreshadowed in the special homage that he has begun to express toward her as a little female: The deprivation for which she feels her mother is to blame is repaired, so far as it can be, by her father.

Early rage at the first parent, in other words, is typically used by the "masculine" boy during the Oedipal period to *consolidate* his tie with his own sex by establishing a principled independence, a more or less derogatory distance, from women. And it is typically used by the "feminine" girl in this same period to *loosen* her tie with her own sex by establishing a worshipful, dependent stance toward men. Just when that boy is learning to keep his feelings for the mother under control, that girl (precisely because her first emotional problems also centered on the mother) is learning to over-idealize the father. This contrast, of course, heavily supports asymmetry of sexual privilege. For without comparably strong, well-defined ways of counterbalancing feelings for the opposite sex with a sense of human identity based on solidarity with each other, women are far less free than men to set their own terms in love.

---

* There is another compensation which the reader might well expect to see included in this list of the future benefits foreshadowed in her relation with her father: the major prospect (heavily emphasized by psychoanalytic writers, and persuasively documented by cross-cultural observations such as those that Mead provides in *Male and Female*) of becoming herself a mother — the bodily creator, and all-providing possessor, of a magically delicious baby of her own.

I believe, however, that this is a murkier and more equivocal prospect (see Chapter 7) than is generally acknowledged: the cherished-mistress facet of woman's status, implicit in the father's courtly homage, has less dirt and dislike in it than the maternal facet does. Also, the compensatory sense of future motherhood, insofar as it *is* positive, draws her closer to the mother as well as to the father (women are largely rivals in courtship, largely allies in childbearing and maternal concerns), and is therefore a neutral factor in her shift of positive feeling from the first parent toward the second.

The nature of the rule

In sum, then: Unilateral male sexual possessiveness rests on strong old feelings, both in men and in women. And so long as the care of the very young remains in female hands these feelings —in which echoes of infancy and of early childhood are fused— will persist.

But before turning to the next part of the higamous-hogamous rule, let me emphasize again the dual sense in which unilateral male possessiveness is in fact a "rule." What I have been offering is a *description* of psychological forces, rooted in mother-dominated childhood, which are widespread enough to make it possible for society to enforce a *prescription* about male and female adult behavior. When I say, for example, that a certain emotional situation, or frame of mind, "as a rule" characterizes father-emulating little boys, or jealous women, I am describing a tendency, a probability: there are many little boys, and many jealous women, whose experiences are quite different from the ones I describe. And it is very lucky that this is so, for if the tensions inherent in the "normal" human situation led uniformly to the same outcome for everyone we would have little hope of outgrowing what is maiming in our sexual arrangements. (See Box D.) As a code of conventionally accepted comportment, on the other hand, the double standard of sexual possessiveness is a "rule" that, whether obeyed or defied, exerts some real coercive force on *every* person. (See Box E.) To survive as this kind of rule, it need not have powerful emotional roots in all of us: just in most of us.

The same is true for the rule —to which I now turn— that female erotic impulse must be curbed: It is a societal prescription, fed psychologically by an amalgam of very early and slightly later experience in enough mother-dominated childhoods to make it generally enforceable.

(Continued on page 59)

Box D

My business here is to sketch out some broad generalizations about differences between men and women who have started out life under mainly female care, rather than to dwell on the many striking exceptions to these generalizations which quite obviously also exist. This is not, of course, because these exceptions seem to me negligible: their significance is clearly enough vital. It is because this significance cannot be appreciated until the diseased norm from which they deviate has been examined at its roots. In choosing this procedure, which relies on the reader's intellectual patience and good will, I knowingly run the risk that some feminists will accuse me, as they go along, of reinforcing socially oppressive sexual stereotypes; and that some anti-feminists will feel free to misuse what I say to support their views. This risk is unavoidable. But it seems sensible to try to reduce mis-understanding at least a little by saying something at this point (now that the reader has an idea of what I am up to) about stereotyping in the perception of human group differences.

All group differences (even differences between non-human groups, like plants vs. animals, or edible vs. non-edible substances) tend to be oversimplified, absolutized, in everyday thought; irregularities, am-biguities, are smoothed over to save mental effort; our view of them is governed by principles of mental economy as inexorable as those that govern visual form perception, or the process of memorizing names and telephone numbers, or the learning of useful habits. Furthermore, in everyday thought about especially complex and emo-tionally charged situations, oversimplified generalizations are apt to be actively treasured, and exceptions to them purposefully under-played.

This tendency can be so destructive socially that people who have seen some of its ugly consequences —for example, in the formation of racial and ethnic stereotypes— often angrily oppose the formula-tion of any group concepts whatsoever. But the fact is that we cannot orient ourselves to social reality without forming hosts of such con-cepts. They are indispensable;* the best we can do is to pay strenu-

* Think —to choose two minor examples— of a woman driver who feels safer picking up hitchhiking adolescents if they are girls rather than boys; or of a black driver who anticipates a pleasanter social encounter if he stops

ously disciplined attention to their limitations. An important expression of such discipline is to keep in mind the presence and the meaning of exceptions to group generalizations.

This keeping in mind is especially relevant, and for most people especially difficult, in the case of generalizations about psychological sex differences. Men and women are not simply two separate groups (like Swedes and Italians, for instance) who happen to have differing distributions of certain traits, distributions which overlap so that some of each are apt to be damaged by social categorizations* which ignore the overlap. Men and women are on the contrary interlocked, symbiotically interdependent, groups; and many members of each, under prevailing conditions, keep pushing hard against the crippling constraints that membership forces upon all members of both. This makes instances of non-conformity to psychological generalizations about men and women peculiarly meaningful. Yet their very meaningfulness, the explosive societal significance of the fact that many people do not fit at all well into their assigned boxes, makes the people who do manage on the whole to stay in such boxes peculiarly unwilling to think about these non-conforming instances in a careful way. A human being who violates "rules of gender" is violating rules — prescriptive and descriptive— to which most others conform at real inner cost, and around which defensive fear and anger are therefore bound to be mobilized. Defensive fear and anger discourage strenuous intellectual activity.

What I hope readers will do, then, is try —despite the variety of emotional sore spots which a discussion like this one bumps into, and which make such an effort difficult— to keep in mind a fact upon which it would be dreary for me to keep dwelling as I go along: it is precisely the existence of many lively exceptions to the generalizations sketched out here (and of the deep human stresses around gender reflected in these exceptions) that makes it necessary and possible to

---

a black rather than a white passer-by for local directions. Both drivers may be guessing wrong in a particular case, but neither is foolish: adolescent boys *do* commit more crimes than adolescent girls; whites *are* likelier than blacks to act tense or rude when approached by a black.

* Such as, for example, ethnic rules of thumb used by potential employers who might pigeonhole Italians into jobs requiring personal outgoingness and Swedes into jobs requiring polished attention to technical detail.

solve the problem around which the sketch is centered. Chapter 10 says something more about this fact.

Also: if keeping the exceptions to my sketch in mind makes the sketch itself seem intolerably rough, I hope readers will ask themselves whether what really distresses them is the roughness of the sketch or (at least in part) the painfulness of the situation to which it points.

Box E

There is a fact that can seem at first glance to belie the general statement about unilateral possessiveness made in this chapter: the fact that there are certain situations, both in our own and in other societies, in which the amicable sharing of women by mother-raised men is a well-established custom. But a closer look at such situations —at least as we meet them in our own cultural mainstream, where we do not need anthropologists to interpret them for us— makes it clear that their emotional atmosphere is wholly compatible with what this chapter describes as the underlying basis for the double sexual standard.

Among us, some women —probably the majority of those who are heterosexually active— are jealously owned by individual men.° And other women —a smaller number— are public property, available on an auxiliary basis to men who also own private women (or could if they wanted to, or will when they are older). Gang bangs and fraternal excursions to whorehouses are traditions that express the emotional flavor of relations with these public women: they are shared not merely amicably but as a group affirmation of common maleness. There is of course no correspondingly recognized population of public men.†

° Usually one per man, sometimes two. I suppose relatively few ordinary Americans manage to keep sole access to a wife and more than one mistress; if there are statistics, I have not seen them.

† Odd women here and there do make use of male whores, but this is a fringe phenomenon. It is not proverbially accepted as an expression of the client's irrepressible, girls-will-be-girls, forgivably naughty sexual high spirits; neither is it a traditional group escapade. It can also happen that women will mention a man to each other, with a certain glee, as a skillful and/or easily available sexual floater. This shows, to be sure, that a reversal

The shared woman and the shared man are as a rule in directly contrasting situations. He can usually command fidelity from at least one of the women who share him, and his relation to her carries an element of triumphant vengeance against the early mother, who was unfaithful to her baby with the father and/or siblings while he depended for everything on her. (She shares him, as a rule, unwillingly; she may not know it, or she may be resigned to it; in any case it is not she, but he, who has decided that he must be shared.) The shared woman, on the other hand, usually has no claim on any man's fidelity. She is the captive and derogated mother, the dethroned tyrant, the defiled goddess, communally possessed in a spirit of ritual counter-assertion against the sexual rivalries that weaken male solidarity. (Think, for instance, of the bizarre emotional familiarity one feels with the atmosphere of male sharing which pervades that disquieting fable *The Story of O.*) She is the mother whose son, putting away everyday childish feelings, ceremoniously abjures his wish to have her for himself in order to cement societally vital bonds with his brothers and father.

Both woman-sharing and man-sharing situations, in other words, are apt under the prevailing conditions to embody male rage at the early mother and female consent that she should be punished or dethroned. In submitting to *either* situation, the woman participates vicariously in the act of humiliating the mother, against whom she also has a grudge: she lends her person to this enterprise. And at the same time, since the humiliated mother is also herself, she has a chance to relive directly the situation of humiliated child, this time of her own accord.

I would be astonished if something of this atmosphere did not surround the sacred prostitute priestess, or the Eskimo wife whose husband hospitably shares her with his guests. (This is, needless to say, a hunch: its verification would be an anthropologist's task.) The in-

---

of the usual pattern is not at all impossible; but what is interesting about it is that it happens so rarely.

The "private" woman who has outside affairs is somewhat less unusual; still, she is significantly rarer in our mainstream than the errant husband, and subject to much more extreme penalties if found out. And she is far less likely than the errant husband either to capture a private concubine or to take up with an amicably shared man (a whore or an "easy lay" whose name is passed around by her cronies).

gredients of defilement and humiliation may be peculiar to our own puritanical, sado-masochistic culture. But it is hard to see how the purposeful sharing of woman by mother-raised men could fail to carry some flavor of ritual conquest over a deep-seated reluctance in the service of a higher purpose.

Woman-sharing ceremonies have another function too: They permit male homoerotic impulse some expression in a safe context of triumphant, harsh masculinity.° The cuckold is threatened by uncontrollable, uninvited, ego-alien upsurges of sexual feelings for the man with whom his wife has thrown him into vicarious contact. The participant in a gang bang voluntarily invokes this inner demon, releasing it into an arena fenced around with dramatic assertions of his intact initiative and his fearsome heterosexual prowess. And the gang bang, of course, is of interest here not as an aberration peculiar to juvenile delinquents and demoralized soldiers, but as the extreme expression of a male tendency that is quite normal in our culture: Ritualized verbal gang banging is so staple an ingredient of ordinary respectable man-to-man coversation that any objection to it is taken as a tasteless assault on an inoffensive form of pleasantry.

° This they have in common with initiation ceremonies in which young males submit to the manhandling of older ones as the price of admission to the adult community. Indeed, initiation ceremonies and woman-sharing ceremonies have several functions in common.

The Muting of Female Erotic Impulsivity

Roots in infancy

Suppression of female sexual impulse has an obvious practical congruence with one-sided male possessiveness: a woman with a strong sexual will of her own may defy a man's wish to keep her for himself. But on the more covert emotional level that we are considering here, there is not only this practical, realistic concern; there is also a different, non-rational kind of fear, a deep fantasy-ridden resentment, directed against her impulsivity itself. Her own bodily pleasure in sex, independent of the pleasure she gives her partner, is the essential threatening fact. It is threatening, first

of all, because it resonates with the distress of a very early discovery, a distress that antedates jealousy since it is felt while the
infant is still too young to notice the existence of competitors for
the mother's resources. This discovery is simply that the infant
does not own or control the mother's body: because this body has
needs and impulses of its own, its responsiveness to the infant's
needs is never totally reliable. (A mother's milk, for example, may
sometimes flow faster or slower than is comfortable for the infant.
She may be sleepy, distracted, or sluggish when it wants to play;
she may alarm it or disturb its peace with over-avid caresses.)
The very same spontaneous, impulsive, autonomous erotic spirit
in the first parent which —as the baby will later find out— allows
her to turn at will to others makes her from the outset imperfectly
subject to its desire even when they are alone.

The significance of this awareness on the infant's part goes far
beyond the purely sexual matters now under discussion. Some
broader consequences of the trouble we have in coming to terms
with the early mother's inconveniently human autonomy are explored in Chapter 6. And much of the rest of this book has to do
with the trouble we have in handling the more general problem
of which this autonomy of hers is just one manifestation: As
Freud pointed out, the fact that human infants receive such
nearly perfect care seduces them into fantasies which are inevitably crushed, fantasies of a world that automatically obeys, even
anticipates, their wishes. The loss of this infant illusion of
omnipotence —the discovery that circumstance is incompletely
controllable, and that there exist centers of subjectivity, of desire
and will, opposed or indifferent to one's own— is an original and
basic human grief.

All of us, male and female, feel this grief. To some degree, it is
irreparable. We manage in part to console ourselves for it indirectly, through mastery, competence, enterprise: the new joy of
successful activity is some compensation for the old joy of passive, effortless wish-fulfillment. This indirect way of handling the
grief is central to the pathology of civilized life, a pathology to
which our male-female arrangements contribute in a way that

will be discussed in Chapters 7, 8, and 9. At the same time, for the sexual situation with which we are concerned here, the important fact is that we also attempt to undo the grief *directly*. Indefatigably, we go on trying to recover what has been lost: We try it first-hand by seeking out situations in which we can re-experience personally, at least for a moment, the infant sense of omnipotence. And we try it second-hand by acting as nurturers, pleasure-givers, empathic wish-granters, by recreating the mother-infant atmosphere so as to relive vicariously some part of the lost delight.

In lovemaking, both man and woman make this direct attempt to repair the old loss. Each of them does so both first-hand, by taking bodily pleasure, and vicariously, by providing pleasure for the other person. But the balance tends not to be symmetrical. She is the one whose physique more closely resembles the physique of the first parent, and who is likely to have incorporated this parent's attitudes more deeply; he is therefore apt to be the one who can more literally relive the infant experience of fulfilling primitive wishes through unqualified access to another body. For her, the vicarious version of this reliving —providing the body through which the other's wishes are perfectly granted — is likely to be a more prominent feature of the interplay. If this symbiotic arrangement is to succeed, the woman's own sexual impulsivity must not be freely unleashed. Unleashed, it can disrupt the recreated harmony; it can revive —in a first-hand way for him and vicariously for her— the first intimations of isolated, non-omnipotent selfhood; it can reactivate in both of them the malaise that originated in the nursling's discovery of the mother's separate, uncontrollable subjective existence.[*]

[*] There are also other, more specific, ways in which mother-dominated infancy makes for the stifling of female spontaneity in adult sex. Psychoanalytic workers infer, for example, that nurslings sometimes frighten themselves with fantasies about devouring their mothers. Having entertained this fantasy, the young cannibal is prey to a number of natural fears. One of these fears is that the mother is destroyed, or too damaged to take care of her baby. Some symbolic adult ramifications of this fear are discussed in Chapter 6. More relevant for sex, however, is the fear that the mother has correspond-

The arrangement, of course, is an unstable one. Vicarious bliss has some advantages over direct bliss (imagination fills in gaps, glosses over blemishes), but no vigorous person willingly makes do with it as his or her whole portion. The infant in every adult wants pleasure unlimited and uninterrupted by the ebb and flow of another creature's impulses. On some level woman, like man, resents the other person's uncontrollable erotic rhythm. This resentment is softened in the mother-reared woman by her greater emotional access to vicarious delight. On the other hand, it is sharpened by the crucial physical fact that in coitus she is far more dependent on the man's erection than he is on her vaginal responsiveness. Men have doubtless always sensed the explosive potentialities of this fact: it feeds into their archetypal nightmare vision of the insatiable female, and deepens their feeling that the unleashing of woman's own erotic impulses would disturb the precarious heterosexual peace.

The independent sexual impulsivity of the female, then, is feared because it recalls the terrifying erotic independence of every baby's mother. To soothe the fear, we subordinte Eve's lust to Adam's, but this cure only makes the sickness worse: subordinated, Eve's lust is more frightening still.

Woman's sexuality is under doubly explosive pressure. Her

---

ing intentions to eat her baby. A genitally demanding woman reactivates this fear. (A genitally demanding man who "uses her up" could also, in principle, reactivate it in a woman. But his bodily dissimilarity to the mother, and the fact that he is trying to push himself into the other person rather than suck the other person into himself, make the fear less literal for her. In any case, what matters is that man's fear can make coitus impossible, so woman is careful to avoid evoking it. Her fear merely results in frigidity, which need not worry him unduly since it does not preclude coitus, or even conception; indeed, frigidity on her part can help to assuage anxiety on his.)

A related impulse —often acted upon by the nursling who has acquired teeth— is to hurt the mother by biting her. The archetypal "vagina dentata" myth (see Hays) embodies the sensible anxiety that she will bite back. Such anxiety, of course, is much less readily evoked by a quiet, passive woman than by an actively lustful one.

One thing women sense —or learn— is that they must avoid behavior which stirs up alarms of this kind in men.

physical situation in coitus, as compared with man's, has in it much more of the infant's dependence on an imperfectly reliable source of fulfillment. Yet it is she who must make reparation to him for what both endured as babies. Coital satiety (to be fucked as the baby would like to be fed: on demand and at the rate one chooses and as long as one wants) is for anatomic reasons a chancier* matter for her than for him; and in addition she is for social and emotional reasons less free to seek it out. Inevitably, like any other suppressed force, her sex impulses come to seem boundless, ominous. And inevitably, this makes it more urgent to suppress them.

Roots in early childhood

The feelings discussed in the preceding section are primarily male feelings. Women share them only vicariously. But there are factors working to mute female lust that stem from a peculiarly female emotional situation. This situation takes shape not in infancy but in very early girlhood.

To repeat what I pointed out above in connection with sexual possessiveness, the mother-father-child triangle that Freud has called Oedipal is apt to arouse much more symmetrically balanced feelings in the girl than in the boy: since the homoerotic side of this triangle is older and more openly acceptable in her case than in his, she is not so purely the rival of the mother as the boy is the rival of the father. (Not only is her own jealousy more ambiguous than the boy's; her same-sex rival is herself more mildly, ambiguously jealous than the boy's is. The mother, to be sure, is an earlier, less rational authority, and in that sense a more formidable competitor than the father; still, competition with her is less apt to feel acutely risky since she is likely to feel less

---

* This chanciness in itself could tempt her to settle for the vicarious (mama) role in the you-be-mama-I'll-be-baby game instead of risking disappointment in pursuit of the direct (baby) one: combined with this temptation, the social and emotional pressures to accept the vicarious role are usually irresistible.

resentful than the father of the claims her child makes on her spouse.)

What is salient for the girl at this stage is not so much rivalry as another, more primitive problem: the realization that she must now, in some basic way, start to renounce, let go of, her first, life-giving love. To yield wholeheartedly to the charm of the opposite sex, she —unlike the boy— must shift a large portion of her early animal-poetic passion away from the parent to whom it was at first exclusively attached. The boy faces a clear crisis of nerve. She must handle a more diffuse, pervasive guilt, a vague sense of disloyalty, an ancient, primal fear of loss.

The sacrifice of sexual spontaneity, the curbing of sexual will-fulness, that men will require of her in adult life can serve her own purposes, too, then: It can serve as a penance for this per-vasive guilt. In turning toward man, but forgoing the vigorous pursuit of "selfish" body pleasure with him, she can achieve some of the heterosexual rapport that her love for her father taught her to want, and at the same time allay this primal fear of loss.

Woman's need for penance and her sense of primal loss are complicated, moreover, by the other large fact about the girl's Oedipal situation that was discussed above: the fact that the infidelity to her first love that began in this period typically went far deeper than her shift toward the second actually required. The sacrifice of full bodily pleasure with man, which I have heard described as "the gift to the mother,"* atones for something more than the partial desertion of her that the girl's growth toward heteroerotic susceptibility would in itself inevitably entail. What the girl has been guilty of is lavishing upon her father —that is, upon man— not only the erotic recognition, and the warmth and trust, that he on his own could inspire in her, but also much of the physical affection and filial-romantic gratitude that would have remained attached to her mother —that is, to woman— if they had been integrated with the child's inevitable antagonisms toward her. What she has done is to give away to someone else

_____
* Annette Overby, personal communication.

love that a part of her knew belonged rightly to the mother, in order to spare herself an emotional effort that seemed —but was not really— unnecessary.* The result is that she has cut herself off from a continuity with her own early feeling, for which she now mourns. It is in part to propitiate her fantasy mother, to punish herself, and thereby to regain some of this inner continuity that she holds back the final force of her "selfish" carnal passion for man. She holds it back out of love for him too, out of unwillingness to alarm him and pleasure in acceding to his wishes; but also out of anger at herself and at him: anger at a gratuitous betrayal of her oldest root in life, a betrayal for which she was responsible but of which he (in the form of his original parental predecessor) was the instrument.

But feelings of guilt and loss connected with her first love are not the only preoccupations that work to take the edge off woman's sensual passion for man. She tends also to feel more preoccupied than he does, while they are making love, with the opportunity to achieve vicarious homoerotic contact, and in this way to steal back some of what life has taken away from her: she is apt to be busier than he is imagining herself in the other person's situation, more engrossed in the other person's access to her own body and thus less engrossed in her own access to the other person's body.† And in the meantime this holding back, this abstention from full use of the male body as a source of direct pleasure for herself, can also express another, related, feeling: a grudge against the male, her rival for her first, female, parent. The grudge is not normally strong enough to make him unattractive to her. But she can reconcile resentment and attraction by embracing him and at the same time vengefully using the embrace for an ulterior purpose: to get access to the mother again after all.

* Recognition of this fact is an important step toward solidarity among women (as well as toward freer, less grudging female enjoyment of male charms).

† There are other forces, too, that converge to push her into this vicarious position, that work to make her use herself as a mirror for other people's experience. These are discussed in Chapter 6.

The mother-raised woman, then, submits to the mother-raised man's demand that she mute her own adult lust; and in submitting she consoles herself by betraying him and going back to her first, infant, love. She avenges herself on him by making him her instrument of re-access to what she has renounced. But it is a weak consolation and a poor revenge. For her re-access is only second-hand, and her old feelings of guilt and loss only feebly assuaged. What she is giving up is the right to use her body's sensuous capacities as directly, concretely, immediately as she did in the original embrace.

Sexual Excitement and Personal Sentiment

Closely related to the two aspects of the double standard of sexual behavior discussed above (at least in our own culture) is a third psychological sex difference: that carnal excitement tends to be more firmly tied to strong personal feeling in women than in men.

This tendency, like some others discussed just above, is supported by a fact that follows inexorably from our prevailing child-care arrangements: since the first parent is female, heteroerotic feeling has deeper roots in infancy for men than for women.

A male disability and a female one

What these deeper roots mean is that in intimate relations between a man and a woman he is in one very important respect more vulnerable than she is: She can more readily re-evoke in him the unqualified, boundless, helpless passion of infancy. If he lets her, she can shatter his adult sense of power and control; she can bring out the soft, wild, naked baby in him.

Men try to handle this danger with the many kinds of sex-segregating institutions that they seem always and everywhere driven to create.* Secret societies, hunting trips, pool parlors,

* As I shall show in Chapters 6, 7, and 8, this male preference for all-male colleague groups has a number of other psychological determinants too, all of them rooted in the fact that women are the first parents. This root fact is

wars—all of these provide men with sanctuary from the impact of women, with refuges in which they can recuperate from the temptation to give way to ferocious, voracious dependence, and recover their feelings of competence, autonomy, dignity.

But they need other safeguards too. Short of avoiding women altogether, the best safeguard is to renounce the opportunity for deep feeling inherent in heterosexual love. One way to do this is to keep heterosexual love superficial, emotionally and physically. Another is to dissociate its physical from its emotional possibilities.

Woman is less vulnerable to this danger: In the sexual recapitulation of the infant-mother interplay, she has more of a sense than he does of embodying the powerful mother within herself; a greater part of her than of his reliving of the infant role is vicarious, through the other person. This makes her less afraid of being plunged back into the atmosphere of helpless infancy, and therefore typically better able to fuse intense emotional and intense physical intimacy.

Unfortunately, however, she is also typically less able to *separate* these two feelings when it would be appropriate to do so. Indeed, the gentlest hint that such separation may sometimes be appropriate is obnoxious to many women. To give way to bodily lust for a man without a sense of magical personal fusion with him seems to them unworthy, or dangerous, or degrading; incapacity to do this seems to them a mark of human dignity, rather than the disability which in fact it is. For this disability, there are many well-known practical reasons (women's economic and social dependence makes them emotionally clingy; sex is a more serious matter for them because it can make them pregnant; etc.). But there are also other reasons, less widely understood and at least as important.

I said above that a woman can assuage guilt about betraying her first, homoerotic, love in sex with a man by renouncing the

---

of course mutable. But the preference is so fierce, and so hard for many people to imagine outgrowing, that theories are spun (see Chapter 4, note 2) to show that it must stem inexorably from something in our species' gene structure.

pursuit of "selfish" bodily pleasure with him. But there is also another way for her to assuage this guilt: she can find that she is unable to give way to sensual delight except when romantic love —love shot through with the flavor of the original blissful mother-infant union— has flooded her being. This solution allows her to reap the joy of heterosexual carnality while keeping some magical, loyal connection to her earliest tie. (In her case, unlike his, the sense of catastrophic helplessness that return to the atmosphere of the old union can rekindle is kept within bounds by her own gender continuity, and her partner's gender discontinuity, with the first parent. And to the extent that she does feel painfully helpless with him, her pain [see Chapter 8] redresses for both of them an old imbalance: now it is mama who cries for baby and baby who lets mama cry.)

The hapless tendency of many women to melt into a feeling of emotional closeness with any man who manages to excite them sexually is related to still another factor: The mother, as a number of writers point out, is likely to experience a more effortless identification, a smoother communication, with a girl baby than with a boy baby. With him, there is more difference and separateness, more of a barrier to be bridged. This means that girls and boys are likely to be treated differently in the prototypic adult-infant situation in which bodily intimacy first occurs. The nature of this difference helps account for the differing degrees of ego-distinctness that they later bring to sex. The girl, as she did at the beginning, melts more easily into the personality of the person to whose flesh she is drawn. Infancy has not taught her, as surely as it has taught him, to feel simultaneously the boundaries of herself and the current between herself and what attracts her.

A male "solution"

For reasons that so far as I know remain to be explored, the degree to which men and women differ in their need and/or ability to dissociate personal love from sex feeling varies from one historical or cultural situation to another. (The present account does not explain this variation: clearly, it depends upon factors that have not been considered here.) But to the extent that it is in fact emotionally feasible for him to maintain such a dissociation, there is one further function, not yet mentioned, that it can always serve for a mother-raised man: It can help him to cope with the problem of ambivalence toward the first parent.

For this problem, as I have been pointing out, the Oedipal triangle offers the girl, but not the boy, a solution of sorts. (To repeat: she can dodge the work of healing the split between bad and good feelings toward the first parent by shifting a substantial portion of the magically good ones onto the second, so that her love for the opposite sex comes to be infused with the infant's grateful passion toward the mother while most of the hostile, derogatory attitudes remain attached to their original object.) The boy cannot use his father in this way without giving homo-erotic attraction a dominant place in his love life. If woman is to remain for him the central human object of the passions most deeply rooted in life's beginnings, his relation to her must embrace, at a primitive level, *both* the worshipful and the derogatory, the grateful and the greedy, the affectionate and the hostile feeling toward the early mother.[3]

(Before going further, it seems best to stop and acknowledge a question that may well, by now, be irking the reader so seriously that a digression which articulates it —even an arbitrarily timed digression— will be felt as a relief: What makes me think that any conceivable child-care arrangement could magically dispel the problem of infantile ambivalence? What good would it do, after all, if fathers were as actively parental from the beginning as mothers and ambivalence therefore extended impartially to all our relations with people instead of focusing mainly on women? Trial readers of this chapter have asked this question with levels of indignation ranging from gentle to vituperative. It is a question that I start answering in Chapter 6, and continue answering in every chapter after that. If I were unaware of it, or had no clear idea what to say about it, indignation would indeed be justified. If you are too impatient to hear me out, skip, for example, to page 93, or 133–34, or 191.)

To return, then, to our discussion of male heterosexual ambivalence: One way a man can handle this fundamental difficulty is to sort out the conflicting ingredients into two kinds of love, tender and sensual. Lust then carries all the angry, predatory impulses from which the protective, trusting side of his love for woman must be kept insulated. He may keep tender and sensual love separate by expressing them toward different women, or toward the same woman in different situations or moods. Or he may largely bury one side of his heteroerotic feeling, giving direct expression mainly to the other.

Another way he can handle the difficulty is to mute all animal-poetic feeling for other people. In this case, romantic and sexual interest play such a minor role in his life that women can remain the central object of such interest without causing any serious inner tumult. The result may or may not be a general constriction of the emotional flow between the man and his world. If not, what happens often enough to color the whole climate of history is that his passion can flow into work —that is, into the exercise of competence in the public domain— while his heteroerotic affection stays absent-minded and tepid, his sex life perfunctory. A man like this need not be literally polygamous: his wife is still apt to feel that he is "married" to his business, to the army, to the sea, to science as much as to her, or more so, while she is married only to him. A sex relation that he finds quite adequate to his needs is apt to leave her dissatisfied in one of two ways: Either it engages her deepest feelings, which she then finds unreciprocated, since his are engaged elsewhere; or it does not, in which case she feels centrally restless, her personal depths untapped, stagnating. It has often been pointed out that women depend lopsidedly on love for emotional fulfillment because they are barred from absorbing activity in the public domain. This is true. But it is also true that men can depend lopsidedly on participation in the public domain because they are stymied by love.*

* Freud, and more recently Marcuse and Brown, emphasize the malignancy (of which more in Chapters 7–9) in the shift of energy away from erotic into "civilized" activity. But they are referring to the general taboo —in part

Consequences for the atmosphere between the sexes

The tendency of the sexes to differ in their ability to integrate, or separate, sensuality and sentiment has the same early origins, then, as the double standard. It also has the same worldly outcome. It originates in mother-dominated childhood and it contributes to the overall subordination of women. A woman's lust for a man is likely to tie her to him emotionally more closely than his lust ties him to her. Affection is likelier to keep her physically faithful to him than him to her. If he has a strong animal passion for her, his human loyalty and protectiveness may well be reserved mainly for another woman. If she is the one he tenderly loves, she may well have to make do with a sexual pittance. If he has not split off affection from lust —and sometimes even if he has— the chances are that he has muted both, turning most of his passion into realms from which she is excluded. His trouble fusing tender and sensual feeling, and her trouble separating them, enslaves and/or castrates her. She is typically dealing with a partner in some way heavily calloused, and he typically lives in an atmosphere of some kind of reproach: he is heartless; she nags and complains.*

The Upshot

The higamous-hogamous adult consequence of mother-dominated childhood maims both sexes. It makes women —for inter-

---

societally imposed and in part intra-psychic— against direct expression of carnal feeling. What I am talking about here is a specific source of tension in the male-female tie, generated by our prevailing early-child-care arrangement, which works to shunt off into compulsive public activity some male passion that could be spent more appropriately and harmlessly in bed. The mid-1960s peace movement slogan "Make Love Not War" refers to this pathological shunting. But how many of the men who shouted it proved friendly to the sudden female demand for re-examination of our sexual status quo that soon followed?

* See Greer's (*The Female Eunuch*) and Firestone's (*The Dialectic of Sex*) recent portrayals of her castration and his heartlessness.

nal, not only external reasons— normally less able than men to
defend their interests against rivals; or to give free rein to erotic
impulse; or to enjoy sex (in the special way that it can be so
enjoyed) without deep personal involvement. And at the same
time, it makes men —for complementary internal reasons—
normally less able than women to accept the fact that it is impossible wholly to monopolize the erotic interest of another person
without crushing the untameable part of that person which makes
her/him erotically interesting; or the fact that the other person's
sexual impulses and rhythms are by no means automatically
synchronized with one's own. It also makes them more frightened
than women of the crucial realm of personal feeling to which sex
offers access.

The maiming of men under higamous-hogamous conditions is
in some respects more cruel than the maiming of women. The
truth of emotional experience —their own and others'— tends on
the whole to be more threatening to them. As a result their freedom to feel emotional intimacy —with themselves and with
others— tends on the whole to be more constricted, hemmed in
by the massive denial which is necessary to keep so much truth at
bay. And their physical sex pleasure —though wider-ranging than
women's and much less likely to be plumb thwarted— is likelier
to be impoverished by dissociation from deep personal feeling.

Nevertheless, both sexes see the double standard —quite correctly, I think— as more damaging to women. Men are on the
whole content with it, and women on the whole pained by it, for
the simple reason that it is women who bear the brunt of the
crudest, most primitive constriction to which the double standard
gives rise: Our sexual arrangements make for a head-on clash
between a fact of human anatomy and the emotional constraints
that stem inevitably from what Washburn calls the "fundamental
pattern" imposed by evolutionary pressures "on the social organization of the human species."*

* This is just one of a number of such clashes. (Chapter 2, for example,
pointed to a corresponding clash between this "fundamental pattern" of
gender organization and the needs of the higher central nervous system.)

Anatomically, coitus offers a far less reliable guarantee of orgasm —or indeed of any intense direct local genital pleasure— to woman than to man. The first-hand coital pleasure of which she is capable more often requires conditions that must be purposefully sought out. Yet it is woman who has less liberty to conduct this kind of search: the societal and psychological constraints inherent in our "fundamental pattern" leave her less free than man to explore the erotic resources of a variety of partners, or even to affirm erotic impulse with any one partner. These constraints also make her less able to give way to simple physical delight without a sense of total self-surrender — a disability that further narrows her choice of partners, and makes her still more afraid of disrupting her rapport with any one partner by acting to intensify the delight, that is, by asserting her own sexual wishes.

The bodily bind in which this contradiction puts women —less leeway to pursue a primitive goal which is itself more elusive— is part (not the main part, but a vital part) of the reason why it is mainly women, not men, who are urging upon our species the terrifying task of reorganizing its technologically obsolete gender arrangements. As everyone on some level really understands, the issue at stake is not only freedom to seek out genital pleasure but something more as well: the sexual realm under dispute is a wildlife preserve in the civilized world, a refuge within which inarticulate, undomesticated private creative initiative is protected from extinction (See Box F.)

What the double standard hurts in women (to the extent that they genuinely, inwardly, bow to it) is the animal center of self-respect: the brute sense of bodily prerogative, of having a right to one's bodily feelings. A conviction that physical urges which one cannot help having are unjustified, undignified, presumptuous, undercuts the deepest, oldest basis for a sense of worth; it contaminates the original wellspring of subjective autonomy. Fromm made this point very clearly when he argued, in *Man for Himself*,

---

It is the tension these inner frictions generate that makes our species' life keep growing and changing in the special way that it does.

that socially imposed shame about the body serves the function of keeping people submissive to societal authority by weakening in them some inner core of individual authority.*

Antagonism to the body is not, of course, simply imposed by society. It does not stem solely from external constraints designed

---

Box F

Women who act openly interested in getting more genital pleasure are suspected of wanting to take the bit in their teeth in a more general way too — that is, of threatening to overthrow the overall human dominance of men. And conversely women who do challenge the overall human dominance of men are suspected of being "frustrated" — that is, of wanting, or at least needing, more genital pleasure. Women are thus taunted into declaring themselves enchanted with their genital situation on pain of being branded emotionally unfeminine (bossy bitches, controlling, assaultive, selfish —in short, man-like— and hostile to the human dignity of actual men). And at the same time they are bullied into certifying themselves delighted with the prevailing male-female power relations on pain of being branded sexually unattractive (bitter bitches, incapable of getting and holding the love of a good man, unable to inspire the kind of phallic servicing that keeps truly beloved women content with their lot).

What everyone correctly senses is that if women are capable of more genital pleasure than they get now, and manage to find it, they will become more willful, less easily subordinated as people; and that, conversely, if they are capable of more human willfulness than they now show, and manage to win a real share of the worldly power now monopolized by men, they will become sexually more demanding. It is hard to tell which threat —the sexual or the worldly one— defenders of our old arrangement find more basically alarming.

---

* This was his simpler, more sunny-minded reformulation of Freud's dark point, in *Civilization and Its Discontents*, about the sublimation of sexual into societally "useful" energy, a process which to Freud meant that the growth of civilization and its increasingly deadly character have been intrinsically inseparable.

to foster social obedience. It is an attitude with deep spontaneous roots in the psychological situation of our species (see Chapter 7). It is often used, moreover, to express not compliance, but defiance, independence, strength of will: fleshly ordeals such as fasting —and celibacy— are typically undertaken by humans in a spirit of willful, autonomous personal choice. But the burden of sensual self-abnegation imposed on women by the double standard is not undertaken in a willful spirit. It is passively accepted; and for this reason it does work as Fromm indicated that sensual self-abnegation can work: it helps make women in a special way humble, dependent, malleable.

The chronic bodily muting accepted by "feminine" women is the opposite of dramatic and self-assertive: it wholly lacks the brightness and clarity of a hunger strike or a religious vow of abstinence from sex. Occasionally women flare up a bit and use it vengefully, affirming it as a sign of their own moral superiority to, and power over, the abjectly lust-ridden male.* On the whole, however, the female burden of genital deprivation is carried meekly, invisibly. Sometimes it cripples real interest in sexual interaction, but often it does not: indeed, it can deepen a woman's need for the emotional rewards of carnal contact. What it most reliably cripples is human pride.

---

* "Idiots, all of them!" cackles Polly Peachum's old mother in the Brecht-Weill *Threepenny Opera*. She is singing a song of triumph over Mack the Knife, who can be trapped because he cannot resist the whorehouse. ("Because he knows what women do to him, he thrusts them well out of his way. He cries, 'I've mastered it, without half trying!' but comes the night and once again he's lying.") But she is singing in the dark. Mack enslaves "good" women more deeply and permanently than they can ever ensnare him: He is polygamous; they are monogamous. He has roots in rowdy male fellowship and in (criminal) enterprise; they brood about him, yearn for his return, and bicker with each other. As for "bad" —that is, shared— women, and the murderous, impotent rage that they feel in the face of man's contempt, think of Jenny Diver's "Black Freighter" song.

Notes Toward Chapter 5

So: as long as it is women who are mainly in charge of children the double standard will survive. The harsh truth is that no societal compromise which changes other features of woman's condition while leaving her role as first parent intact will get at the roots of asymmetric sexual privilege.

Even if this truth were widely understood, however, there are many otherwise staunch feminists who would shrink from acting upon it. It is one thing to want change in the educational, vocational, and legal status of women; it is quite another thing to start tampering with Motherhood.

Motherhood is a subject for countless bitter jokes, and a swelling contemporary folklore is devoted to the baleful effects of mothers. Still, most of us go on feeling that the mother-child tie is in some real sense sacred: whatever else it may be, it is clearly the most fundamental, universal, biologically sturdy tie we have. To conserve the integrity of this tie, many people would argue, some minimal asymmetry in the sexual prerogatives of men and women —especially if hedged about by more humane laws and customs— may be a reasonable price to pay: why jostle the primitive cornerstone of human solidarity precisely at this time, when all the other age-old forms of primary group structure —extended kin groups, permanent intimate work groups, stable neighborhood communities— are menaced by technological change?

The trouble with this argument is that the frightening task

of recreating viable bases for primary group life cannot be approached without jostling just what we feel, in our fright, least willing to jostle. To take on a task of such an order —and we are confronted with a number of tasks of such an order— we must mobilize vast resources of realistic, responsible, adult strength; and this is exactly the kind of strength that we will continue to lack so long as woman-dominated child care continues. We do not in fact have the option of putting up with the higamous-hogamous rule in order to stave off societal chaos. This option is a mirage, for it is precisely in the childhood conditions which make that rule inevitable that our helplessness to stave off chaos is rooted: The primitive cornerstone of human solidarity is also the primitive cornerstone of human pathology.

Central to the structural weakness built into our species' life is an imbalance between the overwhelming sturdiness of the mother-infant pair and the fragility of the father-infant pair. It is this imbalance —given the mental complexity of human young— that makes the internal stresses of the parent-child triangle so fatefully hard to handle. The special and exclusive bond between women and children underlies the half-recognized monstrosity implicit in the mermaid and minotaur myths. We lean heavily on the reliability of this bond; yet it is part of a congenital deformity that we must now outgrow before it kills us off.

What makes Motherhood reliable is that the erotic flow between the child and its female parent is primed by a set of powerful postpartum mechanisms, mechanisms which prompt not only women, but also simpler she-mammals, to nurture and protect their young.* What makes Motherhood monstrous, atavistic, is that we force these primitive biological underpinnings

---

* The reliability of Motherhood is also guaranteed, of course, by the powerful economic, educational, legal, and other societal pressures that force women to accept their traditional responsibility for children. But these pressures are themselves ramifications (to borrow Margaret Mead's phrase) of the mammalian tie, practical ramifications which we are now technologically free to reconsider and reshape.

— which are neither specifically human nor designed to do
more than guarantee the brute survival of the newborn—
to carry a peculiarly human, and wildly disproportionate,
psychological weight. (See Box G.)

The mammalian mechanisms for ensuring adequate maternal
behavior, together with the special emotional repercussions
of these mechanisms in the human mother, do on the whole work
wonderfully well to ensure that women will take good care of
small children. (They work far from perfectly, of course:
the harmonious physiological inter-responsiveness of the
mother-child pair can be disrupted for us by psychological
complications foreign to other mammals. [Cats and rats, unlike
humans, have no prudery about carnal contact, no fear of
parental responsibility, no erroneous learned beliefs about what
is good for babies.] Still, in women not critically thrown off
stride by this kind of complication, the female mammalian
machinery is indeed powerfully reliable: even under adverse
conditions —famine, for example, or parental feeble-mindedness
— which can weaken the more complex human motives, sharable
by fathers, that make adults nurturant toward children, this

(Continued on page 81)

Box G

In women, the bodily based postpartum ties to the newborn that we
share with cats and rats are crucially transmuted —just as sex, defeca-
tion, sleep, and other animal functions are transmuted— by their
setting in the human central nervous system.

Consider the milk let-down and the accompanying uterine contraction that can be triggered in a mother by the cry of a hungry infant.
These responses, which are as automatic as the dog's conditioned
salivation to the sound of Pavlov's bell, help to ensure that a woman,
like a cat or a rat, will feed her young promptly. The simple similarity, however, is overlaid with some vitally significant differences.

On the one hand, the let-down and the contraction are in the
woman's case neither so necessary nor so sufficient to ensure the

feeding of the young as they are in the cat's or the rat's case: Other parental motives make it highly likely that she would feed the baby anyway, and in the absence of these other motives she might well — since human parenthood is a long, heavy responsibility, and humans are able to think about the future even against the pull of strong physical feelings— abandon it anyway.

At the same time, her mammalian bodily responses carry for the human mother emotional consequences that they do not carry for the cat or rat. To begin with, her body sends information about feeling to her conscious self in a way that is possible only in a highly self-cognizant creature. By shivering suddenly, for instance, my body can tell "me" that I am more afraid than I realized; by tingling or bounding forward it can stir in "me" a surprised awareness of joy. In this same way a mother's body tells her, by letting down milk and contracting at its center, how passionately she is connected to the infant. Furthermore, feeling in a woman is shaped by remembrance and anticipation in a way that it is not in a cat or a rat. When the mother felt the child moving in her body, she looked forward to holding it in her arms, and perceived that a *person* was moving inside her. When she now puts this person to her breast, she remembers how it moved in her body. And her future feeling for the child, when this close postpartum tie has been outgrown and it is a rambunctious toddler (indeed even later, when it is a pimply adolescent, or a greying eccentric), will always be flavored on some level —as it could r ot be for a less intelligent mammal— with the memory of the passion which at this moment knots her belly and makes her nipples spurt.

It is in this transmuted form —this humanly self-aware and humanly durable form— that the woman's tie to the child embodies her continuity with far simpler fellow creatures. Yet we act as if this biological continuity in itself makes the tie in some mystic sense sacred, untouchable: to tinker with it, we feel —as if tinkering had not gotten us onto our hind legs in the first place— is to desecrate it. And so, quite blindly, we rely upon it to carry the whole early burden of a parental function incomparably more extensive and demanding than the cat's or the rat's, a burden the main part of which is no more intrinsically male than female, since it consists of nothing less than the first, psychologically most crucial, initiation of a new member of our species into the species condition.

The *absence* of a bodily postpartum tie between a man and his child, moreover, is subject to a corresponding transmutation: the fact that human bodies have human brains in them makes not only motherhood, but fatherhood, too, radically different for us than it is for cats or rats (or even for baboons or gorillas.)[1] *It is as true for men as for women that the question of what constitutes physiologically determined parental behavior must be answered in terms that embrace our own most distinctive physiological properties: the organs that govern our actions as parents include organs of intellect.*

It is precisely *because* he cannot carry the baby in his belly or give it milk from his bosom that the human father —with his capacity to imagine being what he is not, doing what he cannot, seeing what is gone or not yet here or out of sight— feels an especially vivid urge to use his other, more singularly human, capacities to nurture this baby. To him the neonate is not the small, writhing and squeaking, special-smelling lump of flesh that it is for the tomcat. It is a daughter or a son, a being started with his own seed whose long, mysterious gestation in the dark inside of another person he has typically been thinking about —often with impatience and jealousy— for many months; a being whose resemblance to his dead grandparents he is excited to notice, whose future as a companionable child and supportive adult and maker of grandchildren he anticipates, whose bodily growth and steady stream of ordinary achievements will soon be flooding him with joyful pride.

So far, men have had to act on this urge mainly in indirect ways: See Mead's and Hays' accounts, for example, of the various forms of couvade in culture after culture through which men take vicarious part in childbirth; or of the initiation rites through which they symbolically and passionately affirm that it is they who have themselves created human beings, as compared with the mere flesh spawned by woman. Think also of the anxious concern that men have so widely shown for immortality through heirs, and their efforts to control the sexual life of women to make sure that the children they sponsor really do come from their own seed: the tenuousness of their physical tie to the young clearly pains men in a way that it could not pain bulls or stallions.

It is now for the first time possible for us to rearrange the structure of our primary-group life so that men can act directly, rather than indirectly, on this specifically male and human urge of theirs, *this impulse to affirm and tighten by cultural inventions their unsatisfac-*

torily loose mammalian connection with children.° They need leeway to work out ways of making their actual (rather than their symbolic or vicarious) contact with the very young as intimate as woman's. And with the very young, actual contact is the bodily contact that keeps them clean, fed, tranquil, safe, rested, and mentally stimulated. "As intimate," obviously, does not mean qualitatively identical. It is precisely the irreducible qualitative *difference* between motherhood and fatherhood —the physical difference, as it is reflected and re-worked in the parents' thoughts and feelings— that gives men's passion for babies its own special male edge, its characteristic paternal flavor.

Not only is it now possible for us to achieve this rearrangement. For the reasons discussed throughout this book, it is now also urgent: it can, if time permits, make a momentous difference for our collective fate.

° Intrinsically, in fact, this connection may well be far less loose, in terms of capacity for spontaneous physical responsiveness to young, than the exigencies of human life make it seem. Rosenblatt points out, in his paper on the "maternal" behavior of adults other than the mother in rats, that with sufficiently intense exposure to infants males, as well as virgin females, show the same four impulses toward pups —crouching, retrieving, licking, and nest-building— as postpartum females: With appropriate stimulation, they, too, are driven by environmentally guided behavioral mechanisms of the kind that underlie what used to be called "maternal instinct."

bodily machinery of Motherhood works strongly to bind women to their young.)

Unfortunately, however, Motherhood also has another kind of reliability: it gives us boys who will grow reliably into childish men, unsure of their grasp on life's primitive realities. And it gives us girls who will grow reliably into childish women, unsure of their right to full worldly adult status.

Such men and women can be relied upon to seek each other out, for they have proverbially complementary emotional strengths and weaknesses. If we had cause to feel uncertain of the animal attraction between the sexes, and to worry about a falling birth rate, this reliable emotional interdependence might be a precious guarantee of human survival. But in fact we have precisely the opposite worry: not too few babies, but (considering the planet as a whole) far, far too many.

Indeed, the proverbial forms of emotional interdependence between men and women, far from being a guarantee of human survival, are at this point an active menace to it. Together, cozily interdependent male and female quasi adults are letting the fate of our species slip through their fingers: the males —who make public policy— through inadequate emotional contact with survival-essential considerations;* and the females —who have better contact with these considerations— through inadequate authority to make public policy. The terms on which we cohabit are terms that let us go on living as if mama —the fantasy mama of infancy— were still here beside us, breathing, in the room.

* The film *Dr. Strangelove* is a major, comically chilling, contemporary depiction of this male incapacity.

5

"Children!
Every One of Them!"*

In Chapter 4 I mentioned two special ways in which the hand that rocks the cradle helps make girls into childish and submissive women. First, mother-dominated infancy makes the prospect of adult sexual maturity (which in her case means tearing herself away from her first love) more problematic for the girl than for the boy. Second, mother-dominated infancy gives rise later, in sex, to a demand for female bodily self-abnegation, and women's compliance with this demand crucially reinforces in them the "feminine" qualities of obedience, humility, dependence.

But there is also a more general feature of what we think of as normal childhood that helps maintain human infantilism, a feature that underlies not only the pathetically babyish worldly self-insufficiency so widely characteristic of mother-raised women, but also the pathetically babyish bluster so widely characteristic of mother-raised men.[1]

The troubles faced by boys and girls as they try to become men and women differ in a more complex way than common-sense thought suggests: people nod their heads comfortably to the idea that a man must *prove* his manhood, while a woman just *feels* her womanhood. But much of what men are trying to prove (to themselves and each other) is that they are strong enough to withstand the kind of strength they imagine grown-up women possess. And much of what women are trying to feel is that they are really as grown-up, really as strong, as men imagine they are.

* A cliché: Men say it about women, and women about men.

A girl, like a boy, must model herself after the parent of the same sex* in some central respects, and then renounce dependence on that parent, establishing status as an equal and autonomous being. The crucial difference is that the girl's mother, the adult whose authority she must manage to incorporate inside herself, was at the point of first encounter a far more magically formidable being than the boy's father: She had powers more absolute than any that can possibly be encountered later, powers too strong to defy and too awesome to emulate. Her impact, moreover, was felt in that emotionally crucial period when feelings are formed entirely without words, feelings which then survive without ever being touched by words,[2] so that they never fall under the sway of more mature rational processes: The child's superstitious reaction to the first parent's power continues to live a subterranean life of its own, unmodified by that limited part of human sensibility which we call intelligence.

In discussing the boy's worries about becoming an adult, psychoanalytic thinkers emphasize his doubts about whether he can ever grow as large and virile as his father (and whether he can in the meantime avoid the father's vengeance for this and other rivalrous thoughts and achieve solidarity with him as an adult model). It may be that the boy does have more grounds than the girl for discouragement about the discrepancy between his own physique and that of the adult he is expected to become: the father's impressive external genitals, deep voice, heavy musculature, and (in some cases) overall hairiness that may indeed make him seem more drastically different to the boy than the mother's curves and pubic bush can make her seem to the girl.

---

* And/or other same-sex models, if any are available. In this respect, the extended family offers the child valuable alternatives. It does not, however, change the basic necessity to incorporate awesome adult power, and under prevailing conditions it is female adult power that is at the outset more awesome.

As Margaret Mead and others have pointed out, if the child lived in a less rigidly sex-dichotomized social milieu than those that now prevail, it would have still more alternatives, since opposite-sex adults with congenial temperaments or interests could also be drawn upon as models.

Still —as Mead remarks in *Male and Female*— this kind of discouragement is softened for both sexes in most human habitats by the fact that a continuous series of children and adolescents of graduated size and shape is visibly present, spelling out the steps between infancy and adulthood and helping to make this emotionally improbable physical transition intellectually more plausible.

What is far more discouraging, because far less available to objective external scrutiny, is the transition from the child's own world of thought and feeling to the inconceivable inner world of the same-sex adult. And this more discouraging transition is crucially harder to achieve in the girl's case than in the boy's: the inner world that she must come to embrace belongs, on an inarticulate level of awareness, to the magically powerful goddess mother of infancy. In comparison with this mysterious realm, the father's world, encountered later in childhood, is relatively accessible to rational delineation and realistically oriented fantasy. For both the girl and the boy, the power that she must try to incorporate has in it more of the uncanny than the power that he must try to incorporate: she comes to embody female authority less confidently than he comes to embody male authority; but female authority inspires a more primitive awe in him than male authority does in her.

The fact, then, that the infant's first extended encounter is with a woman, rather than with both a woman *and* a man, makes it in some ways harder to become a woman than a man. At the same time, it makes men in some ways more helpless with women than women are with men. The woman feels herself on the one hand a supernatural being, before whom the man bluffs, quails, struts, and turns stony for fear of melting; and she feels herself on the other hand a timid child, unable to locate in herself the full magic power which as a baby she felt in her mother. The man can seem to her to fit her childhood ideal of a male adult far better than she herself fits her childhood ideal of a female adult. This flaw in her sense of inner authority deepens from within a feeling of hers which society at the same time abundantly encourages from the outside: that she is unqualified for full worldly adult status; that she has no right to a voice in consequential public decisions; and therefore that she has no connection with the mainstream of human affairs except vicariously, through a man, so that without some personal alliance with him she can claim no formal place in human life.

In the preceding chapter, I suggested that the greater sexual permissiveness of women —their ability to tolerate the unilateral possessiveness of men, and to find some pleasure in lovemaking despite the requirement that they subordinate their own erotic impulses— rests upon their having incorporated, much more deeply than their partners, the richness of the opulent all-providing early mother. Yet it seems clear that women's acceptance of this kind of sexual disadvantage also rests upon the special female childishness discussed here. A sense of helplessness, of deficient adult authority, of having no right to assert oneself fully, surely reinforces (as well as being reinforced by) acquiescence to the double sexual standard. Can the same sexual permissiveness be an expression of more grown-up and at the same time of more infantile feelings?

Apparently it can: the prevailing atmosphere between men and women does seem to depend *both* on the woman's partial success in coming to feel that she embodies the resources of the original parent *and* on her partial failure to do so. She typically is, in sex, *both* more nurturing and supportive (i.e., adult) *and* more dependent and submissive (i.e., childlike) toward the man than he is toward her. He is likely to have grown, more fully and easily than she has, into a feeling or real possession of the status that the same-sex parent had in the eyes of the child. But at the same time, he feels in a certain sense permanently less adult than she does: the father whom he has more fully become is, at archaic strata of personality, not nearly so powerful a figure as the mother whom she has partly become. The respect this father inspired when he first emerged as a distinct figure had no roots in infancy.

Thus, both the things women say about the childishness of

men and the things men say about the childishness of women have a basis in fact: the boy is likely to succeed more completely than the girl at incorporating subjectively the authority of the same-sex parent; but this authority was at the outset more finite. On a primitive feeling-level, female authority is far more awesome to all of us. For this reason, woman incorporates it with a less thorough sense of inner conviction; and for the same reason, man resents her possession of it more keenly. (See Chapter 8.)

As a result, one important function served by the worldly infantilization of women is to reassure men that they themselves are now at least as grown-up, as tightly in touch with what is really what, as competent, provident, and invulnerable, as the parent who originally and magically embodied these qualities. And women, for their own reasons, comply with this arrangement. Their confidence in their human adulthood is flawed: they cannot fully feel inside themselves (what sane person could?) the supernatural power that the baby in each of us goes on believing a grown-up female must feel. They therefore make an implicit bargain with men: shakily posturing in the mother-goddess role that has been thrust upon them, and trying hard to persuade themselves that they can indeed fill it, they are in no position to quarrel with men's claim on a make-believe grown-up arena of their own. What we have worked out is a masquerade, in which generation after generation of childishly self-important men on the one hand, and childishly play-acting women on the other, solemnly recreate a child's-eye view of what adult life must be like.

Notes Toward Chapter 6

It seems clear enough that the double sexual standard, and the
complementary forms of childishness which our arrangements
foster in men and women, stunt both sexes' capacities for joy
and for dignity, and impair human competence to deal with the
present species-wide emergency. And yet both these features
of our social life are widely and vigorously defended: the
argument that they offer special advantages to women as well
as to men is raised again and again, and the thought of their
disappearance makes most people very anxious indeed. There
remains, even in fairly sophisticated circles, a feeling that in some
way —even if it *is* a neurotic way— these symbiotic emotional
arrangements draw the sexes together; that in tampering with
our traditional forms of male-female interdependence we
risk forfeiting the precious psychological benefits of sex itself.

In the next two chapters, I discuss some attitudes in which
no one can claim to see any glimmer of advantage for women,
attitudes that clearly push the sexes apart, making them enemies
and contaminating their straightforward carnal interest in each
other. The main way, in fact, that people manage to defend
these attitudes is to take them deeply for granted: The hate, fear,
loathing, contempt, and greed that men express toward women so
pervade the human atmosphere that we breathe them as
casually as the city child breathes smog.*

* Men who express these feelings in the conventional ways are not thought
of as woman-haters. But women who note, however mildly, that this is hap-

Most of us are so thoroughly adapted to this pollution of the everyday social medium —so desensitized to it, as one becomes desensitized to a steady rumble or stench— that we can sincerely claim not to be aware of it at all. Much of the work that feminists do is an effort to resensitize us to it: smog has to be identified as a problem before citizens can decide that they would prefer cleaner air. Hays' book provides the best-documented cross-cultural and historical survey I know to illustrate how virulently anti-female feeling has permeated our species' life, from Zulu and Bedouin and Asian folk customs, and Greek mythology, through medieval chivalry and nineteenth-century romantic poetry, to Strindberg's plays and *Look* magazine. Morgan's essay in *Sisterhood Is Powerful* provides a telling synopsis of the same situation in a series of quotations from male writers, from African and Chinese proverbs ("Never trust a woman, though she has given you ten sons"), Greek philosophy, and Islamic, Confucian, Hebrew, and Christian scriptures, through centuries of European literature ("And a woman," says Kipling, "is only a woman, but a good cigar is a smoke") to such moderns as Talcott Parsons, Benjamin Spock, Stokely Carmichael ("The only position for women in SNCC is prone"), Abbie Hoffman, and Eldridge Cleaver. And many other people —for example, Millet and Greer— have been showing how it poisons our present cultural milieu. My object here is not to add proof that this feeling exists, but to analyze its roots in the prevailing childbearing arrangements.

The long-range implication of this analysis, of course, is that no fundamental change in the situation of women can be achieved without full male participation in early child care.*

---

pening are quickly (in tones of heavy blame which imply that they have disqualified themselves as mentally balanced observers) dismissed as man-haters.

* This assumes —an assumption that some contemporary feminists regard as far too conservative— that men and women will continue to live together in mixed groups of some kind, and to beget and bear young through copulation and parturition.

But it also has two short-range implications for feminist activism: First, it is unreasonable to expect men to act as our brothers in the task of changing the sexual arrangements; this is too much to ask, even of those men who know that such change will benefit everybody, and whose outlook is in other respects humane. They cannot be our brothers until we stop being their mothers: until, that is, we stop carrying the main responsibility —and taking the main blame— for their early introduction to the human condition. There is no point at all in reproaching them for a hatred they are bound to feel; when they claim —in many cases sincerely— not to feel it, there is no reason at all to believe them; when they recognize and deplore it in themselves, there is no sense at all in trusting them to keep it under control.

Neither, however, can we go far toward changing the sexual arrangements without focusing on a related fact: What stops men from being our brothers also stops us from being each other's sisters. To ignore this fact —to identify the male as the sole source of our female sense of being hated and despised— is dangerously comforting; it encourages women to suppress important tensions among themselves which are then bound at some point to explode. For sisterhood truly to be powerful, the internal obstacles to human female solidarity must be faced, not evaded. What we ignore or deny at our peril is that women share men's anti-female feelings — usually in a mitigated form, but deeply nevertheless. This fact stems partly, to be sure, from causes that other writers have already quite adequately spelled out: that we have been steeped in self-derogatory societal stereotypes, pitted against each other for the favors of the reigning sex, and so on. But it stems largely from another cause, whose effects are much harder to undo: that we, like men, had female mothers.

6

"Sometimes You Wonder
if They're Human"*

When I was a child, people sang a popular song that foreshadowed for me, in an oddly disturbing way, a certain helpless, resigned adult astonishment.

> I never thought that anyone in his right mind
> Could treat a fellow human bein' so unkind.
> You went away and never left a note behind—
> Was that the human thing to do?

The singer, a woman, is in some muffled way shocked —as women somehow are, again and again, even when they have had plenty of time to get used to it— to find herself treated as if she were not an actual fellow creature. And she wonders without sharp anger whether the man himself is human, whether he is in his right mind. Women friends of mine say to me, in the same tone of dull surprise, "You know, *I think they're all crazy!*" And men draw cartoons like the one on the following page, the meaning of which women understand so immediately and so deeply that acute indignation, for inner reasons which they tend not to explore, is hard to mobilize.

Men's feeling that we are not really human originates in their infancy. It resonates, moreover, with the atmosphere of our own infancy: this is what most centrally muffles our shock, dulls our

* Old saw.

91

This is a classic cartoon, first printed in *The New Yorker* in 1945. Like Andersen's dream-image of the doomed, man-loving mermaid, it formed part of the amalgam of folklore and raw firsthand experience out of which my own early sense of our prevailing male-female situation grew. Another such cartoon, probably from *Esquire* in the late 1930's, sticks in my memory, but I have been unable to track it down for reproduction here. Two elderly men, prosperous dissipated-looking banker types, sit in a nightclub with a trussed-up, ultra-curvaceous young blonde chattel-type, who stares blankly into space. The one whose proud trophy she appears to be is saying to the other (as if she were a moody horse? a gurgling stroke victim? a stone idol that has just fluttered an eyelid and flared its nostril?) "Sometimes I think she's trying to tell me something."

indignation, when we encounter it. Our own reactive feeling —
that it is men who are not really human, "not all there"— comes
later and is far less primitive.

The earliest roots of antagonism to women lie in the period
before the infant has any clear idea where the self ends and the
outside world begins, or any way of knowing that the mother is a
separately sentient being. At this stage a woman is the helpless
child's main contact with the natural surround, the center of
everything the infant wants and feels drawn to, fears losing and
feels threatened by. She is the center also of the non-self, an
unbounded, still unarticulated region within which the child
labors to define itself and to discover the outlines of durable
objects, creatures, themes. She is this global, inchoate, all-embracing presence before she is a person, a discrete finite human individual with a subjectivity of her own.

When she does become a person, her person-ness is shot
through for the child with these earlier qualities. And when it
begins to be clear that this person is a female in a world of males
and females, femaleness comes to be the name for, the embodiment of, these global and inchoate and all-embracing qualities,
qualities very hard indeed to reconcile with person-ness as one
has begun to feel it inside oneself.

One result of female-dominated child care, then, is that the
trouble every child has in coming to see that the magic parental
presence of infancy was human, a person, can be permanently
side-stepped: Women can be defined as quasi persons, quasi
humans; and unqualified human personhood can be sealed off
from the contaminating atmosphere of infant fantasy and defined
as male.

This is why, so long as the hand that has rocked every cradle is
female, psychoanalytic theorists and taxi drivers will go on, in
their respective ways, complaining that the minimal, irreducible
individualism of women is unwomanly, and pontificating about
the masculine protest, and wondering angrily who wears the
pants. Operetta stars will go on warbling about "a little list" of
people who "never would be missed" which includes "the lady

novelist." And restaurants will go on courting customers with signboards like the one reproduced just below. For whatever core of clear self-feeling a mother-raised woman does manage to muster is inevitably perceived by her mother-raised associates as objectionably, presumptuously, male; it cannot possibly be seen simply as human.

When men start participating as deeply as women in the initiation of infants into the human estate, when both male and female parents come to carry for all of us the special meanings of early childhood, the trouble we have reconciling these meanings with person-ness will finally be faced. The consequence, of course, will be a fuller and more realistic, a kinder and at the same time more demanding, definition of person-ness.

Until then, women will continue to bear the brunt of our failure to face this trouble. Our gender arrangements, in other words, will go on making it possible for us to act out our early feelings toward the first parent in terms almost wholly unmodified by what we are later able to learn about this parent's actual human capacities, needs, and boundaries.

The discussion that follows examines the felt quasi humanity of woman from three perspectives. (Some overlap is unavoidable, but each needs separate consideration.) First, she is the object of deeply conflicting feelings toward existence itself. Second, we have trouble perceiving her as either wholly possessing or wholly lacking a subjectivity like our own. Third, she embodies the original non-self, a part of the infant's world which is both "it" and "you," and which feels both vitally necessary and vitally threatening to the formation of the "I."

The Mother as Representative of Nature:
Pre-Rational Ambivalence Toward the Source of Life

One basis for our species' fundamental ambivalence toward its female members lies in the fact that the early mother, monolithic representative of nature, is a source, like nature, of ultimate distress as well as ultimate joy. Like nature, she is both nourishing and disappointing, both alluring and threatening, both comforting and unreliable. The infant loves her touch, warmth, shape, taste, sound, movement, just as it loves dancing light, textured space, soft covers, and as it will come to love water, fire, plants, animals. And it hates her because, like nature, she does not perfectly protect and provide for it. She is the source of food, warmth, comfort, and entertainment; but the baby, no matter how well it is cared for, suffers some hunger or cold, some belly-aches or alarming sudden movements or unpleasant bursts of noise, some loneliness or boredom; and how is it to know that she is not the source of these things too?

The mother, then —like nature, which sends blizzards and locusts as well as sunshine and strawberries— is perceived as capricious, sometimes actively malevolent. Her body is the first important piece of the physical world that we encounter, and the events for which she seems responsible the first instances of fate. Hence Mother Nature, with her hurricane daughters Alice, Betty, Clara, Debbie, Edna. Hence that fickle female Lady Luck.

The envy-gratitude split

Melanie Klein provides an intense, poetically vivid account of this infant situation in her short, profound, controversial psycho-analytic treatise *Envy and Gratitude.**

* Many readers miss the point of this deeply startling little essay, mostly, I think, because it is threatening to them, but partly because of the difficult language in which it is couched. A reader afraid of the essay's emotional chal-

Her efforts to reconstruct "the patient's feelings as a baby at the mother's breast" have convinced her, she says, of the fundamental, lifelong consequences of the simple fact that in this situation, "together with happy experiences" there are "unavoidable grievances." The infant, for example, "may have a grievance that the milk comes too quickly or too slowly; or that he was not given the breast when he most craved for it, and therefore, when it is offered, he does not want it any more."* She writes of "the infant's desire for the inexhaustible, ever-present breast . . ." and of its "feeling that the mother is omnipotent and that it is up to her to prevent all pain and evils from internal and external sources . . ." The resulting attitude of destructive rage, which she calls envy, "spoils and harms the good object which is the source of life," for the child believes —and on some level will always believe— that angry thoughts damage their target. "If envy of the feeding breast is strong . . . full gratification is interfered with because . . . envy . . . implies robbing the object of what it possesses, and spoiling it." As a result, "a part of the self is felt as an enemy to the ego as well as to the loved object" and the child feels "recurrent anxiety that his greed and his destructive impulses will get the better of him . . ."

Envy, in Klein's sense, also engenders another kind of worry. The sense of having harmed "the breast" leads by a process of

---

lenge can easily escape it by ridiculing what is vulnerable in Klein's exposition. A reader interested in facing the challenge will try harder to hear the main things she is saying. The mental processes that Klein seems to attribute to three- or six-month-old infants, for example, should not be taken literally; her formulations are based on the play, dreams, and transference behaviors of older children and adults, who have recast memories of very early feelings into words and images that the infant did not possess. For this same reason, the term "breast" as she uses it must be understood not solely in its literal sense but also as a metaphor for "source of good."

* Interestingly, the experimental psychologist Hebb has made the same observation on a young chimpanzee. Finally offered a cup of milk for which she had been clamoring in vain, she dashed it to the floor. What this anecdote suggests is that as creatures approach the human level of complexity, their behavior takes on some of that destructiveness toward the self and what the self loves that we think of as human.

projection to "persecutory anxiety": ". . . the object that arouses guilt is turned into a persecutor," becomes the "earliest internalized persecutory object — the retaliating, devouring, and poisonous breast."

Threatened by bad feelings from within and (projected) hostility from without, the child is in danger of being cut off from its "good object" — that is, from its sense of connectedness to a benevolent and lovable outside force. The child handles this danger with what Klein calls a "splitting" mechanism: Its hateful feelings are sharply dissociated from its loving ones; the menacing, vengeful aspects of the mother (as she exists in the child's mind) are walled off from her comforting, providing aspects. The child comes to feel "that a good and a bad breast exist." The good breast remains intact, unsullied by badness, but it disappears altogether from time to time and a bad breast is there instead: ". . . early emotional life is characterized by a sense of losing and regaining the good object."

Later, when the infant is more able emotionally to endure the anxiety of experiencing such contrasting feelings toward a single object (and, I would add, more able cognitively to conceive of a single object so complex), the early splitting is to some degree overcome. A patient who has not managed to do this in infancy can sometimes do it afterward, Klein says, in psychotherapy. Such a patient achieves the insight that "the object's badness is largely due to his own aggressiveness and the ensuing projection." It is then possible to realize that the object "is not so bad as it was felt to be in its split-off aspects." This paves the way for "the urge to make reparation," which normally arises when the infant tries to integrate the good and bad "breasts." Reparation "involves counteracting destructive impulses by mobilizing feelings of love."

Klein's reconstruction of very early emotional life does not pretend to bridge the gap between the actual texture of the infant's experience and the terms in which psychoanalytic patients (and psychoanalysts) express themselves. Still, the feeling constellations that she describes correspond recognizably in their quality and their general shape with feeling constellations which are central in adult life, emotional states so inarticulate, so global, so profound that they do —in the same way that sexual joy does, for example, or the sense of desertion, or the experience of beatific mutual gazing— seem clearly to have roots in pre-verbal infancy.

Indeed, one of the core problems with which religion (whether it is labeled "religion" or not) tries to cope is precisely the interplay between "envy" and "gratitude." Dostoyevsky is writing, I think, about this basic interplay when he tells us how Alyosha Karamazov feels after his saintly teacher has died and begun —to the malicious delight of people who have all along been jealous of his sweet, joyous spiritual power— to stink.

> "I am not rebelling against my God," says he to a spiteful friend. "I simply 'don't accept his world.'" Characteristically cheerful, gentle, and mild, he is now irritable and depressed, ironical and reckless. Angrily, he violates his rules of diet with sausage, pollutes himself with vodka, and goes to a woman who in his mind stands for lust and vindictiveness. But while he is there she suddenly shows him her pain, her emotional generosity, and her need. The tide of his feeling for life begins to turn. Soon afterward he dreams of the wedding at which Christ turned water into wine, where his dead teacher, alive, takes his hand and pulls him toward kindness and rejoicing; then he goes out into the autumn night. He stands gazing — "and then suddenly threw himself down upon the earth. . . . He could not have told why he longed so irresistibly to kiss it, to kiss it. But he kissed it . . . and vowed passionately to love it, to love it forever and ever. 'Water the earth with the tears of your joy and love those tears.' His elder's words echoed in his soul."

Though it is seldom felt so purely and directly as Alyosha felt it, his swing between bleak dislike and utter love for what he thought of as God's world is humanly characteristic. Coleridge's Ancient Mariner felt it too.

In his opening comments nature goes back and forth, even within a stanza, from persecutory to alluring: the storm blast was "tyrannous"; but when "ice, mast-high, came floating by" he notes that it was "green as emerald." The companionable albatross, a "sweet bird," is welcomed "As if it had been a Christian soul." But wholly without warning, the narrator is moved to destroy it. Feeling toward him shifts from initial approval to heavy blame; his mates hang the corpse of his victim around his neck. Becalmed, all start to die of heat and thirst, and the horror of nature fills Coleridge's canvas: "The very deep did rot: O Christ! That ever this should be! Yea, slimy things did crawl with legs Upon the slimy sea." An uncanny skeleton ship bears down on them against an ugly sunset, without wind. Her crew, especially its female member, is ghastly: "Is that a DEATH? And are there two? Is DEATH that woman's mate? Her lips were red, her looks were free, Her locks were yellow as gold: Her skin was as white as leprosy, The Night-mare LIFE-IN-DEATH was she, Who thicks man's blood with cold." The two play dice. Death wins his comrades, and Life in Death wins the narrator. Accursed and alone, he loathes the world and himself: "A thousand thousand slimy things Lived on; and so did I." His heart, "dry as dust," cannot pray. "For the sky and the sea, and the sea and the sky Lay like a load on my weary eye, And the dead were at my feet." For a week he yearns to die. But then one night, like Alyosha, he looks at the sky, and suddenly, in what before had been "the rotting sea," in which "death-fires danced at night," he sees the "charmed water" burn red in the ship's shadow; he sees the water snakes that were "slimy things" before, and for him, as for Alyosha, the deep turn toward life begins: "They moved in tracks of shining white, And when they reared, the elfish light Fell off in hoary flakes. Within the shadow of the ship I watched their rich attire: Blue, glossy green, and velvet black, They coiled and swam; and every track Was a flash of golden fire. O happy living things! no tongue Their beauty might declare: A spring of

love gushed from my heart, And I blessed them unaware . . .
The self-same moment I could pray; And from my neck so
free The Albatross fell off, and sank Like lead into the sea."

To me, the passionate depth of this swing away from the world
and back, and its inaccessibility to will or reason, fit well with
Klein's suggestion that it is originally experienced by the nursling,
that it is first felt in relation to a parental being whose human
qualities are sensed, but only indistinctly sensed: an omnipotent
parental being, personal and purposeful enough to earn love for
what she provides and blame for every misfortune, and too vastly
contradictory to make any steady, integrated sentiment toward
her possible. The infant develops strong feeling for this being
long before it is able to recognize her —even partially— as the
finite, limited, vulnerable creature that she actually is. And this
special feeling seems to survive, and to seek an appropriate object, long after its original object has evolved into a mere person
(or in any case into that compromised version of a mere person, a
mere woman).

Rapacity and greed, responsibility and compunction

The early mother's apparent omnipotence, then, her ambivalent role as ultimate source of good and evil, is a central source of
human malaise: our species' uneasy, unstable stance toward nature, and its uneasy, unstable sexual arrangements, are inseparable aspects of this malaise. Both toward women and toward
nature as a whole —as originally toward the mother, who was
half human, half nature— we feel torn between two impulses:
the impulse, on the one hand, to give free rein to the nursling's
angry greed, its wild yearning to own, control, suck dry the
source of good, its wish to avenge deprivation; and the impulse,
on the other hand, to make reparation for these feelings, which
threaten to destroy what is most precious and deeply needed.
The balance between infantile destructiveness toward the
source of life, and the reciprocal surge of anxiety and good will

that keeps this destructiveness within bounds, varies from person to person, and from culture to culture. This balance is sometimes tipped more toward hostility and rapacity, sometimes more toward respect, concern, awe. It need not always be tipped in the same direction for women and for nature. The degree to which destructive and loving impulses are split off from each other is also variable. The main point is that there is always a balance, inherently tense and unstable, and that the destructive side of it is always lively.

What I have just said needs to be qualified in two ways. First, women are obviously not the only human targets of our central destructiveness. Men, and even children, are also treated as natural resources to be mined, reaped, used up without concern for their future fate;* as sources of labor to be drawn on with only our own interests in mind; as property to be seized, held, disposed of for our own profit. Men and children, however, are less adequate targets than women for this kind of feeling: they are not so readily classifiable with the early mother; it is harder — though of course possible— to overlook their humanity.

Men, moreover, are likely to feel internally less identified with the early mother, so that even when they cannot escape being treated exploitatively —indeed, even when they, like women, have been taught by society that as members of a given caste this is their appropriate lot— they are less apt to accept such treatment without clear-cut resentment. Women have, in some deeper sense, expected it all along.

Women, then, are both the most acceptable and the most accepting victims of the human need for a quasi-human source of richness and target of greedy rage. If this were not the case, if

---

* Indeed, women themselves are quite capable of transferring to men some of the attributes that originally belonged to the early mother, and of behaving accordingly. A classic literary example of this voracious using up of a husband's creative resources by a heartless wife is George Eliot's portrait of Lydgate and Rosamond in *Middlemarch*. The point is, however, that what seems monstrous when a wife here and there does it to her husband seems simply male —normally, heedlessly male— when a husband as a matter of course does it to his wife.

there did not exist a special category of human being who seems on an infant level of thought naturally fit to fulfill this infantile need, our species might be forced to outgrow it. Under present conditions, the availability of women as especially suitable victims encourages people to indulge the need, which then extends —since it is inherently insatiable— to embrace other victims as well.

Many other writers have pointed to the connection between the universal exploitation of women and the survival of an atmosphere in which the idea of exploitation in general remains acceptable. What I am trying here to add to this old insight is another, and doubtless stickier, point: The universal exploitation of women is rooted in our attitudes toward very early parental figures, and will go on until these figures are male as well as female. Only when this happens will society be forced to find ways to help its members handle the impulses of greed and rapacity that now make man "wolf to the man." *It is at this point that the human projects of brotherhood, of peace with nature, and of sexual liberty interpenetrate.*

A second qualification must be added to my statement that we all use women as targets of the primitive envy-gratitude ambivalence described by Klein. Both sexes do use women in this way. But the feelings women have about doing so are modulated by the fact that the early mother eventually does, at least to some degree, evolve for the growing child into an actual person. The girl child is likely to come to identify with this actual person more closely than the boy child. She is therefore apt to develop a livelier sense of compunction for her, and also for the figure of the early mother that remains, on archaic levels of awareness, connected with this later, more actual mother. In this compunction —particularly if the split-off antagonism that goes with it is recognized and integrated— lies a strong potential basis for solidarity among women. Men's affection for each other does not include anything like this tender, healing solicitude. They do not need to make reparation to each other for early feelings of greed and rage.

Neither, moreover, are men's solicitous impulses toward women the same as those that women feel toward women. The boy's restitutive urges toward the early mother —as echoed in later relations with her and with other females— are less tinged than the girl's with fellow-feeling. For him, the mother to whom reparation must be made is mainly an idol that has been flouted and must now be mollified lest she exact vengeance, a natural resource that has been assaulted and must now be restored lest it cease to provide, a living source of delight that has been tampered with, perhaps destroyed, and must now be coaxed back to life. For the girl, too, she is all these things; but she is also —more vividly than for the boy— a creature who has suffered injury just as one can suffer it oneself, and who needs to be soothed and protected just as one needs her to soothe and protect one's vulnerable self. (Colette's Renée in *The Vagabond* sees in a lesbian pair "the melancholy and touching image of two weak creatures who have perhaps sought shelter in each other's arms, there to sleep and weep, safe from man who is so often cruel, and there to taste, better than any pleasure, the bitter happiness of feeling themselves akin, frail and forgotten." But what has to be added to her account is that these "women enlaced" are sheltering each other not just from what men want to do to them, but also from what they want to do to each other.)

It seems to me possible that this component of the girl's reparative feeling extends to nature as well as to other women. What has kept women outside the nature-assaulting parts of history — what has made them (with striking exceptions, to be sure) less avid than men as hunters and killers, as penetrators of Mother Nature's secrets, plunderers of her treasure, outwitters of her constraints— may well be not only the practical procreative burden that they have carried, but this special compunction too. Certainly it seems reasonable to suppose that if men had felt all along more closely identified with the first parent —as they will if time permits us to make the necessary change in our child-care arrangements— we would not now be so close to the irrevocable murder of nature.

That we are in fact now so close to this final murder must, I think, have to do with the predominantly self-interested character of male reparative feeling.* Men's exploitation of Mother Nature has so far been kept in check largely by their conception of the practical risk they themselves ran in antagonizing, depleting, spoiling her. (In preliterate societies, we are told, ritual apologies are offered by hunters to the animals they kill, and by woodcutters to the spirits who inhabit the trees they chop down.) As technology has advanced, and they have felt more powerful, one part of this sense of risk —the fear of antagonizing her— has abated. A euphoric sense of conquest has replaced it: the son has set his foot on the mother's chest, he has harnessed her firmly to his uses, he has opened her body once and for all and may now help himself at will to its riches. What remains is the danger that she will be depleted, spoiled. Men's view of this danger has been fatally short-sighted; it has not kept pace with the actual growth of their destructive power. What has kept it so short-sighted has been, at least in part, the strength of their vindictive, grabby feelings. To maintain a longer, more enlightened view, these feelings —unleashed by their sense of conquest— would at this point have to be pulled back in, and kept under control, by a more powerful effort of will than they seem to be able to muster.

But our ambivalence toward the parent who is the first representative of nature consists not only of unstable, conflicting feelings of envy and gratitude, rapacity and compunction. It consists also of unstable, conflicting perceptions of her sentience. A central reason for woman's anomalous image, which (even in her own mind to some degree) combines, or fluctuates between, omniscient goddess and dumb bitch, lies in the trouble we have totally accepting the discovery —which cannot be totally re-

* This is not to suggest that it is *the* explanation, of course. Our predicament clearly also has to do with societal factors of the blind kind that Tolstoy described in *War and Peace* — historical and sociological processes whose overall shape does not at all coincide with any participant's motives, and only fragments of which are represented in any participant's awareness. But psychological processes of the kind referred to here —processes rooted deep in "normal" personality, and mutable only if confronted— must be an important *part* of the explanation.

jected, either— that this parent has definable, understandable subjectivity; that she embodies an autonomous awareness corresponding to our own.

The Mother as Representative of Nature:
The Semi-Sentient "She"

Mead and Hays, among others, have documented the tendency, expressed by people under a wide range of cultural conditions, to see in woman a mystic continuity with non-human processes like rain and the fertility of plants. The question is why this should be so much more the case for woman than for man, who has his own metaphoric continuity with these non-human forces. Rain and sun, for example, have been represented in myth as male sources of life that kindle and fertilize the female earth; the sea and its winds have been thought of as male; the upthrusting of trees and green shoots is often viewed as a phallic event. And yet such metaphors dominate people's everyday sense of what men are far less than their sense of what women are. D. H. Lawrence was right, I think, to complain that the animal mystery of men, the cosmic (or —to use the term broadly— religious) impact of their physical maleness, is on the whole underplayed in our life.

Mead suggests that it is the more visible, sustained drama, the more conspicuous mystery, of woman's role in procreation that makes her concrete presence seem so much more a center of magic non-personal force than man's. To Hays, the superstitious awe, often loathing, that surrounds menstruation and parturition, and links them to wider natural events, expresses the human male's ambivalent response to otherness, a response that connects what is not male (woman) with what is not human (nature). Both these explanations seem true as far as they go.*

What is also true, however, is that woman is the creature we

---

* Hays, though, does not explain how women, to whom femaleness is not otherness, are persuaded to lend themselves to the uncomfortable rituals that dramatize the male response he describes: are they bullied? brainwashed? just humoring their menfolk?

encounter before we are able to distinguish between a center of sentience and an impersonal force of nature: it seems extremely unlikely that the flavor of this early encounter could fail to survive as a prominent ingredient of our later feeling for her. The ambiguity in our perception of the mother's subjectivity is not explicitly mentioned in Klein's exposition, but it is implicit in the emotional events she describes; without it, they could not occur. This ambiguity seems to me an important part of the reason why people —men especially, but women too— have such a partial, unsteady grasp on the fact that women are human, and find it so hard to show ordinary human respect for them.

"It"ness and "I"ness

Every "I" first emerges in relation to an "It" which is not at all clearly an "I." The separate "I"ness of the other person is a discovery, an insight achieved over time. Small children do not completely have it (an example is the tendency of three- or four-year-olds to assume that you, whom they have just met, must somehow already know by name all the people they know) and the reader need not be told that there are many adults who have only a gross, rudimentary mental grasp of it. This fact of infancy, together with our female-dominated child-care arrangements, guarantees a more or less lopsided view of male and female "I"ness. The mother is first experienced by every one of us as "It," while the father, who is a much more peripheral presence at the beginning, becomes a significant figure only after the concept of an independent outside "I" has begun to be established. It would be strange if this early difference did not carry over, on a pre-rational level of feeling, into adult life.

A ship, a city, any entity that we half-seriously personify, is called "she." "She" designates the borderline between the inanimate and the conscious. De Beauvoir splendidly describes this quasi-human connotation of "she." In her account, man's assignment of the role of "other" to woman is a way of mitigating the loneliness of his place in nature. He commandeers woman's services as intermediary between his conscious self and the natural surround. And she accepts the role because it relieves her of primary responsibility for a burden he is willing to assume with her assistance: the burden of lonely subjectivity in a world that is otherwise (except as human imagination inhabits it with phantom subjectivities) soulless.

This analysis of de Beauvoir's seems to me entirely valid, but — like any analysis— incomplete. In Chapters 7 and 9 I try to carry it a step further. Here, what I want to add to it is the observation that woman, no matter what other changes take place in her situation, will remain fitted for this role as half-human "other," and can never escape it, so long as she agrees to go on being the goddess of the nursery.

The girl's difficulty in coming to accept the "I"ness of women is likely in one sense to be less serious than the boy's, since she comes to feel more identified with the first parent, and of course cannot help being "I" to herself. Unhappily, however, this difference also works in the opposite direction: her sense of continuity with the mother —who to some degree, on some level, remains "It" to all of us— makes her seem less of an "I" to herself.

Even to the daughter, the mother may never come to seem so completely an "I" as the father, who was an "I" when first encountered. The "It"ness that colors her perception of her mother colors her perception of every female presence, including her own.* And this view of herself is confirmed by what she sees reflected back in the eyes of others: if she is unamazed, unaffronted, to find herself looked at as "It," the original reason for this monstrous composure of hers (a composure which in turn re-

---

* This outcome is modified to the extent that she manages —as many gifted women do— to preserve her "I"ness by thinking of men, not women, as her real fellow creatures. This is a problem for political solidarity among vigorous women that cannot be wished away by denial or pushed safely underground by moral-ideological disapproval. On the other hand, once recognized for what it is, it may prove easier to surmount than certain obstacles to solidarity among men. For the impulse toward reparation, toward the passionate bridging of rifts, has older roots in infancy between women than between men.

validates the other person's view of her, legitimizes it by failing to challenge it) is the gender of the hand that rocks the cradle.

Conceptions of female sentience and demands on the natural surround

Our difficulty in coming to grasp the fact of the mother's separate human subjectivity (like our related difficulty in outgrowing the early feeling that she is omnipotent and responsible for every blessing and curse of existence) has central consequences not only for the way we look at women, but also for our stance toward nature. Because the early mother's boundaries are so indistinct, the non-human surround with which she merges takes on some of her own quasi-personal quality. In our failure to distinguish clearly between her and nature, we assign to each properties that belong to the other: We cannot believe how accidental, unconscious, unconcerned —i.e., unmotherly— nature really is; and we cannot believe how vulnerable, conscious, autonomously wishful —i.e., human— the early mother really was.

Our over-personification of nature, then, is inseparable from our under-personification of woman. We cannot listen to reason when it tells us that the mother —who was once continuous with nature— is a fully sentient fellow person; nor can we listen when it tells us that nature —which was once continuous with the mother— is wholly impersonal, non-sentient. If we could outgrow our feeling that the first parent was semi-human, a force of nature, we might also be able to outgrow the idea that nature is semi-human, and our parent.

But we will do this only when we are forced to do it, and we will be forced to do it only when both sexes have started to carry the emotional aura of the first parent. When all of us come to carry it, full human status can no longer be reserved for those who do not: Our conception of humanness will have to be expanded to embrace this early emotional aura; and our understanding of what the aura really is deepened to make it compatible with humanness. The feelings we all have toward the magic nurturer of infancy will have to be confronted, because they will have to be assimilated into our sense of what can be expected from, and what is owed to, a human person. *It is at this point that the human project of reconciliation between the rational and the pre-rational layers of our sentience interpenetrates with the projects of sexual liberty and of peace with nature.*

Meanwhile, unfortunately, the basic infantile belief that nature is our parent has not at all abated as our power to grab what we want from her has increased. As science and technology advance, formal theological belief in a parental deity has of course come to seem less plausible. But what has changed in the stance most people take toward nature-the-parent is not the destructive infantilism of this stance. What has weakened is a later-born feeling toward parental authority, a feeling which lies closer to the rational surface of awareness, and which is apt to be focused in good part on the father, who represents the more mature human world: that a parent can state valid moral imperatives, and impose predictable penalties if they are not met. The fading away of God the Father, the righteous judge, should in principle motivate his lopsidedly developed offspring to learn how to judge and govern themselves, but so far this has not happened. The loss of supernatural moral guidance in the light of scientific reason has not made people more grown-up; it has only unleashed the amoral greed of infancy.

Inextricable from the notion that nature is our semi-sentient early mother is the notion that she is inherently inexhaustible, that if she does not provide everything we would like to have it is because she does not want to, that her treasure is infinite and can if necessary be taken by force. This view of Mother Earth is in turn identical with the view of woman as Earth Mother, a bottomless source of richness, a being not human enough to have needs of an importance as primary, as self-evident, as the importance of our own needs, but voluntary and conscious enough so that if she does not give us what we expect she is withholding it on purpose and we are justified in getting it from her any way we can. The murderous infantilism of our relation to nature follows inexorably from the murderous infantilism of our sexual arrangements. To outgrow the one we must outgrow the other.

There is an additional way in which the early mother's continuity with nature contributes to our sexual situation. Not only is her own "I"ness ambiguous in the mind of the child; she also acts, for the child, as a central representative of that from which the self must be carved out.

The Mother as Representative of Nature: The Non-Self

Woman and the formation of the self

Each subjective self starts forming itself in a world which is both a stimulus and an obstacle to the self-forming venture. In this world, the mother is the most vivid and the most active presence.

On the one hand, her interested awareness is essential to the child's developing selfhood, which finds its own existence reflected, confirmed, in her recognition of it. The child's first experiments in action, its first efforts to see how its own voluntary behavior can bring about change in the environment, are crucially supported by her response to them. It discovers on its own that it can make something interesting come into view by moving a limb, make interesting sounds happen by exercising its vocal apparatus, and so on. But with her it discovers that the movements, sounds, and so on that it is able to produce at will can elicit different, but meaningfully related, movements, sounds, and so on from another creature: it can initiate events in which she will participate. Just as importantly, the way in which she initiates events assumes, recognizes, invites exercise of, the child's capacity for active, conscious, voluntary response. The child thus becomes aware of itself as an influential social being, important and attractive to those who are important and attractive to itself.

As Asch shows in eloquent detail, the human self develops in a social field consisting of mutually interpenetrating subjectivities: there can be no full-blown "I" without a "you" which is perceived as recognizing the "I," and as aware of being recognized by it as another "I." Paradoxically, the mother is never an unqualified "you" in this sense because she always retains some of the "It"ness that she had at the outset; yet she is the first —and for the original formation of the self the all-important— "you."

On the other hand, even while she provides this vital support for the early growth of the self, the mother is inevitably felt as a menace to that self. She is the outstanding feature of the arresting, sometimes overwhelming, realm within which the self's boundaries must be defined. The multiple rhythms of this outside realm, its pulls, pressures, and distractions, can threaten to swamp the nascent self's own needs and intentions, to blur its perception of its own outlines, to deflect its inner sense of direction and drown out its inner voice.

There is also the fact that when the active project of selfhood feels too strenuous or too dangerously lonely the temptation is strong in all of us to melt back into that from which we have carved ourselves out. The mother supports the active project, but she is also on hand to be melted into when it is abandoned. She may, indeed, even encourage the child's lapses from selfhood, for she as well as the child has mixed feelings about its increasing separateness from her. There is of course no such thing as a wholly benevolent mother, with no antagonism whatsoever to the child as an autonomous being.* But even if there were, she would be experienced by the child, in its struggle to become such a being, both as an interfering influence and as a lure back into nonbeing.

Adult consequences

So long as the first parent is a woman, then, woman will inevitably be pressed into the dual role of indispensable quasi-human

---

* Quite apart from the ultimate impossibility of human perfection, our gender arrangements militate in an immediate way against the chance that such a mother could exist. The early developmental situation under discussion here makes it hard for any of us —and mothers, too, were infants once— to come to real terms with the independent existence of other subjectivities.

supporter and deadly quasi-human enemy of the human self. She will be seen as naturally fit to nurture other people's individuality; as the born audience in whose awareness other people's subjective existence can be mirrored; as the being so peculiarly needed to confirm other people's worth, power, significance that if she fails to render them this service she is a monster, anomalous and useless. And at the same time she will also be seen as the one who will not let other people be, the one who beckons her loved ones back from selfhood, who wants to engulf, dissolve, drown, suffocate them as autonomous persons.

In adult life as we know it, it is of course women who are in reality most likely to be distracted, drowned, suffocated as individuals. What they are expected to provide for others, and to suppress in themselves, makes this axiomatic. Yet even so, it is they who are perceived as the naggers and the engulfers, the main menace to the autonomy, the human selfhood, of others. It is true, and by now widely understood, that woman's limited opportunity to develop her own self does in fact often make her batten on, and sabotage, the autonomy of others. But what I am pointing to is another, deeper-lying truth: that the threat to autonomy which can come from a woman is felt on a less rational, more helpless level, experienced as more primitively dangerous, than any such threat from a man.

The possibility that a man will interrupt a woman's train of thought, interfere with her work, encourage her to sink back into passivity, make her an appendage of himself, does not engender the same panic in most of us as the possibility that she will do this to him. The original threat that we all felt in this connection was felt as emanating from a woman, and we lean over backward in our heterosexual arrangements to keep this original threat at bay. We will have to continue to do so, in some way, until we reorganize child care to make the realm of the early non-self as much a male as a female domain.

New Ways

When we have achieved this reorganization, men will be less afraid of being drowned by women; but a fact which must be faced —and probably few of us are ready to face it without some sense of painful loss— is that they will not need women in the same way either. The precious captive female "other" that de Beauvoir has described and that men now need is the maternal "you" of infancy, kept on hand to go on helping the "I" in its continuous rediscovery and redefinition of its boundaries, but penned in, bottled up, so that it cannot suffocate or swallow the "I" as it once threatened to do. When the early parental "other" is no longer exclusively female, woman will no longer be peculiarly qualified to provide this kind of company.

Correspondingly, woman will be freed of her dependence on the vicarious experience of "I"ness now provided by man. She will be released from her present obligation to recreate in herself the maternal "you," and to lavish its benefits on man, whose need to protect himself from its dangers she is then forced to respect out of concern for his autonomy, which she is in turn privileged to enjoy second-hand. She will be no more worried than man about the possibility of drowning out or engulfing another person.

Under these conditions she will be as eager as man is to find some direct re-access to emotional contact with the original "other." The nourishment of individuality offered by this magic non-self will inhere as deeply in men as in women, and so will its dangers; new ways will therefore have to be found for coping with these dangers — ways less expensive, and less explosive, than banning the selfhood of half the members of our species.

We already have inklings of what these ways will be. When the magic richness and the magic dangerousness of the first parent are embodied inside every person, male and female, when they are contained within the same skin that contains the subjective, vulnerable, limited human "I," the emotional uses of this magic will change. What now serves as a chronic focus of greed, a chronic source of terror, will be transformed into a wild place to be visited for pleasure, a special preserve where old, primitive regions of human personality can be rediscovered. The "I" will turn to this part of itself, and of the other person, as it turns to forest or flame or moving water: to replenish its energies in contact with something less tidy and reasonable, more innocent and fierce, more ancient and mystifying than itself.

The ways we find, then, will be ways of drawing more flexibly on the emotional resources of infancy, of dealing more openly with our need to regard each other half as fellow creatures, half as magic parents. Our concept of the human person will deepen to do justice to the complex truth of human experience. The actual finite individual in each of us will learn to affirm itself to other people while still allowing them, on some playful level, to endow it with early parental magic.

Until we learn to do this, what should be felt as play will continue to be self-deluded play-acting, lived out in grim earnest. And in this living out we will continue to prey on and terrorize each other; also to gobble up, poison, and chop to lifeless bits the world that we nevertheless love, the world that nurtures us, the only world we have.

Notes Toward Chapter 7

The human sexual situation, I have been saying here, has laws of its own, laws that cannot be extrapolated from observation of behavioral differences and social interactions between males and females in other species. It is of course built upon a mammalian base. But what it has in common with the sexual situations of other mammals is transformed, transmuted, by what it does not have in common with them. Our life engenders motives for a profounder, more intricate interdependence between the sexes, and a correspondingly profounder, more intricate subordination of the female, than would be possible in any other animal. At the same time, it engenders powerful motives, also uniquely human, for withdrawing our consent to this subordination and modifying the nature of this interdependence.

So far, the human peculiarities on which I have focused are the intelligent, inventive, self-creative character of our species and the overriding psychological importance of the fact that our infancy is so long. From here on, I must focus also on another cluster of peculiarities: our way of coping with the knowledge that we are mortal; our complex sense of the meaning of the flesh; and the uneasy obsession with enterprise and mastery that has prevaded our communal self-creation.

The bearing of our sexual arrangement upon these peculiarities lies in the crucial part that infancy —this is to say, female-dominated infancy— plays in shaping them. But before this so far

unexamined bearing can be discussed I must start —at the risk
of irking the reader with a restatement of the obvious— by
marshaling some familiar facts about our adult life.

The human being, so far as we can tell, is the only animal
who knows it is going to die, and the only animal who knows
that anything happened before it was born. Alone among the
beasts, we can conceive of our individual lives as finite[1] and
recognize a reality that extends beyond them. We are able to
imagine a future that will not start until after we have stopped
imagining it. We enjoy inherited products, work at inherited
projects, and sense ourselves inhabiting —preserving,
replenishing, extending— a shared world, a world that others
have cared for and cumulatively created, a world in which what
we do can exist after we have left it for people who have not
yet entered it.

On the one hand, attachment to this ongoing world helps
make our awareness of mortality painful. Our sense of personal
significance is assaulted by the thought that this massive, vivid
human reality, in which we cannot help being passionately
engrossed, has managed before and will manage again to get on
without us. Added to the bitter grey riddle of abrupt
nonexistence, and to plain grief at being cut off from the tangible
moment, is a longer-range sense of interruption: Rooted in our
species' cumulative, self-created world, we live enmeshed in
events, in enterprises, in ties among persons, that evolve over
long periods of time. Our past-remembering, future-anticipating
feelings of responsibility, of purpose, even of passive suspense,
form the very stuff that these events, enterprises, ties consist of.
Being humanly alive means, by definition, taking intentional
part —as initiator, as collaborator, even simply as witness— in
what will happen next.

On the other hand, our attachment to the ongoing world can
also help make mortality more bearable. Since the influence
we have exerted outlives us, we are not —at least not in the
most immediate way— wholly mortal. Neither are we wholly
helpless in our mortality, since we have a chance to determine by

our conduct how durable this influence, which extends our connection with life, will be.

These features of our adult sense of mortality would be enough in themselves —and I have not yet turned to the contribution of infancy— to induce in us a deeply mixed set of feelings toward the flesh. Inescapably, the link between mind and its organic incarnation both absorbs and disorients us. The living presence of the simplest sentient creature seems to us unbridgeably discrepant with its corpse. And in the case of a human presence, this discrepancy is magnified beyond measure by the huge reservoir of socially pooled intelligence that stretches the range of any individual human sentience, and by the awareness of individuality —the "I"ness— that burns at its center. The patterned societal processes into which this "I" is woven, the domains that it inhabits, extend so far into time and space beyond its carnal center that its dependence on such a center eludes our mental grasp. No matter how hard we force ourselves to look at it, death remains in a basic way mentally unassimilable, uncanny, a cold, crushing enigma. When we let ourselves feel even a small part of the weight of this enigma, the body whose collapse is destined to extinguish the living self loses its homely, everyday, secular status. It becomes sacred and blasphemous: a marvel, and at the same time ghastly, repellent. Its life looks inevitable; we know that this look of inevitability is a lie, that the burning, breathing flesh lies; but we cannot believe what we know. And this mysterious body, this body whose transcience we try so vainly to feel as a fact, is loved with a special reverence for continuing, miraculously, to live, and hated with a special loathing for promising, incredibly, to die.

These facts of our existence are obvious. They are not, however, the real trouble, the trouble that forms part of the central malaise with which this book is concerned. The real trouble —by its very nature far from obvious, since its existence rests upon our failure to apprehend it— is not death's enigma, but our inability to carry the full emotional weight of this enigma; not our mix of love and hate for the flesh, but our

inability to endure feeling fully the actual sharp edge of this
carnal contradiction; not the ambiguity and frailty of our hold on
the communally created continuum from past to future, but
our inability to try assessing open-eyed how much and what kind
of a hold this is and how much and in what way it matters to us.

In discussing this central trouble, I shall draw heavily on
Norman Brown's recent extension, in *Life Against Death*, of
Freud's big insight into the pathology of our organized social
life.* The gaps in Brown's argument that I think need filling, and
the changes in its direction that would then follow, are referred
to presently. But what I see as its immensely useful crux is this:

We have been using our capacities for enterprise and mastery,
Brown says, primarily to suppress —to shut out of real emotional
awareness— our sense of mortality: Civilization has so far been
shot through with neurotic denial of the fact of death. And
what this means is that it has also been shot through with
neurotic rejection of a joy that cannot be felt while death
is denied: the direct joy of our perishable fleshly individual
existence.

In making history, he begins, what mankind is doing is "making
itself more unhappy and calling that unhappiness progress."
Man is "the restless and discontented animal," with "desires
given in his nature which are not satisfied by culture. From the
psychoanalytic point of view, these unsatisfied and repressed but
immortal desires sustain the historical process. History is
shaped, beyond our conscious wills, not by the cunning of Reason
but by the cunning of Desire." This desire is something "over
and beyond the 'economic welfare' and 'mastery over nature'"
emphasized by Marx, who "though always complicated, is not
free from the tacit assumption . . . that the concrete human needs

* *Civilization and Its Discontents* is devoted to the explicit statement of
this insight, but it is implicit throughout his work. It —taken together with
his elucidation of the interplay between the rational and the pre-rational
layers of our sentience— makes possible a giant step forward in our communal effort to diagnose our situation. Brown refocuses and deepens this contribution of Freud's; he forces the energy that is in it out into a new growing
edge.

and drives sustaining economic activity are just what they appear to be and are fully in consciousness": For "categories like 'economic necessity' and 'human needs' " are naïve, and Marx, in the absence of a psychoanalytic perspective, was forced into "a psychology of history which condemns man to be eternally Faustian and precludes any possibility of happiness." To explain "the unceasing bent for technological progress sustaining the dialectic of labor in history" he had to postulate as "an absolute law of human biology that the satisfaction of human needs always generates new needs." And what such a law means is that "human discontent . . . is incurable."

Freud's approach, on the other hand, if synthesized with anthropology and history, offers what Brown sees as the possibility of "a way out of the nightmare of endless 'progress' and endless Faustian discontent"; man can wake up from the nightmare and start to live. "Civilization," Brown summarizes, "is an attempt to overcome death." And this attempt he equates with what Freud called the death instinct.* Our obsession with it is "the core of the human neurosis. It begins with the human infant's incapacity to accept separation from the mother, that separation which confers individual life on all living organisms and which in all living organisms at the same time leads to death. . . . Humanity is that species of animal that cannot die. This decisive posture in the human animal is grounded . . . in the biology of prolonged infancy; it is grounded in the social correlate of prolonged infancy, the human family. This incapacity to die, ironically but inevitably, throws mankind out of the actuality of living, which for all normal animals is at the same time dying; the result is denial of life. . . . The distraction of human life to the war against death . . . results in death's dominion over life. The war against death takes the form of a preoccupation with the past and the future, and the present tense, the tense of life, is lost."

---

* As Freud used it, this controversial term was multi-dimensional. Brown focuses on, and brilliantly reinterprets, what I think is its most substantial dimension.

The life that is being rejected, moreover, is centered in the
body: not in the compromised body of the adult, but in the pure
one of the infant, whose bright sentience is inseparable from
its bright flesh. He quotes Coleridge's remarks on "the seeming
identity of body and mind in infants, and thence the loveliness of
the former" — followed by steadily increasing separation, so
that later the body becomes "worse than indifferent" without "the
translucency of the mind," and at last "body as body" is
"almost of an excremental nature." This happens, Brown says,
because "Man's incapacity to live in the body . . . is also" —that is,
it both stems from and underlies— "his incapacity to die."

*The real trouble, then —the trouble whose bearing upon our
gender arrangements is discussed in Chapter 7 and 9— is this:
Our love and our hate for the body remain inaccessible to and
unreconciled with each other so long as the full recognition
of mortality that would bring them together remains beyond our
emotional strength.* And the pooled inventiveness and striving
which constitute our species' self-creation† have been from
the outset contaminated* (I say contaminated; Brown, I think,
would say generated) *by these unreconciled feelings for the flesh:
the basic way of life that distinguishes us from other creatures is
distorted* (I say distorted; he, I think, would say dominated) *by
this refusal to face death.*

The link between this trouble and our female-dominated
child-care arrangement lies precisely in the fact that it is a trouble
based on something more than the familiar adult feelings

---

* Brown says —and I agree— that the love is suppressible and distortable,
but not wholly extinguishable; that the hate corrupts and debases the flesh;
and that this is part of the process which we must overcome or die off like
dinosaurs. What he does not point out is that in a less morbid form some pull
between delight in and antagonism to the body is an inevitable ingredient of
our lives; it follows from the "familiar facts" I marshaled above. Brown
— either because he does not think that this irreducible pull exists, or because
he sees it as irrelevant to his argument— never makes the distinction between
it and the pathological ambivalence with which he is concerned. But the
distinction will be relevant for what I have to say.

† This process Brown describes as a "nightmare of infinitely expanding
technological progress." So it is. But Chapters 7 and 9 suggest a way out
of the nightmare that is different from Brown's "way out."

—pain at separation from the ongoing world; bafflement at the dependence of sentience on flesh— that I reviewed just above. The link lies in the fact to which Brown points: that what makes these adult feelings so hard to come to terms with is the infant background against which they are experienced.

Death is an enemy that we meet, in a different guise, long before we know that the ongoing human world exists and that the transience of the flesh will cut us off from it. We meet it during our long infancy, during that period of dependence on adult care that, for our species, continues well into a stage when we are mentally developed enough to perceive this heavy dependence and to have highly complex reactions to it.

As Brown, following Freud, maintains, the adult's grief at mortality is preceded and preformed by the infant's grief at its lost sense of oneness with the first parent: The later knowledge that we will die resonates with the pain of our earliest discovery of helplessness, vulnerability, isolation; with the terrified sorrow of the first, and worst, separation.[2]

Correspondingly, the adult's ambivalence toward the mortal flesh is preceded and preformed by an ambivalence that takes shape in infancy. Freud has pointed out how the child tries to console itself for the first great loss by mastery, by the exercise of competence and will: Torn from what he calls the "oceanic feeling" that it enjoyed at the outset, from the passive infinite power that lay in unity with the all-providing mother, it explores the active, the finite but steadily growing, powers of its newly isolated self. And what it learns, as it starts to affirm itself as a willful, enterprising "I," is that its body, precious vehicle of the "I," is also the "I" 's hateful jailer and saboteur: through the body the "I" learns how puny it is in the face of inanimate obstacles; how limited its power is to make what it wants happen; and most humbling of all, how deeply it can be forced to knuckle under to another, alien, will. The later discovery that the flesh is transient and will finally cut the "I" off from the world resonates with this earlier discovery of the flesh's treachery, made as the "I" first starts to form itself.

As for our adult failure to seize straightforwardly the hold

on the human future that in some measure mitigates our mortality
—our failure, that is, to use this hold in full awareness of its
limitations— this too echoes an infant impasse.* What Brown
spells out —and in doing so he is pruning and extending
Freud's line of thought— is how in our very early use of
enterprise to cope with the pain of the first separation we
preform the core of the pathology that will later on emerge in
our use of enterprise to cope with the pain of the last separation.
The core of this pathology is denial that either of these
separations actually takes place. And for such a denial to be
achieved a fateful renunciation must be made, one that in turn
adds another, more malignant, component to the rejecting side of
our inevitable mix of feelings for the flesh.† What must be
renounced (because we cannot experience it sharply without
acknowledging vulnerability, isolation, loss) is the fundamental,
primitive joy of the body, the irreplaceable joy part —but only
part— of which we must in fact irrevocably lose when infancy is
over and all of which does in fact inevitably end with death.
The denial that this renunciation makes possible allows the child,
and later the adult, to maintain an illusion of total control: the
illusion that in exercising competence we can exert absolute
power over everything that matters. If we can feel that there
exists no precious thing that we must inevitably lose, no real pain
that we cannot hope to prevent, then we can re-establish in
fantasy the omnipotence we originally knew.

But as I shall try to show in Chapter 7, renunciation of life's
original joy in the service of this fantasy undercuts the only way
—the real but limited way— in which the exercise of competence

---

* Brown, as I read him, would probably not agree that arriving at the
ability to seize and use this hold is a valid goal of adult development. But
that disagreement rests on issues that we will get to later. His spelling out of
the infant impasse is in my view accurate anyway.

† This is my formulation. Brown's implies that once we surmount the need
to deny death we can inhabit our bodies as simply and comfortably as our
fellow creatures do. Indeed he commends us, as the Bible does, to the lilies
of the field (for they take no thought of the morrow, and they toil not,
neither do they weep).

can in fact (and here my view differs from Brown's) help ease the pain of isolation and mortality. It spoils the actual, finite pleasures that successful enterprise can carry. Indeed what Brown, following Freud, makes clear is that it even hollows the triumph of ersatz, fantasy, omnipotence: Such triumph is hollow because it can never repay its price in older and simpler pleasures; this it is intrinsically unqualified to do.

Brown's reformulation of what Freud had to say about this fundamental predicament, and related diagnoses of civilization's disease by Marcuse in *Eros and Civilization* and Mumford in *The Pentagon of Power*, have a bearing on our sexual situation which their authors cannot be expected to have seen. Cut loose from some of the tacit male assumptions that tie them down, these diagnoses have explosive implications for change in our gender arrangements. Amended and extended, they permit us to step into territory that even de Beauvoir's searching analysis of these arrangements never touched.

What Brown spells out for us is that the basis for our adult refusal to face death —the basis for our contaminated, compulsive adult involvement in enterprise and our unresolved adult mix of feelings for the flesh— is laid down early. What I want to add here is that it is laid down under a particular condition, immutable till now, which deeply affects the way it is later elaborated: under all-female auspices. Change in this condition will undo the most pernicious aspect of the prevailing ' symbiosis between men and women: collaboration to maintain the central human neurosis that ties together mortality, carnality, and enterprise.

7

The Dirty Goddess

The fact that woman serves her species as carnal scapegoat-idol in itself needs no exposition at this point. The face of this fact is a folk cliché; as for the depth of its emotional charge, and its wide-ranging presence in culture after culture, these have already been made clear enough by other writers. What I want to do here is explore the childhood roots of this familiar fact, and the part it plays in the larger disease that all our central human projects are efforts to outgrow.

In the words of de Beauvoir, to whom we owe the classic statement of this aspect of our situation: "The adolescent is discountenanced, he blushes, if while roaming with his companions he happens to meet his mother, his sisters, any of his female relatives: it is because their presence calls him back to those realms of immanence whence he would fly, exposes roots from which he would tear himself loose." "The Earth Mother engulfs the bones of her children. . . . Death is a woman." Woman is "night in the entrails of the earth. Man is frightened of this night, the reverse of fecundity, which threatens to swallow him up . . . in many a legend do we see the hero lost forever as he falls back into the maternal shadows — cave, abyss, hell." Yet at the same time, "Embracing her, it is all the riches of life that the lover would possess. She is the whole fauna, the whole flora of the earth; gazelle and doe, lilies and roses, downy peach, perfumed berry, she is precious stones, nacre, agate, pearl, silk, the blue of the sky, the cool water of springs, air, flame, land and sea. . . .

Nothing lies deeper in the hearts of men than this animism."
(*The Second Sex.*)

De Beauvoir herself, and Margaret Mead (whose cross-cultural
Male and Female was published at about the same time), and
also H. R. Hays (who provided devastating documentation of this
aspect of human anti-humanity in *The Dangerous Sex* about a
decade later) have offered explanations which begin diagnosing
—but which need to be extended now if we are to get on with
changing— the part that this carnal ambivalence toward woman
plays in the more general ambivalence that permeates our attitude toward central features of our condition. So far as I know,
no really new light has been shed on the matter since then.*
What all three of these writers have pointed out is that man has
magic feelings of awe and fear, sometimes disgust (also, Hays
adds, destructive rage), toward all things that are mysterious,
powerful, and not himself, and that woman's fertile body is the
quintessential incarnation of this realm of things. Alien, dangerous nature, conveniently concentrated near at hand in woman's
flesh, can be controlled through ritual segregation, confinement,
and avoidance; it can be subdued through conventionalized
humiliation and punishment; it can be honored and placated
through ceremonial gifts and adornments, through formalized
gestures of respect and protectiveness. History and ethnography
abundantly illustrate human use of this opportunity.

De Beauvoir, as part of her many-faceted concept of woman as
"other," makes the additional point that woman acts as an intermediary, conscious and at least partly controllable, between man
and unconscious, uncontrollable nature. What she helps him contact and cope with, in this capacity of intermediary, is not only

---

* What is new in more recent feminist accounts of woman's carnal status
is an abruptly accentuated sense that this status is intolerable — a groundswell of anger. Why this kind of anger is surfacing so markedly just now is a
question that Chapter 10 takes up. My intent here is to help make sure that
the eruption turns out to be part of a genuine revolution: a fundamental reorganizing event embodying the clearest possible insight into the process that
is being reorganized; a revolution conceived in such a way that it will not
reverse itself.

brute nature as it surrounds him, but also brute nature as it exists inside him, in his own mute unfathomable body. That body is in some intimate sense himself; yet it is not himself: it is in many ways the arch-enemy of his long-range, distinctively human, concerns.

This meaning of woman, as representative of the body principle in all of us that must be pushed down when we embark on any significant enterprise, clearly underlies many of the rituals surveyed by Hays and by Mead. People under the most diverse cultural conditions seem to feel an opposition, an antagonism, between what is humanly noble, durable, strenuous, and the insistent rule of flesh, flesh which is going to die and which even when death is remote makes humbling demands: we must feed it, we must let it sleep, we must get rid of its smelly wastes. This opposition expresses itself in a variety of ways: People fast, dance till they drop, go sleepless, in rituals of defiance against the flesh that wants to humiliate them as they embark on undertakings that will dramatically tax the body's strength and skill and/or draw on the utmost resources of the higher central nervous system. Anti-female measures are prominent among these body-defying rituals: sexual abstinence is a common precaution when men are getting themselves ready for enterprises like hunts or wars or full-scale appeals for supernatural guidance; care is commonly taken to seal off from the contaminating touch of woman objects that will be used in this kind of solemn endeavor — weapons like bows and spears, for instance, and religious paraphernalia like the medicine bundles men flourish in pre-literate rites and the scrolls and cups and cloths and sticks they flourish in synagogues and churches. Such measures are not solely a means of protecting the higher life of men themselves from corruption by the female body principle; they are a means of safeguarding the efforts that men make on behalf of the whole community. Women as well as men want these efforts to succeed.

In principle, to be sure, man can embody for woman just as she does for him the dangerous carnal pull away from high and strenuous things. The virginity of such figures as Joan of Arc and

Artemis, goddess of the hunt, the asexuality of Athena, goddess of wisdom, and the celibacy that nuns, like monks, must practice, point in a qualified way to this principle. But these are exceptions, for the ordinary human female has been excluded from the kind of enterprise for which the flesh must be formally defied. Until now, this exclusion has been in any case a practical necessity, and the fact that it was mobile man who did the defying and eternally pregnant or lactating woman who stood for what must be defied could be seen as hinging simply on that necessity. But the changes that have now made that necessity obsolete will not in themselves lift off woman the curse of carnality, any more than they will in themselves make her man's accepted peer in the world of enterprise. At this point the reasons for the curse, as for the exclusion, lie mainly not in objectively unavoidable procreative demands on her adult energies but rather in the meanings that her gender has carried, for man and for herself as well, since their own early childhood.

De Beauvoir's account puts heavy emphasis on one such meaning: Our resentment of mortal fleshliness, she says, is aimed with special force against the flesh from which our own has emerged. "From the day of his birth man begins to die: this is the truth incarnated in the Mother," she says. And this resentment, in man, extends to the flesh he impregnates. "In procreation he speaks for the species against himself: he learns this in his wife's embrace; in excitement and pleasure, even before he has engendered, he forgets his unique ego. Although he endeavors to distinguish mother and wife, he gets from both a witness to one thing only: his mortal state. He wishes to venerate his mother and love his mistress; at the same time he rebels against them in disgust and fear."

Maternity, Mortality, Carnality, and Enterprise

This observation of de Beauvoir's is a pivotal one. If it could not be extended, we would face a sad choice indeed: either to accept woman's scapegoat role as to some degree inevitable or to

reject (as certain feminists have recently been feeling angry
enough to say we should) our status as a live-bearing species.
For so long as we hold on to this status, how can the meaning of
the female body fail to be permeated in some special way with the
meaning of mortality?* The fact that we are born is one with the
fact that we die; we are born as one proverb says, between piss
and shit; and it is between female piss and female shit that we
are born.

Luckily, the situation is far less stark than this way of putting it
suggests. De Beauvoir's observation can, I think, be extended in a
fundamental way: What matters is not the sheer fact of a link
between mortality and maternity, but the emotional meaning of
the link; and what I want to show is that this emotional meaning
is more profoundly mutable than her account indicates.

It is mutable because the meaning of mortality itself can (indeed now must, since the meaning it has had so far drives us to a
kind of "progress" that cannot go on much longer) change. For
this to happen, the meaning of maternity itself (its present meaning, which is by no means eternal, by no means intrinsic to or
inseparable from our status as live-bearing mammals) must also
change. And for this in turn to happen, man's hand must be as
firm on the cradle as woman's.

It is the hand on the cradle that in fact shapes our feeling for
the mortal flesh. What we learn about the flesh in the cradle,
before we have any way of knowing that the flesh was born and
will die, is incomparably deeper and denser, more immediate and
vivid, than the abstract notion of nonexistence will ever be. What
eventually gives mortality its emotional flavor, what lends real
and substantial form to the thin, impalpable, deniable certainty
of death, is the concrete atmosphere of our introduction to carnal-

* She calls upon women to surmount this meaning by declaring themselves
more firmly as "subjects," as "essential," as free "existents" who are more
than mere body and for whom man in turn is also "carnal prey"; prey that
can deteriorate with age and whose incipient "decrepitude is terrifying." And
of course women do have to do this for decisive change to begin. But how
is such change to be carried through if what is crucial after all is the inherent
connection between womb and tomb?

ity. This introduction starts in the first minutes, weeks, months of life; it is in some essential ways complete by the end of the first two years.

Our knowledge that the flesh is transient does not begin to take shape, then, until we have already been accumulating body-emotional experience for some time: we are apt to have been living for three years or so before we start to believe that there were real events flowing when we ourselves did not yet exist, and to start struggling slowly with the fact that a creature's existence at some point ends, that there is such a thing as a formerly alive and now lifeless animal body. This knowledge, moreover, is only part of the insight that makes death's bearing on our own life different from its bearing on the lives of other animals; the other part of this insight takes even longer to become a real part of our awareness.

We have been immersed in the human realm well into middle childhood before we fully sense that humanness is a matter of transcending one's own life by using what has been learned or made by others in the past so as to learn or make —preserve, replenish, discover, create— what will be used by others in the future. (The acquisition of this understanding is what we call education: it is the child's taken-for-granted but in fact staggering feat, the feat of coming to apprehend the main outlines of a culture, which means coming to feel oneself as a participant in the ongoing societal process.) It is only as this happens that we can start to feel the final edge of what de Beauvoir calls our "carnal contingency": the relation between membership in humanity and life in the flesh; the fact that the susceptible, ephemeral body, enabling vehicle of our participation in the maintenance and enlargement of human reality, is also the day-by-day antagonist of this participation and its final interrupter.

What that full sense of the nature of our mortality means to us, when we finally do achieve it, inevitably grows out of what the body has come to mean already. It is the significance the flesh already has —the import it has acquired in infancy and very early childhood— that determines how the prospect of the final interruption, undreamed of by the infant, will later be faced. It is this import that determines the spirit in which the self-transcending enterprise of membership in a culture is undertaken, and the spirit in which the flesh is then inhabited. What the flesh has come to mean at the outset lays down the terms, in other words, that the entrepreneur in the person eventually makes with the day-to-day limitations of its agent, the body. It lays down the rules, moreover, by which the demands of enterprise, enterprise that extends the aura of a living self beyond the body's space and time, will eventually be balanced against another demand of the living self: the demand for delight that goes nowhere, simple delight, narrow and acute, repetitive and timeless.

Under present conditions the meaning that the body has already acquired for the child, by the time it discovers the human facts of mortality and cumulatively pooled enterprise, is a meaning half drowned in unresolved contradictions. That these contradictions remain unresolved has to do with the female monopoly of early child care, and with the adult emotional arrangements that therefore prevail between mother-raised men and mother-raised women. Let me consider first a relatively simple layer of this ambivalence: that the flesh is both vehicle and saboteur of human wishes; and then a more complex, more malignant layer: that our original interest in the flesh is repressed, but irrepressible, and re-enters awareness in an altered form.

The Flesh as Vehicle-Saboteur of Human Wishes

The relation between our sexual arrangements and our unresolved carnal ambivalence begins with this fact: when the child first discovers the mystical joys and the humiliating constraints of carnality, it makes this discovery in contact with a woman. The mix of feelings toward the body that forms at this early stage, under female auspices, merges with our later-acquired knowledge of the body's transience, and the flavor of this early mix remains the most vivid ingredient of that unassimilable eventual knowledge.

Woman and the early self-discovery of the body

The mother is in a literal sense, not just a figurative one, the intermediary that de Beauvoir describes, for she is in charge of the most intimate commerce between the child and the environment: the flow of substances between the flesh and the world. The infant gets from her the stuff that goes into its body and gives to her the stuff that comes out of it. And the sense of her presence —carnally apprehended in rocking and crooning, in cuddling and mutual gazing— is what makes the world feel safe. Separation from the touch, smell, taste, sound, sight of her is the forerunner of all isolation, and it eventually stands as the prototype for our fear of the final isolation. (This is why the song says ". . . Over these prison walls I would fly Straight to the arms of me mudder And there I'd be happy to die." It is why people cling to other people when bombs are falling: the knowledge that they are present and conscious of course helps, but access to their flesh helps more.) The mother's too tight, rough, or jerky handling of the baby's body, her delay in feeding its mouth or cleaning its skin, are the forerunners of all human insensitivity, callousness, treachery. In the body's pain, which it is up to the mother to prevent, is all the terror of annihilation. The sinking sense of falling —loss of maternal support— is the permanent archetype of catastrophe. During the time, then, when the great passions of life are carried in the joys and vicissitudes of the helpless flesh, this flesh is in the hands of a woman.

And it is not only the helpless flesh that first knows itself, for better and for worse, in woman's hands; it is also the active, striving flesh. In these same hands the body starts outgrowing its helplessness, starts becoming the agent of the child's developing will: It holds and squeezes the breast or bottle, and its sucking makes milk come. It reaches out to grasp objects that invite examination. It turns itself over and lifts itself up to see or hear better. It crawls, then toddles. It explores its own capacities as a sound-producing instrument, for self-entertainment and for purposeful communication. It finds out how to contain or expel its excrements voluntarily, for its own pleasure or to defy or please the mother. In these ways we originally learn the triumph of purpose fulfilled. In these ways, too, we learn the chagrin of failure, for the human infant's intelligence makes the gap between what it can actually do and what it can think of doing immense. And it is woman who presides alone over this self-discovery of the proud, active, and enragingly puny flesh.

It is in interaction with woman, moreover, that the child makes another basic carnal discovery: that the body's love of pleasure, and its vulnerability to deprivation and pain, can subject the person who inhabits it to the domination of another person's opposing will. The least coercive of mothers must sometimes restrain an infant's movements, or make it wait against its wishes; and many mothers, of course, purposefully use corporal punishment —in a formal way thwarting bodily impulses or inflicting bodily pain— to teach the child obedience. The rewards of submitting to the mother's will are correspondingly carnal —body warmth, food, caresses and soothing sounds, ravishing smiles and glances— and teach the child that the flesh can be ignominiously bribed.*

Adult consequences

De Beauvoir correctly insisted that human resentment of the body is inevitable, and that this fact has central relevance for our male-female arrangements. What must be added to her formulation if we want to change these arrangements, I have been saying, is the distinction between female *bearing* and female *rearing* of the resented body.

But there is another distinction, also central for our sexual situation, which must be added as well: the distinction between split-off and integrated resentment. It is split-off resentment that is

---

* Here we are concerned with what this means for our resentment of the flesh, which comes out in our feeling toward woman's body. In Chapter 8 we will consider what it means for our resentment of female will, and the consequences of that resentment for our relation to authority in general.

poisonous. Integrated resentment gives life depth and bounce. To achieve this integration, however —to overcome the splitting process that is a spontaneous early defense against chaos, to reconcile the delights of the flesh with its anguishes, its victories with its mortifications— is no casual task. And what allows us to evade this task[1] and leave them permanently unreconciled is the fact discussed in Chapter 6: The being who is the focus of these mixed feelings is not —even in retrospect— a unitary fellow creature; not an "I," but an amorphous, sub- and superhuman, "she." She can remain amorphous, a bodily and emotional intimate whose own selfhood is inconceivable, unacceptable, because an innocent and dignified "he" is there to represent the part of a person that wants to stand clear of the flesh, to maintain perspective on it: "I"ness wholly free of the chaotic carnal atmosphere of infancy, uncontaminated humanness, is reserved for man. And the integrity of this artificially pure, artificially simplified male humanness is preserved by projecting the magical charms and joys of the body, and its mucky, humbling limitations, onto the ambiguous goddess of the nursery.

Woman, by and large, meekly carries this burden of shame and sacredness, relying on man to represent matter-of-fact spiritual self-respect, clean* world-conquering humanity. Man's hungry, worshiping enjoyment of her body, his dependence on her presence and on her comforting physical services, allow her to relive vicariously through him her own old love of the maternal flesh and her own old, luxurious dependence on physical care, while he relives his directly. His contempt for and cruelty to her body allow her to relive directly, with masochistic pleasure, the fleshly humiliation that both endured as infants, while he relives it vicariously through her. At the same time, through identification

---

* The messiness allowed men in our own culture does not really contradict this point. Their proverbially unfastidious lust, their tolerance of filthy public toilets, their foul language and slovenly ways, all of this is accepted precisely because it does not touch upon their central, clean humanity. It is washed off, like dirt off healthy skin, when they turn to serious matters. In woman messiness of this kind would convey that an intrinsic, inherent uncleanliness, which she is counted on to keep under control, had broken out of bounds.

with his impulse to punish her she can vent vicariously —while he vents directly— vengeful anger at the mother for this early humiliation.*

If there were no longer a special category of person available to absorb our split-off feelings of love and anger toward the flesh —if man could no longer rely on woman to absorb them and woman could no longer rely on man to embody for all of us a humanness spuriously free and clear of the aura of instability and contradiction that they carry— these feelings would have to be integrated within each individual person. It is possible, needless to say, that we will prove unable to marshal the strength for this integration. And it could be argued on the basis of this possibility that we ought to let well enough alone: better to have somebody who represents unqualified humanness than nobody at all; better not to lose what we have by trying for something more. But in fact what we have to lose by trying is nothing. For what has by now become obvious to whoever is really willing to think about it is that if we do not outgrow our present stance toward the perishable flesh the sickness of which this stance is part will quite shortly kill us off anyway.

But let me turn now to what is most actively lethal in this stance of ours; for the ambivalence that I have just discussed is only a part —and a relatively harmless part— of the trouble.

The Flesh as "Return of the Repressed"

The mixed feelings for the body that are now projected onto woman include something more, and worse, than simple love for it and simple anger at it for sabotaging our projects and making us abjectly open to outside control. They include also burial and

* For a surrealistically accurate portrait of this interplay, look again at Réage's *The Story of O.* The reader who would rather not understand what that strange story says can object here that it expresses a fantasy and should not be seen as bearing on people's actual conduct. But the truth is that the most lurid fantasies, if looked at intelligently, have a lot to tell us about "normal" everyday behavior; not, to be sure, about the literal forms it takes, but about its emotional mainsprings.

denial of this simple love, and its return in the form of a morbid, ashamed obsession which then complicates the simple anger. No one, to my knowledge, has described this process of burial and return so well as Norman Brown has; and no one —certainly not Norman Brown— has seemed inclined to look at the way this process is supported by our male-female division of responsibility, opportunity, and privilege.

Brown's account

The process consists on the one hand, Brown says, of a pushing out of awareness of our early delight in the vulnerable body's joys, and a compulsive concentration of attention and energy on that which can be predicted, controlled, manipulated, possessed and preserved, piled up and counted. And it consists on the other hand of the ashamed eruption of a dirty interest in this rejected body, an interest that is a deformed version of our original delight, dirtied and deformed by the crooked paths that a feeling must take to break through repression, smelling of its opposite. The loathing and disgust that we feel for what we cannot help being interested in is our homage to the reasons we had for burying the interest.

Brown's view of how this process starts is summarized above.* What he goes on to say is that the "ever increasing denial of the body is, in the form of a negation, an ever increasing affirmation of the denied body. Sublimations are those negations of the body which simultaneously affirm it: and sublimations achieve this dialectical tour de force by the simple but basic mechanism of projecting the repressed body into things. The more the life of the body passes into things, the less life there is in the body, and at the same time the increasing accumulation of things represents an ever fuller articulation of the lost life of the body." And this projected life is dead life. "What the psychoanalytical paradox is asserting is that 'things' which are possessed and accumulated,

* See pages 118–123.

property and the universal condensed precipitate of property, money, are in their essential nature excremental." But "repudiation of the body does not and cannot alter the fact that life in the body is all we have, and the unconscious holds fast to the truth and never makes the repudiation. . . . Thus the morbid attempt to get away from the body can only result in a morbid fascination (erotic cathexis) in the death of the body. In the simple and true, because bodily, language of the unconscious, Eros can be deflected from the life of the body only by being deflected onto the excremental function. . . . To rise above the body is to equate the body with excrement." Furthermore, "as long as humanity prefers a dead life to living, so long is humanity committed to treating as excrement not only its own body but the surrounding world of objects, reducing all to dead matter and inorganic magnitudes." And what is true of things is true also of modes of language and thought, categories of time, approaches to science. To survive, he urges, we need to move toward "an erotic sense of reality, rather than an aggressive dominating attitude toward reality."

Brown's point, then, is that we bury our attachment to the life of the body at the outset, when we recognize how vulnerable, how isolated and finite, it —the living body— is. This burial allows us to deny the loss of omnipotent infant unity with the first parent —to deny, that is, our dependence on what we cannot control— by ignoring the (fluid and permeable, but never wholly breachable) borders that imprison the weak self in its separateness. We manage, in other words, to maintain a fantasy of being safer and more self-sufficient —because less limited and distinct— than we would know ourselves to be if we kept full emotional contact with the needy, imperilled flesh. And later, when we learn that the body is mortal (that this happens later is my point, not his; for his argument it is unimportant), this same burial of feeling helps us to deny death; it lets us avoid the deepened awareness of unique individuality —unique because each individual is transient— that goes with wholly passionate awareness of the body's ephemeral life. As he puts it, an organism "has individuality because it lives its own life and no other — that is to say, because it dies"; and "the precious ontological uniqueness which the human individual claims is conferred on him not by possession of an immortal soul but by possession of a mortal body." What Brown does *not* say is that this pathological burial —and our consequent fascinated abhorrence for what we have buried— would be far less feasible if our sexual arrangements did not provide us with a special, permanent, quasi-human target for the fascinated abhorrence, along with a special permanent class of human who is exempt from this role of target.

Extension of Brown's account

Brown's diagnosis needs extension, then, to embrace the implications of a vital fact whose existence he takes for granted but whose actual relevance for the situation he describes he fails to note:* the fact that the early carnal interaction whose joy we partly bury is interaction with a *female* body; that the loss we deny by burying this joy is loss of unity with a *woman;* that the efforts we make to console ourselves for this double bereavement, through the exercise of will, competence, mastery, are efforts made at the very outset with the support of —and in opposition to— not a father *and* a mother, but a mother only. What this fact means is that the pathology embodied in the burial of joy and the denial of loss and the attempt at self-consolation is a pathology

* He does discuss, and attempt to extend, Freud's view of the "pre-Oedipal mother," especially in his chapter "Death and Childhood." But, like Freud, he is unable to surmount the assumption that woman is an auxiliary, background, figure: that *the* human situation is essentially a male situation. For example, he repeatedly describes the infant's (pre-Oedipal) effort toward magic self-sufficiency as "the child's project of becoming its own father." But at this stage, as he himself realizes, the father is not yet emotionally real for the child. Why not, then, "its own mother"? And why is the child, except in rare parenthetical excursions into "the psychology of women," always conceived of as a boy child? Without thinking about the girl child whose personality is developing out of the same family conditions in a way that will fatefully complement his own, we cannot grasp what will make it possible later on for Brown's little protagonist to sustain his male side of the collective neurosis that will be their joint strategy, and that will depend heavily on her female contribution. See Chapter 9.

that interpenetrates intimately with our prevailing male-female arrangement: neither can be understood, or changed, without the other.

But before the bearing of Brown's argument upon our problem can be fully grasped, there is another source of distortion in his account that needs to be considered.

Enterprise and the body: the sacrifice of delight and the poisoning of work. The malignant aspect of enterprise on which I have just touched —the "aggressive-dominating," excrement-hoarding, life-denying component of human culture that Brown describes— has a relation to our gender arrangements that will be discussed in Chapter 9. What Brown has to say about this side of our species' life —the side that makes us most actively dangerous to each other and to the web of life of which we are part— needs, in my opinion, no important internal amendment. All that needs adding to his superb account of it is one crucial fact: that it will necessarily continue until female-dominated child care (a fact of life that he never questions) ceases to be the basic condition within which "normal" personality develops.

When I do turn to that aspect of enterprise I will treat his, and related, statements about it (statements, that is, about the existence, and escalating destructiveness, of a collective human neurosis) just as I have so far treated some other writers' statements about the need for change in our gender arrangements. My discussion will take it as axiomatic that these statements are in their main outlines valid, and that anyone who is not already acquainted with them should be; and my aim will be not to repeat or defend them, but only to point out to the reader who has already assimilated them —and who agrees with me that they are mainly valid— some additional considerations which are vital for our understanding of them.

What needs analysis in this chapter, however, is not that intrinsically deathly side of human effort but its more affirmative side, the side embodying the spirit that Brown (when he does on and off allow himself to use this term for anything rational, planful, or strenuous) calls "erotic." The way in which potentially "erotic" effort is compromised, soured, turned into a form of slavery by its relation to our stance toward carnality and mortality is a matter that Brown does not examine in detail. This is partly because such examination is not vital for the main point he has to make; but it is also partly because his view of human activity itself —his view of the relation between the human brain and the human body— needs extension and internal rearticulation before such examination is possible.

As Brown describes the child's attempt to substitute control of the environment for full experience of "the life of the body," one cannot escape the dual implication (a) that efforts to control the environment are in themselves pathological, since we do not see such efforts being made by "healthy" —that is, non-human— organisms; and (b) that the true, ideal life of the human body is discovered once and for all in infancy and would, if we were not afraid of it, be kept essentially unchanged, intact, thereafter. What (b) blurs is the distinction between those qualities of the body's early life which we must leave behind to discover the essence of the human condition and those which we bury out of terror of that essence. And what (a) blurs is a related set of distinctions: distinctions among the varied needs that enterprise in fact expresses.

Correspondingly, in discussing the infant's impulse to console itself, through affirmations of its self-sufficiency, for its loss of felt continuity with the mother, Brown gives us no hint at all that this impulse can have anything but a life-rejecting meaning. But of course both the impulse to console oneself for a loss and the impulse to affirm self-sufficiency can in themselves be wholly and sturdily benign. That they nevertheless do appallingly often take a pathological form is a fact requiring explanation: they do so under particular conditions which need to be specified. If we do not specify these conditions, we miss their relation to female-dominated child care and thereby miss seeing how they can be changed.

Consider what it means that when our early delight in omnipotent unity with an infinite source of richness can no longer be maintained we turn from it to a new delight, as peculiarly human —that is, as rooted in complex sentience— as the old one: delight in conscious planful competence, in self-contained finite power that springs from inside one's own skin. This turning is in itself a simple, affirmative step: renunciation of what has been inexorably outlived is by definition affirmative. (We give up the intimacy of childhood family ties for the poignance of adolescent sexual adventure; we let go of youth's acute, hopeful excitement for the richness of sensibility, the easy exercise of nurturant strength, that middle age carries; finally, to do what Brown insists we must become strong enough to do, we will loosen our fulfilled hold on life to embrace death as a friend.) That this simple step, once taken, subverts itself finally into a complex renunciation of delight itself is an upshot facilitated under present conditions by the fact that the parental being toward whom we are oriented when we first take it is always and only female.

To show that this renunciation need not be the upshot, that mutable circumstance enhances the probability of its happening, let me start by reminding the reader of what is after all intuitively obvious: that enterprise has more than one psychological function.

To begin with, pleasure in the effortful achievement of purpose is an intrinsic part of our species' own variant of the broad activity impulse* that we share with other, less self-conscious creatures: the impulse which —together with our feelings of attraction to "objects in the world," and our efforts to pull them closer to ourselves and to each other— is precisely what Freud meant by Eros. It is part of this broad impulse, in our case, for the simple reason that we are neurally —that is to say, organically— capable of planning: of intending, in other words, to bring about a presently nonexistent state of affairs. For us, conceiving a purpose and going to the trouble to achieve it is the enjoyable exercise of a physiological capacity, just as soaring is for a bird

---

* See the admirable collection of papers entitled *Functions of Varied Experience* (Fiske and Maddi, editors), which fascinatingly illustrates the existence and discusses the meaning of this broad impulse.

or burrowing for a rabbit. And it is an exercise that we start enjoying very early (just how early is a matter, I think, of definition,
and also of guesswork about the subjective life of the nursling) in
infancy. For more detailed comments on the relation between this
point and Brown's view of the bearing of Eros on enterprise, see
Box H.

Beyond this *primary*, direct, value that it carries for humans,
however, enterprise fulfills *secondary*, compensatory, functions
too. These compensatory functions are salient in determining the
actual forms that enterprise takes, so salient that psychoanalytic
thinkers (starting with Freud, to whom we mainly owe our present sense of this problem's shape) have tended to focus upon
them as if they were the whole story. The tendency is understandable, but it has resulted in a gravely skewed perspective on
the meaning of human effort. Substantial counterstatements have
all along been made toward the correction of this skewed perspective,[2] but it persists widely anyway.

Brown's account misrepresents the significance of enterprise,
then, by ignoring the simplest motive underlying purposefulness
in humans: that it gives us pleasure as straightforward as the
pleasure of lovemaking, or looking, or listening; and for the same
phylogenetic reason (which can sometimes betray itself, but on
the whole works well): that this pleasure induces us to act in
ways that turn out to keep us alive. As a result, Brown's account
also misrepresents the significance of enterprise in another way: it
examines the secondary, compensatory, functions of purposefulness in overly global terms. There are two such secondary functions; one is straightforward, constructive, feasible; the other is
unrealistic, maladaptive, self-stymieing. Brown, like Freud, refers
in a way to both, but he does not —as Freud did not— distinguish clearly between them. (Indeed, as the following discussion
tries to show, it is not possible to make the distinction clear if
the importance of the primary, capacity-exercising, function is
slighted.)

The *constructive* secondary benefit that enterprise *genuinely*

(Continued on page 144)

Box H

Brown follows Freud in insisting that "infantile sexuality is the pursuit of pleasure obtained through the activity of any and all organs of the body," and that it constitutes "the ultimate essence of our desires and our being," which is "nothing more or less than delight in the active life of all the human body." But what he says next makes it clear that he does not really mean delight in *all* the active life of the body, or pleasure in the exercise of *all* its organs. Reason, he tells us, is rejected in the unconscious because man is "secretly faithful to the principle of pleasure, or, as Blake calls it, delight." The *Homo sapiens* higher central nervous system, then, that most human of organs, does not count in his view as an organ.

Again: "The ultimate essence of our being is erotic and demands activity according to the pleasure principle"; but this does not include, apparently, the reasoning, self-reflective, inventive activity of the brain. His explanation of why "man never unfolds the mode of being which is proper to his species and given in his body" rejects precisely that feature of what is given in our bodies that makes the unfolding of a mode of being proper to our species a problem for us and not for our animal relatives: It leaves out the considerations that are forced on thinkers about this problem by what is now being discovered about the transition from ape to human (see Chapter 2), considerations that were anticipated by Darwin and discussed tentatively even by Gordon Childe (*Man Makes Himself*), whom Brown quotes in other connections. His account of what "generates the compulsion to change the internal nature of man and the external world in which he lives" — in other words, what made the *Homo sapiens* physique evolve— omits planfulness, adventurousness, imagination. The sole motivating force to which he points is "repression," which in "giving man a history" subordinates "the life of the individual to the historical quest of the species." By "the" life of the individual he seems to mean the part of that life which is unconcerned with transcending itself, untouched by what I described above as education: the vital part that, as he puts it, "in infancy . . . tasted the fruit of the tree of life, and knows that it is good, and never forgets." But of course there are other vital parts: if there were not, the temporally extended consciousness implicit in "never forgets" could not exist. "Human sociability," he sums up —that is, the pooling of intelligent effort that shaped our bodies— "is a sickness."

The conjecture that sickness —psychopathology— has most likely been an essential factor in the evolution of our capacity for intelligent effort (and of the other physical traits that go with this capacity) seems to me, unhappily, all too well founded. Brown has vastly deepened my —our— appreciation of this likelihood, which is fundamental for an effort to come to terms with our situation: having said this, one has said the main thing about his book that needs saying. But the problem that defeats many readers —and complicates the work of people like me, who want to assimilate and extend his argument, as he did Freud's— is how to avoid entanglement in another aspect of this argument.

What is there to say about Brown's assumption that psychopathology is not just a factor in, but the central source of, intelligent effort? that we can and should cut such effort out of our lives? in short that we can live happily in the human body only by somehow getting rid of those features of the human central nervous system without which that body could not have come into existence in the first place, and could not sustain itself now?

To choose just one example of this feature of his argument: Nietzsche seems to Brown to have put his finger on a central problem when he defined man as the "animal that can promise," and asked how such an animal could have come into existence. "The ability to promise," Brown paraphrases, "involves the loss of the natural animal forgetfulness of the past, which is the precondition for healthy living in the present. Man's ability to promise involves an unhealthy (neurotic) constipation with the past (the anal character!): he can 'get rid of' nothing." So the mental competence to project an intention into the future, keep it in mind, and focus one's energies upon its fulfillment —the competence whose evolution is at the center of the evolution of the human body itself— is dismissed as stemming from nothing but pathology, as reflecting nothing but the loss of some former health. It has to do less with proper use of the higher brain centers than with improper use of the lower gut.

offers us —a gift stumbled upon by the human baby as it becomes engrossed in the sheer animal delight of doing what it finds out it can do— is the benefit of a form of compensation that no other animal baby is mentally complex enough to need: compensation, partial and indirect but avidly grasped, for the carnal joy —the unqualified pre-verbal euphoria, the timeless, effortless bodily bliss— that is peculiar to infancy, and implacably lost to us once infancy is over. The constructiveness of this extra benefit lies precisely in its realistically limited nature: an old, irreplaceable good is on some level never forgotten, and a new good —different, incommensurate— is therefore good not only in itself but also because it is discovered just as the other is being relinquished.

The *maladaptive* secondary "benefit" that enterprise *falsely seems* to offer us —or rather that we hopelessly try to make it give us— is compensation for something else, something which we have largely renounced in order to escape full awareness of that other, implacable, loss. What we try to make enterprise replace is not only a kind of joy that we have necessarily lost but also a kind of joy, central and primitive, that we could in fact still have.

This joy that we could have, and renounce instead, is the later counterpart of the early carnal joy. It is not the original ecstatic union with the world, the early state of grace that later stands as religion's prototype of divine presence and universal all-pervasive love. It is, rather, the joy of a creature who knows time and senses its own separateness, who has become familiar with striving and with the ebb and flow, the melting together and drawing apart, that form the living tie between its fragile individual existence and the existence of the hurtful, entrancing surround; it is the joy of a creature who remembers and anticipates less primitive ways of feeling and, suspending what it knows, what it remembers and anticipates, surrenders itself to the melting, flowing moment. So while this joy is not the lost pure euphoria of infancy, it does echo that euphoria clearly enough to offer us episodic, momentary recapture of its flavor; and it therefore also echoes it clearly enough to remind us of what we lost when we found our solitary mortal selves.

We largely spurn this possibility of direct recapture, then, out of lack of strength to endure the pain that it carries. But what we give up in doing so is the only real means we have of supplementing the indirect and incomplete compensation that enterprise can legitimately, feasibly offer in exchange for the early magic of the body: the pleasure in exercising our talents for cerebration and complex effort, and in using our power to make at least some things happen, which in part does genuinely console us for outgrowing the pre-mortal omnipotence of infancy. By spurning the direct access we still have to more primitive delights, we lean too heavily on this partial indirect consolation. We put too heavy a burden on successful effort's modest capacity to make life feel worth living. This is what makes effort —the kind of effort we would be apt to engage in for its own sake anyway— feel like work. So: the aspect of enterprise that is as intrinsically enjoyable to us as hunting is to cats or galloping to horses has in addition two extra, compensatory, emotional uses. Of these the constructive, potentially adaptive one is undercut, sabotaged, by the false, unrealistic one. And this undercutting is facilitated by our prevailing male-female arrangement. *It is at this point that the project of healing the split between work and play, and the project of sexual liberty, meet.*

The way they meet is this: The joy of enterprise really can console us, though only in part, for the inexorable loss of our pure infant sense of omnipotent oneness with the world. Since we are remembering and mourning creatures, this is a consolation that would (if pathological complications did not interfere with it) inevitably deepen for us the emotional value of enterprise. And this partial, indirect consolation could (if we would let it) be vitally supplemented, in turn, by the opportunities that life now and then offers for direct recapture of the earliest mode, the unqualified animal-poetic mode, of erotic intercourse with the surround. But we try to make enterprise repay us also for a loss that is not inexorable, and for which nothing can really console us: our own cowardly repudiation of these redeeming opportunities. (Art and religion offer us opportunities of this kind, and so does pleasure in nature, if we allow them to touch us at the relevant level of feeling; but we rarely do. Parenthood makes possible a vicarious reliving of life's subjective beginnings; but the possibility —because we fear it and because it involves strenuous empathetic effort— is often wasted. Sexual feeling, and the wider emotions with which it can resonate, provide uniquely literal re-access to the original body-erotic realm of passionate contact; but these depths of direct sexuality, for reasons explored throughout this book, are kept largely dormant.) The pleasure of enterprise is deep-rooted, sturdy, essential to our humanity; but it is not built to carry the burden of repaying us for such a renunciation.

In trying to make enterprise carry this *unfeasible* compensatory burden, we forfeit the only possible chance we have to help it carry its *legitimate* compensatory burden, which it cannot carry alone. In this way we poison, in turn, the direct primary pleasure it provides: the pleasure of erotic use of the higher central nervous system. We are disappointed in it for not doing what it is inherently unfit to do: it cannot suffice unaided to console us for a kind of joy that we have implacably outgrown; neither can it succeed —no matter how deeply it exhausts, distracts, and bribes us— in quelling our longing for the version of this old joy that we still could have. *The underlying grudge that embitters our organically based love of enterprise, sickening our zest to live out this vital part of our species' nature, is central to human malaise. It is the other side of our sickened zest for the life of the flesh, and our fear of the realms of feeling to which the flesh originally introduced us.*

The relevance of female-dominated early child care. Our sexual arrangement bears on these matters as follows: The implausible burden assigned to enterprise —the burden of repaying ourselves through exercise of power, control, competence for a vital happiness, within reach, that we cannot grasp without feeling the pain that goes with it— needs somehow to be experienced as plausible.

Otherwise we would be forced to chuck the burden and brave the pain. What makes it possible for this hopelessly heavy burden of renunciation to be experienced as plausible is that under present male-female conditions the kind of happiness we are renouncing is a happiness that we can teach ourselves to be ashamed of. We can be ashamed of it —and thus dodge the challenge of claiming it— because the person in whose arms we felt the original version of this happiness belongs to a category of human being that we can afford to despise, to abandon our early respect for, as we grow: The boy can start to despise femaleness as he grows toward competent membership in the male fraternity (see Chapter 4); the girl can start as she grows toward her love of man, her gratitude to him for embodying uncontaminated clear humanity, her duty to be his competent supporter and assistant, his loyal helpmeet whose "desire shall be toward him."

Gender Arrangements and Ambivalence to the Flesh

To recapitulate: The dirty goddess is dirty not simply because the flesh that she represents is the vehicle-saboteur of our wishes, and because its meaning as hateful saboteur —split off from and thus unmodified by its meaning as lovely vehicle— makes our tie to it feel degrading. She is dirty also, more deeply dirty, for another reason: the positive side of what she embodies —our old joy in the flesh and the capacity we still have to feel the kind of contact with life that the flesh originally carried— has been largely suppressed. The side of what she embodies which, when it emerges, gives her real, radiant goddess status —the mystic carnal truth that underlies the biblical use of the verb "to know" and makes the nude body in art the most telling visual symbol of full human majesty— is not only dissociated, compartmentalized; it is also in large degree denied and discounted.

Our stubborn interest in this discounted carnal truth forces it back into consciousness, but in debased form. The love of the flesh that woman stands for thus includes (in varying degrees, of course, depending on personal and cultural differences) an ashamed love for something actively loathsome. The flesh carries this loathsomeness not because it humbles us with its hungers, reminds us of our tie to the earth, makes us fall asleep when we want to go on playing: these distresses are inherent in the flesh's beauty as a miraculous temporary organization of inorganic matter; our failure to integrate them with our sense of the flesh's beauty keeps our feeling for life shallow, but it is not what makes the flesh loathsome. What debases the flesh is our repression of our sense of the flesh's beauty so as to avoid the pain that this sense carries, and the return of the repressed in a form that includes our reproach to ourselves for failing to bury it altogether.

We are able to go on debasing the flesh in this way, and to live on without rebelling constructively against what we are doing to ourselves, only because woman is available for the dirty-goddess role, and man can thus be relatively exempt (an exemption that comforts her as well as him) from the baseness that she carries.

In sum, human ambivalence toward the body of woman arises from, and at the same time helps perpetuate, incompetence to reconcile our inevitable mix of feelings for the flesh itself. The unreconciled mix is projected onto the first parent. Worse still, much of the positive side of this ambivalence is suppressed and what has been suppressed is converted into an obscene preoccupation; this means that even the love that is part of the prevailing attitude toward woman's body is to some degree a dirty love. The shame that for many people tinges carnal attraction is made possible by, and at the same time deepens, woman's general human degradation.

Both this failure to integrate our feelings toward the flesh and this debasement of what is positive in these feelings express our helplessness to cope with carnality, a helplessness that has so far permeated the death-denying, and therefore death-dominated, life of our enterprising species. Woman's status as scapegoat-idol is maintained by, and at the same time works to maintain, this helplessness. And what keeps her available for this status is her child *rearing*, not her child *bearing*, contribution.

When the child, once born, is as much the responsibility of man as of woman, the early vicissitudes of the flesh —our handling of which lays the basis for our later handling of mortality—will bear no special relation to gender. Both sides of the double fact that we are born mortal and born of woman will then change their meaning.

That we are born mortal now gets its meaning from other grievances against the body, which develop before we discover that it was born and will therefore die, and which later melt together with this discovery into one global rage. For this rage woman, who both bore and raised the body, is at present the natural target. When these early grievances develop as much under male as under female auspices, when they can no longer be foisted off on the female and must be integrated instead, their character, and therefore the character with which they later endow the fact of mortality, will be cleaner, less necrophilic. When our love for the mortal flesh has learned to incorporate our hate for it, we will have learned to live without marching to meet death halfway.

That we are born of woman now gets its meaning from other features of our early relation with her, which take shape before we absorb the strange news that we came out of her belly. Woman's prenatal and postnatal parental contributions are at present so deeply fused together in our thinking that a grievance which in fact stems from the latter can seem connected to the former. When the early experience that later gives mortality its meaning has been discovered not solely in contact with the sex that turns out, amazingly, to have borne the child, but also in equally intimate contact with the sex that turns out to have played an equally amazing part in its conception, the special link between woman and death will dissolve. This link has depended on our child-care arrangements, not on the sheer abstract fact that those who are born die.

Motherhood and Fatherhood

Because pre- and postnatal mothering are now fused in our thinking, the former now has an exaggerated emotional weight for us, as compared with prenatal fathering (which normally includes not only the initial planting of seed but a long period of protective, expectant, imaginative waiting afterward). It is true that man's procreative role is less visible and tangible, and in a physical sense immeasurably less strenuous, than woman's. But it has for that very reason its own specific poignance. When males are as directly involved as females in the intensely carnal lives of infants and small children, the reality of the male body as a source of new creatures is bound to become substantial for us at an earlier age than it does now, and to remain emotionally more salient forever after.

I see no reason to doubt that woman's body, even after it is freed of its special tie to the conscious self-discovery of the mortal flesh, will still have a special post-hoc significance for us as the original nurturer of that flesh, as the heart that sent blood through it before it saw light. But this significance will be changed once the body, and therefore birth itself, no longer seems obscene. The change will not make woman's procreativity less miraculous than it is now, only less horrifying to the spirit that wants to assert its bright distinctness, its non-identity with mucus and blood; the spirit that at present still resonates to the image of Athena springing (fully formed and presumably dry) from the forehead of Zeus. And there will be another change as well: once fatherhood, like motherhood, means early physical intimacy, man's procreativity will seem in its own way as concretely miraculous, as fraught with everyday magic, as woman's. For man's body will carry for us as intense an emotional charge, a charge as pervaded with primitive pre-verbal feeling, as woman's.

We know very well already what this charge will be. We already recognize, though so far in principle only, the symmetry between man's peculiar procreative magic and woman's. Her breast, her hidden womb and the dark grotto that leads to it, are dramatic, in a sense sacred: powerful, yet vulnerable, violable. Her superfluous clitoris, vividly alive on its own, is uncannily moving. But so are his superfluous nipples strangely moving. His proud, vulnerable, untamable external genital is no more and no less dramatic than the belly it fertilizes and the breasts that need it to make them flow. And it is no more or less a sacred carnal truth, for his burst of fertile fluid is as powerful, and at the same time as vulnerable and violable, as the part of her that it bursts into: The fragility of his tie to the seed that he buries for so many months in the dark center of another, independent, body balances the fragility of her claim on him to help take responsibility for the child she carries. His life-extending biological link with the past and future rests with her. If he cares about this link, he can be betrayed, just as she can be betrayed if she relies on him to act as a parent to the child. But see Box I.

We are aware of this potential emotional balance, but we do not live by it. If we did, woman would seem no dirtier and no more sacred than man, man no more a human authority than woman. The sexes would be drawn to each other's bodies, and respect each other's personalities, symmetrically.* Women would

(Continued on page 154)

---

* De Beauvoir is eloquent about the special magic of female flesh, and as she describes it this magic seems an inevitable aspect of our situation as self-aware mammals. But in fact it is inevitable only to the extent that our greater early intimacy with woman makes her body more significant to us than man's is. And it is from this fact that our more intense and ambivalent awe of her procreativity follows. We put more energy, under present conditions, into imagining just what it takes less energy to imagine. Our genesis in her loins preoccupies us more passionately than our genesis in his because her body has mattered to us more than his since long before the question of genesis could occur to us. And so the more strenuous leap of imagination that is needed to take emotional hold of our bodily link with him is just the leap for which early childhood has prepared us less well.

Yet this is a leap that we badly want to make: Since we, unlike other creatures, are able to know intellectually that the procreative link between fathers and children exists, the felt abstractness of the link is painful to us: Its emotional inaccessibility makes us suffer. Its unsubstantiality drives men to unsatisfying and therefore escalating compensatory measures, and makes them seem, to each other and to women, in a certain animal sense nearly reachable yet always out of reach.

This is a dilemma that exists only because we are intellectually complex enough to experience it; and we arrived at this complexity, as a species, as an adaptation to an environment that our own inventiveness was cumulatively creating. So it is a dilemma that our own inventiveness is called upon to solve.

Box I

It is true that woman can betray man by carrying away in her body —or denying that it is his, or not knowing whose it is— the seed that he has to trust her to carry, and that if the bodily link with the dead and the still unborn which this seed represents is important to him, this betrayal can be as hurtful to him as his refusal to act as father to the child can be to her. But these two possibilities cannot really be regarded as evenly balanced unless additional, more subtle matters are taken into consideration as part of the balance.

The imbalance in an immediate sense is that, though both are vulnerable, his situation is by and large much easier to slip out of, psychologically, than hers is. The difference, of course, is that if he betrays her it is because he is choosing not to be emotionally a parent on that particular occasion, while this is a choice that she, regardless of who does or does not betray whom, is less free to make. It is easier, in other words, for him to impregnate her and then dodge the emotional significance of fatherhood than it is for her to get pregnant and then dodge the emotional significance of motherhood. Even in cases (and these are still rare) in which she avails herself of freely accessible abortion and feels no conscious heaviness of heart, what she is refusing to let herself feel solemn about is a process that is going on in her own body, not in someone else's. And needless to say if she bears the child she can neither abandon it nor keep it without heavy, lasting personal consequences.

This is part of what underlies the problem that Margaret Mead considers in her wonderfully lucid essay "Fatherhood Is a Social Invention," in *Male and Female.* That essay is oriented mainly to those social conditions (virtually universal in our species' past, and still in force for most humans now) in which the only reliable alternative to uncontrolled fertility is abstinence from copulation. But even under our own conditions, where parenthood is (relatively) optional, its emotional meaning remains in some irreducible way harder for woman to side-step than for man. Even if she is celibate, or homosexual, she is the one who bleeds every month, and this bleeding (with the uterine contractions and the swelling and tenderness of breasts that often go with it) is more directly tied to gestation and gestation only than any purely bodily experience of his can be. And if they do copulate it is of course she who —if precautions fail, or are not taken— can find herself pregnant. What this means is that so long as we continue to be live-bearing mammals, she has to be more callous than he does to escape experiencing the impact of parenthood. And experiencing this impact (whether we choose or refuse to be parents) means feeling through in a peculiarly primitive and intimate way what it is to be human: to be knowingly part, that is, of a process that started before we were born and continues after we die. Humanness itself, then, is in this particular sense more firmly forced on woman than on man.

But there is another sense (and here it is she, not he, whose link with the past and future is in greater danger of being stunted or mutilated) in which humanness is more firmly forced on him than on her: If he *does* allow himself to feel the impact of parenthood, he (since he does so under less direct, bodily, duress) is more surely bound than she is to recognize that he has done so voluntarily.

An anthropologist once told me about a talk with a Puerto Rican cane cutter whose young manhood was being poured into grueling labor to keep his family alive. He thought, this trapped father said, about just taking off; but he did not do it: "I'd miss the kids" was his rueful explanation. He and the anthropologist then shared a sentimental moment of feeling what it is like to be male and human. The kids' mother, I assume (it is implied in the way he explained himself: not that they would die but that he would miss them), never dreamed of taking off. Women sometimes do, but not often: as *they* are apt, ruefully, to remind each other, when a creature has spent nine months inside your body, it is possible, but more difficult, to consider leaving it to starve. Life, then, neither left her so free as her man was to toy with inhumanity nor pushed her so hard into clear awareness that on balance she chose —preferred— to be human. Again, a symmetry of differentness.

But it should be added that the difference between these two parents was enhanced by the fact that she had not only borne, but also spent more time afterward in intimate contact with, the children. The more contact the father has, and the more helpless his attachment to them becomes, the smaller this difference becomes. It is not, then, only the attractiveness of the young (which male baboons, for instance, also seem strongly to feel) that makes men want more contact with babies. It is also their need to share the opportunity this contact offers for consolidating one's *involuntary*, un-thought-out, humanness.

Conversely, women also wish, from their direction, to reduce this difference. They need to share the opportunity for developing the *voluntary*, conscious side of the humanness that parenthood carries: this (together with the more often expressed feeling that control over one's body, to the full extent that existing technology makes such control possible, is a basic human right) is what makes women want safer, less troublesome birth control, and free —that is, unquestioned, dignified, respected, as well as economically non-punitive— access to abortion. It is also what makes them want child-care arrangements that let the time they spend with their children feel as optional to them as it does to men.

Such changes would surely not erase all difference between male and female parenthood. But there is no reason to want such erasure: the bodily contrasts between the sexes, and many of the ramifications of these contrasts, are a source of joy that we do not need to give up to achieve what is essential in the project of sexual liberty. All we need to make sure of —and this is a matter of social inventiveness, not of renouncing cherished features of our physique— is that what is the *same* in men and women can be freely and fully lived out by both. What they share is a capacity for the kind of intelligence, imagination, and will that draws on many layers of sentience at once; the capacity to be abstractly reasonable and at the same time intuitively empathic; the capacity, in other words, to contribute to the self-maintenance and self-creation of human life in two ways that interpenetrate only as they can be contained within a single personality: on the one hand planfully, deliberately, and on the other hand involuntarily, inarticulately.

be overtly, not secretly and half-contemptuously, protective of what is vulnerable in men. And men would protect what is vulnerable in women in a spirit of mutuality, not of condescension, since they would be conscious of, and unashamed of, needing the protection they were getting from women.

Possibilities

It is true, then, that we are born mortal and born of woman. But it is also true that we are born ignorant of both these facts. What we make of each of them, and of the connection between them, depends on what happens before we discover them. Woman is now the focus for our ambivalence to the flesh not because she gives birth to it but because she is in charge of it after it is born. This mutable fact is by far the more important one, for it impinges upon our awareness at an earlier, less rational, more impressionable stage of development, and we are coping with it long before we can learn, or even wonder, where babies come from.

When woman's lone dominion over the early flesh is abolished, she will no longer be peculiarly available as a dirty goddess, a scapegoat-idol, a quasi-human being toward whom we have no obligation to make the painful effort to see her steadily and see her whole. Once we give up this easy way out, we will have to try to reconcile, and live out more directly, the mixed feelings about carnality which we now handle in a split-off, life-denying way. This in turn will help force us to come to more conscious terms with death. Not only the meaning of death, but death's relation to birth, and the meaning of birth itself, will change. Because of our increased early contact with him, man's procreative role will become real for us sooner, and therefore more deeply, than it does now. That rounded complementarity of the male and the female in the production of children toward which we have all along been groping —a complementarity resting on mutual awareness of feeling that only an imaginative, reflective, purposefully procreative species could want to achieve— will start coming into stable focus for us. Woman and man will start at last stably to share the credit, and stably to share the blame, for spawning mortal flesh. *

* This changed meaning of femaleness and maleness will of course extend then, as the meaning of gender extends now, to people who do not in fact spawn flesh. People's bodies have procreatively tinged significance for us mainly because we all *had* parents, not because we all *are* parents.

For our sexual arrangements, the main point here is that we become aware both of mortality and of birth against a prior emotional background whose nature bears crucially upon their impact; and that woman's role in this background, and therefore the meaning-link between mortality and the maternal flesh, is now open to radical change.

For human malaise, the main point is that when this change has been achieved, we may find ourselves able to free the potentially pure human joy in exercising competence, exerting will power, making things happen, from the joyless, corrupting burden of carnal denial that it now carries. We may find out how to handle the memory of the first separation without rejecting the opportunities for direct, effortless erotic flow between the self and the environment that life continues, episodically, to offer; and how to handle the prospect of the final separation without despising the body's simple wishes, without robbing the body of the poignant, cherished status that rightly belongs to loved and perishable things. We cannot be sure that we will be able to do this. But we can be sure that we will remain *unable* to do it until children's first efforts to cope with the irreducible isolation of individual existence, their first steps toward independent enterprise, their first discovery of the mixed blessings of carnality, are felt through as intimately in relations with male as with female adults. At that point, we will have a chance.

Notes Toward Chapter 8

There is a kind of woman who resents and resists the aspects
of our sexual arrangement that I have discussed so far, and at the
same time accepts quite cheerfully the aspects to which I am
about to turn now. She finds ways of defending herself —of
eluding, refusing, defying— the erotic disadvantage that man
expects her to accept, his indifference to her thoughts and
feelings, the contemptuous homage that he pays to her body. But
she feels —with disdain, with gratitude, or with some
combination of the two— that he is entirely welcome to rule
the world: welcome to preside over public life, and welcome to
"wear the pants," to be at least nominally in charge, at home.
   "Boys will be boys" is what women like this have a way of
saying to each other, in one language or another, about politics
and war, about technology and high finance, about the organized
power that administers religion, art, science, and scholarship.
What they mean is: "Let the big babies play their pompous,
dangerous, stupid games. Luckily we are here to handle the
sensible, the real and human, side of life." And about who wears
the pants, they are apt to say something like: "Oh, yes. Yes. He's
the big boss, all right," sometimes meaning: "But who actually
runs this house, who keeps it *alive?*" and sometimes: "That
male ego! If we don't protect the delicate thing, who will?"
   Two streams of feeling feed into this female position, this
position that is the informal counterpart of what men
ceremonialize as chivalry. One is the feeling that the world men

rule is a crazy mess, silly and pompous when it is not cruel
and ugly, and that women counterbalance its foolishness and/or
hatefulness by cultivating and defending for everybody's
benefit another —a more solid, anti-historic— world: a sane
world of food and flowers, houses and children, weddings and
wakes, friendship and love. To say how this feeling actually
bears on history (and its bearing is far grimmer than these
pleasant women, and the men who are pleased to have them
there making their counterstatement, would like to think) is this
book's most central intent: I get to it in Chapter 9.

What has to be discussed first, however, is the other stream of
feeling that feeds female consent to male rule: Women —not
only weak, timid, conventional women, but also many who are
proud, adventurous, iconoclastic— are apt to be guided by a
sense that there is some justice, some mutual protection and
comfort, some necessary balance of power built into this feature
of our "fundamental pattern." (George Eliot's Maggie and
Dorothea [*The Mill on the Floss, Middlemarch*], and Eliot
herself, are examples of this personally bold and worldly
unassuming type of woman. So are Virginia Woolf's Orlando,
when she turns female, and Woolf herself. So are Kawabata's
geisha [*Snow Country*] and Stendhal's Clelia and Mathilde
[*The Charterhouse of Parma, The Red and the Black*]. And
Stendhal himself, as well as Kawabata and Leonard Woolf, are
examples of the kind of man who loves and honors the humanity
of such women without ever dreaming of them as tycoons,
or generals, or heads of state.)

It is a balance that is now under broad attack: reasonable as
it seems to many women, and emotionally essential as it is
to most men, it is still this aspect of our arrangement that is
most obviously, simply, measurably unfair. The implicit, unofficial
indignities that women suffer for the reasons reviewed in
Chapters 4–7 have begun to be challenged by contemporary
feminist activists in a newly explicit ideological language and a
newly unladylike vocabulary of public behavior. But these
are the indignities against which personally untamable women

(alone, often inarticulate, and thus not of widespread help to each other) have always waged guerrilla war. On the other hand there is a much broader, personally more conservative, segment of our population right now for whom the most blatant, officially indefensible injustice, the one that seems most open to attack, is just the one that many a free female spirit has been content in the past to leave unchallenged: male rule of the world.

There is an odd split, then: In contrast to the privately insurgent kind of woman I have been discussing, and the kind of man who is her friend, there is another kind of woman for whom it is the formal, not the informal, side of our sexual situation that is intolerable. To her (and to the kind of man who supports her position), the male-female atmosphere against which guerrilla war has always been waged may seem sacred, not to be tampered with; or alternatively, it may seem secondary, a mere outgrowth of more basic —i.e., economic and political— factors.[1] What she cannot accept is the overt male monopoly of public power.

I am not sure what this split means, but I know that its existence keeps people blind to an essential fact: the private and public sides of our sexual arrangement are not separable, and neither one is secondary to the other. Both have their psychological roots in a single childhood condition. Both will prevail in essential ways as long as that condition prevails, and both will melt away when that condition is abolished.*

---

* This is not meant to deny the importance of fighting each of them on its own level. On the contrary: only as part of this fight is it possible to start changing the childhood condition that supports them.

8

*The Ruling of the World**

Most men —even most men who believe in principle that this "right" is unfounded— cling hard to their right to rule the world. And most women —including many who are ashamed of the feeling— feel deep down a certain willingness to let them go on ruling it. People balk, brazenly or sheepishly, candidly or with fancy rationalizations, at any concrete step that is taken to break the male monopoly of formal, overt power. They have immediate practical reasons for balking. (Both the rulers and the ruled enjoy familiar privileges, and feel committed to familiar responsibilities, on which their sense of worth, safety, and competence rests; they shrink from novelty that could endanger, overtax, and humiliate them.) But they have older, longer-standing reasons as well.

Men's balking, I think, could hardly matter now if women were not balking too. Without substantial female compliance, male rule would at this point be a pushover. And what makes woman comply —indeed, what has doubtless always made her comply, apart from habit and tradition— is something more than the obvious physical fact of her procreative burden, which, together with man's greater muscular strength, has usually, until now, made her look to him for protection and put him in a position to demand her obedience. As modern technology undermines his

* See Preface, page xv, for my grateful acknowledgment of Joan Herr-mann's contribution to this chapter.

sheer biologically given power to bully her, the importance of this something more becomes clearer and clearer.

The crucial psychological fact is that all of us, female as well as male, fear the will of woman. Man's dominion over what we think of as the world rests on a terror that we all feel: the terror of sinking back wholly° into the helplessness of infancy. As the folk saying insists, there is another realm that interpenetrates all too intimately with what is formally recognized as the world: a realm already ruled, despotically enough, by the hand that rocks the cradle.†

Female will is embedded in female power, which is under present conditions the earliest and profoundest prototype of absolute power. It emanates, at the outset, from a boundless, all-embracing presence. We live by its grace while our lives are most fragile. We grow human within its aura. Its reign is total, all-pervasive, throughout our most vulnerable, our most fatefully impressionable, years. *Power of this kind, concentrated in one sex and exerted at the outset over both, is far too potent and dangerous a force to be allowed free sway in adult life. To contain it, to keep it under control and harness it to chosen purposes, is a vital need, a vital task, for every mother-raised human.*

The weight of this emotional fact is so familiar to us, we carry it so universally and its pressure is so numbing, that to be vividly aware of how it crushes us —or to imagine not being crushed by it— is almost impossible. We can refer to it with the elliptical offhand intensity of that folk saying, or describe it with the sustained poetic lucidity of de Beauvoir, and still never focus on how the possibility of living free of it can be concretely realized.

Pre-Christian goddesses, de Beauvoir says, "were cruel, capri-

° Sinking back *partly*, on the other hand, is delicious; it is the basic form of play that makes the adult human condition tolerable. This is the problem that our male-female arrangements are in large part an unconscious attempt to cope with. It is a valid enough problem; what the project of sexual liberty requires is not that we suppress it but that we find better, more conscious ways to handle it.

† I am by no means the only writer who is now urging that this fact be confronted. See, for example, Janeway's *Man's World, Woman's Place.*

cious, lustful; in giving birth to men they made men their slaves. Under Christianity, life and death depend only on God, and man, once out of the maternal body, has escaped that body forever. For the destiny of his soul is played out in regions where the mother's powers are abolished . . ." But having said this (and she says it in many ways), de Beauvoir rests her case. Her implication is that in the very act of recognizing its truth, we will have started to surmount it, and of course she is right. What I am adding is that having started we must carry through what we have begun; and that to do so we must look hard at what is very hard to look at: the precise feature of childhood whose existence makes the adult situation de Beauvoir describes inevitable, and the consequent necessity for female abdication of unilateral rule over childhood, which she stopped short of facing.

Let us look at it, then. The nature of female power over early life has been discussed at length here in earlier chapters, but its meaning for the formal allocation of adult societal authority has not been made explicit. What follows is an attempt to spell out this meaning. First it is spelled out in a summary account of the contrast between maternal and paternal authority in childhood°

° As I said in an earlier chapter, this book takes as its main literal referent the middle-class American situation that I know best. It is meant, however, to point in a schematic way to what are so far as I know very nearly universal human conditions: that women are the first parents, and that they and children coexist in primary groups with men. I must count on the reader to make the necessary intercultural translations or transpositions.

The main point of this account, for instance, does not depend on the existence of the tight mother-child dyad that is common among us: it applies equally to childhood in extended families. It is really concerned only with the most general differences between the prevailing roles of females and of males in early child care: the authorities referred to here as "maternal" and "paternal" need not always reside in the child's biological parents; other females and males can be involved in addition or instead.

Correspondingly, this account has basically to do only with the most general features of male dominion. It does not try to deal with differences in the extent or specific nature of this dominion from one society to another. (Differences of this kind are related, I suspect, not only to economic and political factors, and guiding value systems, but also to differences in the extent and specific nature of male participation in early child care. But checking such a hunch is a task for which I am unsuited.)

and our consequent preference for male leadership in adult life. And then it is spelled out in an account of a further outcome of that human preference, an outcome whose implications reach far beyond our gender arrangements themselves in a direction that I believe has not yet been at all adequately explored: *Male worldly rule is linked to a persistent drift in our species' life that has so far prevailed again and again against our equally persistent impulse toward what men call brotherhood: the drift —in part unwilling but on the whole inexorable— toward despotism in societal authority.*

If people could come widely to see just what this link between societal despotism, female rule over childhood, and male rule over the historical process really is, the result could be fundamental, since it is lack of insight into the nature of this link that makes possible the shared self-delusions on which the historical process now rests. Action embodying such insight might even now make a difference for the possibility that a human future is not, after all, out of the question.

Roots of Adult Male Dominion

The nature of maternal authority

Maternal will emanates, first of all, *from a subjectivity that we encounter before our own sense of subjectivity is at all clearly established. It is the first separate subjectivity of which we become aware, and its separateness* (see Chapter 6; also Chapter 4) *is a fact to which most of us are never fully reconciled.* To recognize the actuality of any subjectivity outside our own —which means recognizing the actuality of our own as well— is a momentous intellectual step. It would be a huge, difficult step in any case: the discovery that any fellow creature exists revolutionizes the nature of existence. And the difficulty is immensely complicated by the difference between the mother's adult sentience and our own infant one, and by our grief at the separation, at the cutting off of our initial sense of fusion with her, that this step involves. We necessarily take this step so far as we must. But few of us carry it to its logical conclusion, which is a matter of coming to see in retrospect that the first parent was after all no more and no less than a fellow creature. To come to see this is not a task wholly beyond human strength, even under present conditions. But it is a task that is rarely taken on, since it is arduous and our male-female arrangements make it easy to shirk.

Female sentience, for this reason, carries permanently for most of us the atmosphere of that unbounded, shadowy presence toward which all our needs were originally directed. And the intentionality that resides in female sentience comes in this way to carry an atmosphere of the rampant and limitless, the alien and unknowable. It is an intentionality that needs to be conquered and tamed, corralled and subjugated, if we (men most urgently, but women too) are to feel at all safe in its neighborhood.

It needs to be corralled, controlled, not only because its boundaries are unclear but also because its wrath is all-potent* and the riches it can offer or refuse us bottomless. *What makes female intentionality so formidable —so terrifying and at the same time so alluring— is the mother's life-and-death control over helpless infancy:* an intimately carnal control exerted at a time when mind and body —upon whose at least partial separability it later becomes a matter of human dignity to insist— are still subjectively inseparable. This *power* that the mother exerts is felt before the existence of her *will* can be perceived.

---

* See, for example, the comments quoted by Wolf in her essay on Chinese women to show the intimidating impact of female rage even in social settings where a woman's temperamental capacity to raise a row is her one and only weapon of defense.

See also the memorable scene in Schell's *The Village of Ben Suc*, in which a tiny and helpless Vietnamese peasant housewife managed to alarm, abash, and for a moment stymie the tall soldier who (representing U.S. armed might, and self-righteous male conviction of historical necessity) had come to demolish her home: What intimidated him was her angry "What the hell do you think you're doing in my kitchen?" clearly understood across the language barrier. This archetypal assertion of the sacredness of the hearth carried for him, one gathers, a tone of not-to-be-trifled-with female authority despite his overwhelming physical advantage over her and despite the fact that her kitchen was by his standards pathetically, outlandishly meager and fragile.

When the child, in the process of coming to know itself as a center of will, starts to be aware of hers, it faces the will of a being at whose touch its flesh has shuddered with joy, a being the sound of whose footsteps has flooded its senses with a relief more total than it can ever know again.* For a long time to come, her kiss will still make bumps and bruises better; her voice will still dispel terror. Yet she is a being who on other occasions has mysteriously withheld food, who has mysteriously allowed loneliness, terror, and pain to continue. She is still —and will be for years to come— a being whose moods of inattention or indifference cast an ominous shadow over existence, a being whose displeasure is exile from warmth and light.

But *what makes female intentionality formidable* is something more than the mother's power to give and withhold while we are passive. It *is also the mother's power to foster or forbid, to humble or respect, our first steps toward autonomous activity.* It is just as we begin to discover the drastic limits of our own will's scope that we start to be aware of her separate intentionality, and this awareness is inevitably pervaded with the feeling evoked by that discovery. We meet her will just as we start to struggle with the human chagrin of confinement in a circumscribed body, a body whose efforts to impose the wishes of its imaginative adventurous inhabitant on the indifferent physical world prove enragingly puny. And this outside will of hers easily prevails, when it so chooses, over our own emerging will: it prevails not only through passive resistance to our wishes, as the physical world does, but also through personal and purposeful force exerted upon this weak, circumscribed body. This coincidence multiplies the newly discovered bodily chagrin, makes it intimate and social, transmutes it into humiliation.

---

* Infant relief is infinite because infant despair is infinite. Hungry or wet, itchy or cramped or cold, responding to pain in the gut or trouble breathing or a thwarted hunger for skin contact with an anxiety so acute that it is itself gut pain and breathing trouble and hunger for skin contact, the despair we originally suffer has no limits that we can conceive of, no end that we can foresee: it is eternal despair, precisely the timeless carnal soul agony recalled in the Christian vision of hell. Correspondingly, the bliss we originally enjoy is eternal bliss, the prototype of heavenly bliss.

Woman is the will's first, overwhelming adversary. She teaches us that our intentions can be thwarted not only by the inconvenient properties of objects but also by the opposed intentions of other living creatures. In our first real contests of will, we find ourselves, more often than not, defeated:* The defeat is always intimately carnal; and the victor is always female. Through woman's jurisdiction over child's passionate body, through her control over what goes into it and what comes out of it, through her right to restrict its movements and invade its orifices, to withhold pleasure or inflict pain until it obeys her wishes, each human being first discovers the peculiarly angry, bittersweet experience of conscious surrender to conscious, determined outside rule. It is against this background that child's occasional victories over woman are experienced, and its future attitude toward contact with her formed.

Mothers vary enormously, to be sure, in their use of force; some use it in only the gentlest and subtlest way, and some deny that they use it at all. But inescapably, they do use it: the adult must act to ensure the infant's survival, and to protect its growth, without applying beforehand for the infant's consent. At the same time, it is not only through force that female will is imposed. Even without setting herself to secure the child's surrender, the mother, because she loves the child, prevails through the happiness that she is able to bestow. In gratitude for this happiness, and out of the wish to cause, to call up, expressions of this vital love —to exert some control over its flow— the child voluntarily undertakes to do what will please her. It takes the initative, anticipating her wishes and making them its own. In this way it changes submission into mastery, is ruled at its own behest, ruled by a powerful and loved creature whose power and love it thereby incorporates within itself.

---

* This is not to say that infants have no power, or negligible power, over their mothers: they are as a rule highly persuasive little creatures. It is only to say that since they want everything, most of what they want they do not get; and this fact they perceive —often wrongly, but often rightly too— as willed by the mother.

But the victor we go out halfway to embrace is still a victor. Some core of voluntariness in the self is still violated. Voluntary surrender is still surrender. Inside the toddler who hugs the woman's knees —living cheerfully within the framework of each day as she defines it, eating what she sets out and handling the objects she leaves within reach, moving inside the safety barriers she provides, learning to keep in and let out at times and places of her designation the excrement that is so continuous with its innards and so symbolic of all control and possession, releasing its hold on life to sink into sleep at her soothing command— inside this toddler, some center of will is suspended, tensed for a necessary confrontation. (As de Beauvoir puts it, the being whom you are responsible, as a mother, to nurture is at the same time "an independent stranger who is defined and confirmed only in revolting against you.") The child feels confidence within the predictable, customary shape of the life over which she presides; it feels power in joining forces with her power; it feels pride in acquiring the self-command (control over its muscles and its sphincters, ability to contain its own angry or grabby or otherwise importunate impulses) that will win her approval. But all of these feelings of strength are inseparable from the sense of obeying, or collaborating with, her female will. It may be a gentle or a harsh will, a sympathetic or an overbearing or a woundingly indifferent will, but it is in any case a uniquely potent will. And the vital strengths that are developed under its auspices must be tested out against it; otherwise they remain the mother's strengths, not the child's.

The child's will, then, is poised, for dear life's sake, to confront and resist the will of woman. But to live up to this challenge is to contend with appalling complications. For woman is not merely the first, permanently nebulous, outside "I" and the first, all-giving, provider, not merely the first, all-mighty, adversary and protector, lover and ruler. *She is also the first "you,"* and this "you"ness of hers contributes in a number of ways to the lifelong emotional impact of female intentionality.

It means, first of all, that her weight as an adversary rests not just on her strength in contrast with the child's puniness but also on the child's realization that she is consciously aware —and aware of the child's awareness— of this contrast. *In confronting her the child faces an old, devastatingly knowledgeable witness.* It is pitting its young initiative and resolution, testing its young mettle, against the very being in whose consciousness the primitive carnal limits of this initiative, resolution, mettle are most vividly reflected, the being who was most steadily there while the child, in its first enterprises, began to discover these limits. Not only does the child feel on some implicit level the fact that she remembers —and knows that the child remembers— the many times that its will in the past has been subordinated to her own. Its sense of her also reflects the occasions on which she has been there when it stretched to get hold of a bright thing that stayed out of reach; when it tried to walk and fell on its face; when it got too tired to play before it was tired of playing; when —after starting to take pride in using the toilet— it made an accidental puddle or an accidental mess. Female will is for each of us the will of the human presence in whose sentience our own will's earliest, most intimate, defeats have been reflected. When humiliation was new to us, and we had no defenses against its sting, our humiliations —not only those of which a female was the agent but many others as well— were seen by female eyes, recorded in female memory.[*] Woman, de Beauvoir says, "knows everything about man that attacks his pride and humiliates his self-will."

But woman is also the audience who has acclaimed our first triumphs ("Look!" my mother and my aunts would cry out to each baby in turn as it shook a rattle, stood up, peed in a pot,

---

[*] Can this be why men are so especially incensed when women "drag up the past," or "harp on things"? The things the woman harps on are often assaults against herself for which she is still hoping for some reparation or some reinterpretation that will help her accept them. She drags them up because she believes he could provide this if only he wanted to. But a man's assaults on a woman tend to be acts which he cannot in fact satisfactorily interpret or repair: he therefore feels not that he is being asked again for something she needs and he can give but rather that he is being reminded again of a failure.

took the cover off a box and fitted it on again: "Look" —in joyous amazement, as if such a thing had never been seen before— "what the baby can *do!*") and the invincible ally whose help made possible our first landmark achievements. What we feel, along with vulnerability in the face of woman's old awareness of our weakness, is a deep sense of need, rooted in her old support of our nascent strength. *It is woman's will that nurtures* —celebrates, stimulates, shelters— *the growth of the child's own will.*

The child, then, in purposefully opposing the mother, takes a double risk. On the one hand she can retaliate by crushing her opponent's pride as only she is in a position to do: she can point up, dwell upon, the child's early failures instead of minimizing and smoothing them over; she can make the child knuckle under again as it has done before instead of acknowledging its growing strength, and its right to win sometimes, by compromising with its wishes. But on the other hand she can give way too far: she can leave the child in possession of an empty field; she can abandon it to a hollow victory, bereft of its mighty sponsor.* Faced with this double risk, a naturally keen childhood fantasy-wish (lived out widely by adult men with the women whom they rule) is to keep female will in live captivity, obediently energetic, fiercely protective of its captor's pride, ready always to vitalize his projects with its magic maternal blessing and to support them with its concrete, self-abnegating maternal help.

In facing the mother as adversary the child confronts the external consciousness in consensus with which its own consciousness first formed and became real to itself. Her will is part of this external consciousness, in whose aura the child's own will, as a force confirmed in the awareness of another person, first took articulate shape. The confrontation is vital, but it is dangerous. For to set oneself against this outside will is to risk losing emotional contact with the outside awareness in which it is embedded. If the mother is defined too sharply as the antagonist against whom the child tests its strength and sharpens its sense of

---

* This must be why saying in a certain flat tone of voice, "O.K. Right. You win," is such a hostile, angering tactic in a quarrel between intimates.

conscious, intentional self, she cannot be fully the witness who
nurtures that strength and that sense of self: who nurtures it by
recognizing and supporting and applauding the child's early
purposeful accomplishments; by recognizing and comforting the
child's terror as it becomes aware of its own separateness; by
recognizing and defending and affirming the child's new, unique,
autonomous life.

The mother's sentient presence while the child starts to feel out
its own status as a purposeful self, a center of will, draws extra
emotional force, moreover, from the fact that she has been present all along: she was there while the child's sentience itself was
first starting to form. As de Beauvoir says of the child, "Adults
seem to him like gods, for they have the power to confer existence
upon him." And the adult who most crucially conferred existence
upon the child in each of us was the female adult in whose
awareness our own was mainly mirrored when we were still in
the process of discovering it (when we were still learning, for
example, that the world which appeared and disappeared and
swam around us in erratic ways was seen through our own opening and closing and roving eyes, that the limbs we stared at or
sucked when they came into range were our own limbs, and
could be brought into range through our own exertions). At this
stage we surely existed for her, and she probably existed for us,
more clearly than we existed for ourselves. Her firm gaze and her
sure touch mobilized the wandering gaze, the unsteady gestures,
of a subjectivity still uncertain of its own center. To this confident, steadying gaze of hers, to this radiant, reliably responsive
gaze and this calm, reliably responsive touch, the new subjectivity clung with a dependence that was uniquely profound. The
gaze and the touch of mutual recognition for the rest of our lives
carry the charmed intensity of this early exchange between the
first "you" and the nascent "I," the exchange in which the "I" was
born.

When this critical initial stage is over —when the child's sense
of "I"ness is established enough so that it can refer to itself by
name, and it undertakes increasingly voluntary activity, increas-

ingly conscious experimentation with the world— it is to a "you"
continuous with this earliest "you" that it must turn for support.
The will that moves the maternal "you" now begins to be identified as an intentionally opposable force. But this force that the
child must start mustering the courage to oppose is the same
force that shed its infectious assurance over the child's earliest
explorations six or twelve or eighteen months earlier, when it was
a still younger, more tentative animal in still newer, less familiar
and marked out, surroundings. (It is the same force that gathered
up this young consciousness each morning as it emerged from the
soft disordered world of sleep and set it down among bright solid
things, in the clear brisk world of daylight. The willful female
who must be confronted by the enterprising toddler is the female
who handed it entertaining objects before it could reach for
them; who placed it in a convenient position for sitting and
watching, or a safe one for crawling and puttering, before it
could walk; who engaged it in conversation before it had words,
and lured it into learning the rudiments of what we call its
"mother tongue"; who has all along radiated helpful awareness of
its expanding curiosity, and corroborative delight at its expanding
grasp of social truth.)

Our later response to woman's intentionality is shaped by the
pressures of this early dilemma. Woman feeds and confirms the
child's existence from without. But that existence needs also to be
affirmed from within. To do this —to test the reality of itself as a
separate creature— the child, despite its fear of alienating her,
must court some conflict with woman: she is the principle "you"
against which the new "I" can try itself out. Maternal will must
be challenged or something in the child stops growing. But the
sentience in which maternal will is centered must not be allowed
to close in upon itself or something in the child goes dead, for it is
in loving interpenetration with this sentience that the child's own
sentience flowers.

It is during this same period of purposefully expanding competence and knowledge, when our willful "I"ness is growing
sharp and distinct, that we discover an additional basis for that

combination of resentment and need which is destined* to form part of our permanent stance toward female authority: *Woman is the first teacher. She is our first guide into the realm of socially pooled experience that constitutes the human world.* As the small child becomes more mobile, active in a wider sphere, it becomes more aware of depending on the mother for second-hand information, experienced advice, to guide its activities and protect them from unpleasant outcomes. ("Watch out, you'll spill it!" "Careful, you'll fall!" "That will give you a bellyache." "If you don't go to the bathroom now, you'll wet yourself in the car." "You *think* you don't need shoes. Wait till the rocks start hurting your feet!" "Lie down now, or you'll be too sleepy to wait up for Daddy tonight." "Leave that cat alone. She scratches." "Let me put that away before Susie comes. You know she breaks things. You'll play with it tomorrow.") Young failures too often coincide with her predictions. In the slow test of our confidence against hers, she is too often the one who can say, "I told you!"

Unreasonably but dependably, the rage that we feel toward the first teacher for this "I told you!" has, plowed into it, an extra and secret ingredient: rage against the misfortune that hit us when we didn't listen to her. When the child responds to "Don't touch it! It's hot!" by reaching out a rebellious hand, what happens is not only what the proverb promises. The burnt hand does of course come to dread the fire. But what also happens is that the pain that follows the warned-against act is blamed on the authority who warned against it: it feels like a punishment imposed by her for the disobedience. The old feeling that she is omnipotent rises up again in the face of her apparent omniscience, deepening and complicating both the respect and the fury that this omniscience itself evokes. (See Box J.)

The first "you," then, in addition to its other vital functions, is

---

* For men in particular. Women, as I said in Chapter 6, are in a position to redirect much of the sense of need to man, leaving mainly the resentment attached to woman: this helps explain why we see in some women a hostility to female authority that seems purer, more virulent, than the hostility of most men.

the original wellspring of pooled, stored, communicable experience upon which each child draws for its fundamental orientation
to communally tested and communally created human reality, for
its fundamental leap into civilization. The child must balance
against each other two considerations vital to its success in making this leap. On the one hand, to ensure steady access to the
content of the social environment that its body and its nervous
system are built to inhabit, it needs harmony with the first "you."
On the other hand, to assume active membership in the human
species —to play a living part in this social realm that (as Asch
makes elegantly clear) is constructed out of the give-and-take
between differing points of view— it must assert itself against,
challenge the supremacy of, this archetypal female "you."

(Continued on page 174)

Box J

Mothers, I think, sense that they are the targets of unjust blame for
misfortunes that they have warned against, as well as for all of the
other vicissitudes of the human condition that children discover under
female auspices. If they unduly relish the proverb about the burnt
hand, if their "Mother knows best" has a gloating ring to it, the
reason may be something more than sheer pride° in their own right-
ness. It may also be that the surplus, irrational rage directed at them
by their children evokes a dimly felt vengeful response. The response
is dimly felt because to feel it out articulately would be unbearable:
its implications go too far.

There is a general fact that women must manage not to see clearly
if they are to stay rooted in the intimate relations which feel, to most
of them, like the only alternative to emptiness and chaos: they bear
the brunt of a profound, many-faceted early filial spite, and they bear
it alone. If this spite were directed simply at parents, not just at
female parents (and subsequently at their gender as a whole), it
could be more consciously identified for what it is —a childish, out-

° This not to deny that mothers with nothing else to be proud of do in
fact often feel this silly pride. It is the inordinate, self-important pride of a
person maimed by limiting responsibilities, by narrowed opportunities for
personal expression.

growable feeling— and endured, forgiven. But under prevailing conditions it is impossible to forgive, and too painful to be squarely identified, because although it is childish it is never outgrown: the availability of woman as target makes outgrowing it unnecessary. Women meet it not only in their children but in the world at large. They start meeting it long before they are mothers. It is a pervasive societal motif.

Just as the rash child's rage, then, at the mother's "I told you!" has in it an extra, secret ingredient —a stubborn sense that she *caused* the setback against which she warned— so does the mother's resentful response to this rage have in it an unacknowledged ingredient. What gives maternal resentment its own special edge is that the filial hostility which evokes it is massively replicated throughout adult life. It is replicated so massively that numb denial and covert revenge, masked in complacency, are for most women the only feasible emotional recourse. (See also Box P, pp. 234–8.)

In this challenge there is an inevitable strain of vindictiveness: to insist on the validity of our own perspective, of our own feelings, we must vent the rage that we feel in the face of early parental power. And under present conditions, the vindictiveness does not have to be —and therefore typically never is— outgrown. If we are men, we are invited by the world's ways to express it directly, in arrogance toward everything female. If we are women, we are encouraged to express it both directly and indirectly: directly in distrust and disrespect toward other women; and indirectly by offering ourselves up to male vindictiveness, the satisfaction of which we can then vicariously share. In either case, we go on all our lives asserting ourselves against the first parent — with a vengeance.

The vengeance throws us, male and female alike, upon the mercies of male tyranny. What will be pointed out presently is that patriarchal despotism is a booby trap into which humans must keep jumping until female monopoly of early child care — the arrangement that keeps us all childish— is abolished. But what needs to be reviewed first is the childhood experience of paternal authority that makes this trap so alluring, and the solid adult consensus about the necessity for male dominion that makes us jump so helplessly into it.

The nature of paternal authority

To mother-raised humans, male authority is bound to look like a reasonable refuge from female authority. We come eventually, of course, to resent male authority too: regardless of its gender, or of our gender, authority generates resentment. But the primitive swing between need and rage described just above is oriented originally, and stays oriented mainly, toward the will behind the hand that rocks the cradle.[1] On the whole, our attitudes toward the second parent —the parent who ordinarily orbits, at the beginning, outside the enchanted mother-infant pair, and who then enters it so gradually that it remains for a long time a very lopsided triangle indeed— are far less infantile, far less inchoate, than our attitudes toward the first.

We do, needless to say, both love and fear a father's strength, both need and resent his feeling of responsibility for us. But his strength and his feeling of responsibility do not ordinarily become tangible to us until after the world has started to lose its initial magic. His presence is apt to be relatively peripheral until after we have started to organize the realm of inner feeling into reasonably discrete regions or units, and to recognize that a creature can have multiple aspects, shifting moods, and still be a permanent, unitary individual. For this reason he is perceived from the beginning (unless, of course, he is an abnormally rejecting or frightening person) as a more *human* being than the mother, more like an adult version of oneself, less engulfing, less nebulously overwhelming.

Even if a father inflicts corporal punishment, it is punishment endured by a body that we perceive as clearly separate from his. We experience opposition between his will and ours, even if he is autocratic and even though he easily wins, through an awareness that we have come to recognize as uniquely our own; and he experiences this opposition through an awareness on which we do not centrally depend to keep us oriented to the environment.

What he mainly inspires is not so much ambivalence as a mixture of sentiments. The mixture can be disturbing, but the disturbance cannot come as close to the heart of our sense of existence itself as the ambivalence of the earlier, more vital, maternal tie.

A father can be quite tyrannical, then, and still be felt as in some sense a refreshing presence. His power is more distinct and clearly defined than the mother's, his wisdom less eerily clairvoyant. Because he is a creature more separate from ourselves, our resentment of him is less deeply tinged with anxiety and guilt. And our love for him, like our anger at him, lies outside the shadowy maternal realm from which all children, to grow up, must escape.

The father, as de Beauvoir has pointed out, is respected for an achievement to which every child, with some part of itself, aspires: He moves in a world that lies safely outside the maternal aura. His spirit eludes, and even partly controls, that wilderness of forces which is both nature and feminine. Even if his work in the world is menial, he has the status of a participant in history, because he is above female authority: he has identity outside the immediate family circle.

So the essential fact about paternal authority, the fact that makes both sexes accept it as a model for the ruling of the world, is that it is under prevailing conditions a sanctuary from maternal authority. It is a sanctuary passionately cherished by the essential part of a person's self that wants to come up (like Andersen's mermaid) out of the drowning sweetness of early childhood into the bright dry light of open day, the light of the adult realm in which human reason and human will —not the boundless and mysterious intentionality, the terrible uncanny omniscience, of the nursery goddess— can be expected, at least ideally, to prevail.

Adult male dominion

In sum, then, male rule of the world is not a conspiracy imposed by bad, physically strong and mobile, men on good, physically weak and burdened, women. Male rule has grown out of bio-technological conditions which we are just now, as a species,

surmounting, and out of the psychological impulses that inevitably develop under those conditions. In an outer, objective sense,
given the practical pressures that have until now enforced female
care of the young, predominantly male responsibility for extra-
domestic endeavors has been a matter of sheer economic necessity. And in an inner, subjective sense, given the feelings of adults
who have been young under female care, male dominion (the
position of men as the main representatives of societal will; the
main managers —as Margaret Mead points out— of whatever the
community sees as its central concerns; the main wielders of overt
power in their private relations with women*) has been an inexorable emotional necessity.

Male dominion violates some basic human inclinations; it has
been a chronic strain on both sexes, a chronic drain on our species' energies: but on balance —even if the balance does fail for
most people some of the time and for some people most of the
time— it has met for both sexes some urgently felt needs. These
needs are pathological, but the pathology is built into the prevailing division of labor between men and women; and the structure
of this division has been mandatory, given our physical past (see
Chapter 2), just as its dissolution is now mandatory if we are to
have a physical future. Male dominion after early childhood is on
balance psychologically essential so long —but only so long— as
female dominion during early childhood is bio-technologically essential. The problem we now face is a problem of transition.

At present, our concrete situation is that the right to be
straightforwardly bossy —the right to exercise will head-on, in
collision with or frank guidance of the will of another adult—
cannot reside as comfortably in a woman as in a man. This is as
true on the level of world politics as it is across the breakfast
table. It is the prevailing consensus in a world of mother-raised

* Ethnographers describe situations in which it is mainly uncles and/or
brothers, rather than husbands and fathers, who exert this personal male
power. Where other aspects of social structure permit, however, sexual love
and domestic relations built around sexual love provide the theater in which
our species' "now it's mama's turn to be baby" drama can be enacted in its
most intimate, literal, form.

adults; it prevails despite wide situational variations in the leeway that exists for such bossiness, and in the manner of expressing it that is acceptable. Among us the rule, inside certain class and caste limits, is this: A man is entitled to issue blunt orders, contradict people flatly, instruct or command or forbid outright, without apology or circumlocution. Another man is entitled to respond in kind; if he is less powerful, physically or socially, it can be unwise for him to do so, but it is not unmanly: indeed, it can enhance his standing. A woman must not respond in kind, or she is unwomanly. She may offer some countersuggestion or protest to the substance of the man's pronouncement, but she must not reject in principle his right to make it, nor may she claim the same kind of right for herself. If she breaks this rule —except in an experimental contest of strength, which she hopes he will win — she can expect trouble.* And if another woman addresses her in the spirit that she takes for granted in him, that woman in turn can expect trouble from her.

It may be trouble that she can cope with, but it is bad trouble. It includes the penalty that men suffer for unvarnished meekness and mildness, a penalty that few men have the courage voluntarily to face: to be seen as sexually ineligible and uninteresting, even absurd, by most people of the opposite gender, and as sexually inferior, inconsequential, by most people of one's own.† And in addition she meets in both sexes a kind of rage that no man, blunt or mild, bold or meek, has to worry about facing: a desperate, primitive, merciless rage, somewhat modulated by fear since it was originally directed toward an infinitely powerful tyrant, but unmodulated by fellow-feeling since that tyrant was not a fellow creature.

In fact, there are women who do cope with this trouble. Natu-

* The reader may object that there are innumerable families —even whole subcultures— in which men are routinely henpecked. But a henpecked husband *is* trouble, in a way that a submissive wife (given the normal psychopathology of our species' life) is not.

† This threat is in a way mitigated —though not really abolished— among homosexuals of both genders. But I cannot go into that complex matter in this volume.

rally bossy women do manage, here and there, to rule some part of what men call the world. Some of them command respect and loyalty, even gratitude, for the way they do it. But they are few.

They are few. It is hard for mother-raised humans to see female authority as wholly legitimate, for to be legitimate authority must rest, in adult life, on consent that can be withdrawn. It must be vested in a fellow creature whose qualifications can be judged, and whose will seems in some way to represent the common will. For reasons that will be discussed shortly, authority that fully meets this criterion of legitimacy —genuinely democratic authority, delegated by freely acting peers— remains an ideal. Still, despotic authority, which is the prevailing form under present human conditions, meets the criterion better in male than in female hands. On the whole, despotism —male despotism, that is— does reign by a kind of common consent; the consent is often uneasy, often withdrawn for a while, but always in the end re-established.

Almost without exception, then, bosses are men. It is clear why they cannot easily be women. The question we have not yet considered, however, is why adults must have bosses at all. Having deposed the first despot, the parent who with the best will in the world could not avoid being a despot, since her power lay in our biologically given neonatal helplessness; having launched ourselves with her help into the human condition and declared our independence of her; having achieved this, what makes us set up another despot in her place?

The original failed revolution, the prototype, recreated in each life, for every self-betraying revolution in our history, lies here. The father-son drama that Freud saw as basic follows it, and is shaped by it. To break our recurrent cycle of rebellion and capitulation, to expunge tyranny from our species' life, we must address ourselves to this prototype.

The Problem of Patriarchal Despotism

The central lure of patriarchal despotism —the opportunity for self-deceit that has so far allowed every big revolution against tyranny to give birth to a new tyranny— first arises in each life out of a set of pressures that psychoanalytic theory cannot be expected to have identified at all clearly, since these pressures are intrinsic to a division of parental responsibility between men and women the necessity for which this theory never really questions. The booby trap that makes it possible for adults of both genders to submit to autocracy without a saving sense of intolerable shame will lie open for us, I believe, as long as motherhood (female motherhood, with a capital M) is a taken-for-granted background condition of childhood.

 Some steps toward solution, and their limitations

The initiative for sealing off this trap will not be taken by men. Still, men suffer in it. Freud's suffering in it made him take giant steps in a direction that bears closely on the relation between human gender arrangements and human malaise.

He himself did not see this bearing: his own male need to delude himself about the nature of these arrangements was too strong. At one point, for example, in *The Future of an Illusion,* he remarks, in connection with the psychology of belief in God the Father, that the mother, who feeds the child and "becomes its first love-object," is also "its first protection against all the undefined dangers which threaten it in the external world — its first protection against anxiety . . ." But he quickly dismisses the threatening weight of this fact. Instead of seeing that it is precisely this weight which makes us turn to male authority and endow even our ruling deity with maleness, he makes light of — flatly denies, really— the lasting emotional residue of the mother's early power: "In this function [of protection] the mother," he smoothly assures us, "is soon replaced by the stronger father, who retains that position for the rest of childhood." His inability to

tolerate the thought of female power once infancy is over comes
out again, in the same work, in a petulant reference to that hateful American novelty, female suffrage: he blames "the influence
of petticoat government" for the illegalization of alcohol which
was briefly complicating our life here at that time. The phrase
simultaneously derides the notion of female participation in politics and exaggerates the power that females can thereby exert: if
the petticoats have a voice at all, it implies, their voice is bound
to take over altogether.

What struck Freud as a problem requiring explanation was not,
then, male autocracy over females. He saw this as inevitable, to
begin with, because of women's built-in unfitness for extra-
domestic responsibilities: "The work of civilization," he says in
Civilization and Its Discontents, "has become increasingly the
business of men, it confronts them with ever more difficult tasks
and compels them to carry out instinctual sublimations of which
women are little capable." In addition, the subordination of the
female seemed to him inevitable because of the lifelong repercussions of our early response to her lack of an external genital
organ*: The permanent contempt people feel for what is female
stems, he says (insofar as it is not already justified, one gathers,
by woman's natural inferiority), from the small child's impression
of the female as a mutilated creature. (Norman Brown's discussion of this question is —in some ways at least— another matter.
See Box K.)

What Freud did see as an interesting problem was the stubborn resurgence of male autocracy over males. This resurgence he
tried to explain, in the same germinal essay, as follows: when
rebellious subordinate males overthrow a dominant male (originally, as he puts it in mythic-metaphoric terms, when prehistoric
sons in "the primal horde" banded together to kill their oppressive

---

* It is interesting that he wants us to note the lasting effect of children's
fantasy (some children's, let me add, not necessarily all) that the mother
must have had a penis once and lost it. At the same time, he needs not to
see the correspondingly lasting effect of the still earlier —and deeper, more
universal— fantasy that the mother is omnipotent.

father), what inevitably happens as soon as the sting of the deposed patriarch's immediate presence has died away is that other feelings —formerly counterbalanced by the hatred this

(Continued on page 184)

Box K

Brown comes much closer than Freud to seeing that male dominion over females, and female acceptance of that dominion, is a function of female control at the outset. The over-valuation of the penis, he says, is a matter of "revolt against biological dependence on the mother," which "is transposed, by collision with the fact of sexual differentiation, into the desire to be of the opposite sex to the mother." In girls this desire is penis envy; in boys, it is anxiety that one can be castrated as the mother seems to have been.

"What is given by nature, in the family," he continues, "is the dependence of the child on the mother. Male domination must be grasped as a secondary formation, the product of the child's revolt against the primal mother, bequeathed to adulthood and culture by the castration complex." He very nearly sees, then, what I consider the real point. But he falls back, after all, upon a version of Freud's "castration complex."

It is the child's wish to "become father of itself" —that is, to be self-sustaining, not dependent on the mother— that underlies, he says, the incest wish toward the mother, the guilt attendant upon this wish (for which castration is imagined as the obvious punishment), and —stemming from both wish and guilt— the horror of being without a penis. To him, this is why people feel "a preference for masculinity so strong as to see femininity as castration." It is after all the mother-fucking impulse —an impulse based not on sexual attraction to her but on the fact that the child both repudiates its dependence on her and "feels separation from the mother as death"— which makes it "likely that a tendency toward patriarchy is intrinsic to the human family."

This reinterpretation* of penis envy and the castration complex

* It is a reinterpretation that should, he suggests, make these concepts less obnoxious to critics of Freud who "are afraid of any implication that women are by nature and by biology the inferior sex." But why "afraid"?

has the advantage of bringing the question of patriarchy and the question of our struggle against early maternal power into some juxtaposition. But the juxtaposition remains blurry. First of all, Brown skirts the issue of whether, or in what way, male domination is *per se* a mutable and undesirable condition. Secondly, he obscures the simple fact that our resentment toward early female power makes us prefer later-met male power by explaining this preference in much more involuted terms, as the outcome of complex, obscure bodily fears and fantasies: those specifically genital anxieties and yearnings (quite apart from the objection that they do not universally form) in no way embody the direct gist of what is accomplished, emotionally, by the shift of authority from the mother to the father. And finally, no one would be moved to suspect, on the basis of his account, that a central difficulty lies in the early parent's gender; no one would dream, in other words, that if we are to resolve the difficulties which patriarchy is our neurotic attempt to handle, a necessary condition is total male sharing of the "maternal" burden.

More generally, Brown does see that Freudian thought "opens up the question of how the psychic dynamism inherent in the human family might, in the fullness of time, produce the antinomy between Master and Slave . . ." And out of interest in keeping this question open for further examination he does criticize Freud's analysis of the family for its "presupposition that the antinomy between Master and Slave is given by Nature." He does, moreover, recognize the "deep conflict between the erotic aspirations of mankind and the institution of the human family." He agrees with Freud that this conflict lies, partly at least, in the fact that the penis is "desexualized" by feelings of fear and inhibition generated by the prevailing parent-child triangle (an emotional pseudo-solution which in Freud's words, quoted by Brown, "on the one hand preserves the genital organ, wards off the the danger of losing it; and on the other hand . . . paralyses it, takes away its function from it"). What he himself emphasizes, however, is the fact that the broader life of the body is suppressed, muted, by the over-rigid channeling of our eroticism into

---

If those critics had more courage, would they be undisturbed by such an implication? His reference notes indicate that he means Fromm and Horney. Does he feel that they are too shallow to face the grim truth of inherent female inferiority?

"genital organization": that is, into forms which are dictated by the structuring of human life along exaggeratedly gender-differentiated lines.

Brown sees, in other words, that the prevailing structure of the human family both underlies societal despotism and constricts sexuality, and that these two effects interpenetrate. He is wonderfully eloquent, moreover, about "the androgynous or hermaphroditic ideal of the unconscious" and about the necessity to fuse maleness and femaleness within each self. But one feels —and I must count on the reader to go to Brown's text to confirm this feeling; it is too subtle and pervasive to be documented here— that this ideal emotionally androgynous humanity he prescribes is still, physically and literally, *male* humanity. In the world he evokes, one does not sense the presence of ideally androgynous but physically *female* humans. On the contrary, one senses mothers and their offspring still somehow tucked away together in nurseries while men roam about enjoying the polymorphous eroticism that is their birthright. Surely one cannot imagine Brown's emotionally hermaphroditic men burping and diapering babies. I would be glad if this impression of mine were, after all, wrong. But what is clear is this: he nowhere indicates that the early parental figure whose importance he so heavily emphasizes can or should be an androgynous figure. Neither does he indicate that the femininity of this figure under present conditions has anything at all to do with the main problem he discusses: that is, with the present dominion of death in life.

presence aroused in the rebels— rise up and swamp them.* The reverse side of their ambivalence takes over —the loving guilt and dependent identification that make parricide an inherently self-reversing impulse— and sooner or later they move to recreate, reinstate what they have destroyed. The remorse behind this self-reversal is "the result of the primordial ambivalence of feel-

---

* This cycle often turns without even reaching the level of overt rebellion. An adolescent boy once complained to me that although his father beat him often he could not sustain anger against him: "While he is actually beating me I really hate him. But as soon as the sensations of the beating die away, I love him more than ever."

ing towards the father." The sons of this primal father "hated him, but they loved him, too. After their hatred had been satisfied by their act of aggression, their love came to the fore in their remorse for the deed. It set up the super-ego by identification with the father; it gave that agency the father's power, as though as a punishment for the deed of aggression they had carried out against him, and it created the restrictions which were intended to prevent a repetition of the deed. And since the inclination to aggressiveness against the father was repeated in the following generations, the sense of guilt, too, persisted, and it was reinforced once more by every piece of aggressiveness that was suppressed and carried over to the super-ego."

This account does focus our attention on the part that ambivalence plays in a failed move against tyranny: it is a landmark account of the vacillation at the heart of rebellion. But we still need to know what imprisons the sons in this ambivalence. What makes it impossible for them to stop hating what they need and needing what they hate in the old man? Why must they kill him again and again, instead of integrating their resentment with their affection and coaxing him into an honored place by the fireside? Why, in other words, can't they grow up?

Freud of course sees this question. His account includes an attempt to answer it. Oppression, he points out, is not wholly obnoxious to us. Identification with a powerful authority is a fatefully seductive position. Through identification the child "takes the unattackable authority into himself," thus acquiring its power; and this power the child then exerts against a safely attackable target: himself. He has the pleasure, then, of being the one who is entitled to inflict pain. But he is also the angry victim of the pain. This escalating cycle of satisfaction and rage is alternately comfortable and untenable enough, Freud implies, so that the temptation to abandon rebellion and return to it needs no further explanation.

Fromm has developed this partial answer with an optimism that would probably have made Freud sigh. In *Man for Himself*, he stresses the self-delusion —the spurious sense of strength and

competence, when one is in fact ignominiously capitulating—
that is achieved by aligning oneself with what he calls "irrational" authority. He directly urges social change: he exhorts his
readers to examine and overcome in themselves their chronic,
hopeless yearning for a kind of protection and guidance that does
not exist, to face the lonely responsibility for human fate that in
fact lies in human hands. But he does not (any more than Freud
did in his own gigantic final efforts to make people look at the
same problem) touch upon the way our gender arrangements
make it easy to go on evading this responsibility. Indeed, he takes
a step backward from Freud by playing down the untidy details
of infancy. This is about as serious a step backward as one could
take, if what I am saying here is right. It is in infancy that our
yearning for protection and guidance is rooted, and this much,
naturally, Fromm sees, even from a distance. But the relation
between infancy and our feelings about gender, which begins to
emerge from Freud's closer view of the parent-infant tie, does not
strike Fromm as relevant for his re-examination of the problem of
tyranny. So he is even further than Freud was from seeing what
now needs to be seen: for *it is as we leave infancy that the
possibility of transferring dependent, submissive feeling to the
second parent —whose different gender carries the promise of a
new deal, a clean sweep— entices us into the trap of male dominion.*

Fromm does focus, more steadily than Freud did, on two observations: first, that societal necessity does not have to be opposed to the interests of the individual; and second, that it does
not have to be embodied in despotic rule. More recently, in *Eros
and Civilization,* Marcuse has restated the first of these observations in greater depth than Fromm's cleaned-up psychoanalytic
framework allows; on the other hand, Marcuse does not seem
prepared to deal with the problems raised by the second one.
Both Fromm and Marcuse insist, more emphatically than Freud
did, on the distinction between an oppressive, exploitative social
order and a pro-human one; Fromm insists in addition upon the
distinction between autocratic ("irrational") and democratically

judged and chosen ("rational") societal authority. Both affirm a kind of hope which Freud, harshly honest, at the end allowed himself to affirm only tentatively, and which I suppose I share, or I would not be writing this book: hope that the big self-deceptions that cripple our species' life can be undone, or at least substantially undermined, if their nature is illuminated; and that this can happen in time to make some difference in the impending outcome.

The self-deception about societal authority that Fromm worked to undermine has a crucial aspect which he, like Freud, completely overlooked. It is true that the more wholeheartedly we knuckle under to despotic societal authority the stronger and more in control of life we manage, at least superficially, to feel; and that this is so because in knuckling under we dodge the challenge of freedom. (Subordinate and shackled, we have no way of knowing what our autonomous competence, unleashed, could be. We can imagine whatever we like: that it would be negligible, and we are wise to have taken shelter: that it would be enormous, but we do not condescend to exert it. Indeed, drawing a sense of power from the more inclusive will in which we have chosen to submerge our own, we need not wonder at all what our competence might prove to be if we had made another choice; free, we would soon learn its painful limits.) All this is true. But neither Freud nor Fromm recognized the feature of our situation that makes it so easy to hide this truth from ourselves, the massive feature in whose absence the malignant self-deception that supports autocracy might well be impossible to sustain: *what they ignored is the fact that as we rush into the trap of male tyranny the big, immediate thing we are feeling the need to escape is not freedom. It is an earlier, more total tyranny: female tyranny.*

De Beauvoir, from a different direction, also takes major steps toward this problem's solution; and she too stops just short of what seems to me its heart. She has described superbly the variety of ways in which man uses woman to support him in his free —autonomous, unguided, unprotected— creation of his own existence; the need he has to keep her unfree for this purpose; and the fact that woman accedes not only because she is forced to, but also because it is hard to be freely self-creative, easier — since this role is offered to her as an honorable alternative— to take the supportive role and experience his effort vicariously. But free self-creation is only part of man's overall program, a small green frightened part blocked and buttressed all around with the machinery and maneuver of self-maintenance, self-shelter, self-defense. De Beauvoir sees this; but what she does not emphasize is the variety of ways in which man uses woman to help him cope emotionally with *un*freedom, with oppressive societal authority: the ways he uses her to help him deal with the prevailing patriarchal organization of social power which though it places him over her also places him under (or —even if he is at the very summit of his system— potentially under) other men.

The heart of the problem

The main use man makes of woman in the face of unfreedom is to hide from himself the depth of his capitulation to societal coercion, the depth of his failure to leave childhood behind and take his fate in his own hands. Woman uses woman in this way too; her mechanism for doing so is not so different from his as it looks on the surface.

For both, the essential fact is this: Few of us ever outgrow the yearning to be guided as we were when we were children, to be told what to do, for our own good, by someone powerful who knows better and will protect us. Few of us even wholeheartedly try to outgrow it. What we do try hard to outgrow, however, is our subjugation to female power: the power on which we were dependent before we could judge, or even wonder, whether or not the one who wielded it knew better and was bossing us for our own good; the power whose protectiveness —although we once clung to it with all our might, and although it was steadier and more encompassing than any we are apt to meet again— seemed at that time both oppressive and imperfectly reliable (see Chapter 6).

Having escaped that power, or at least learned how to keep it within bounds, all but a few of us have exhausted our impulse toward autonomy: the relatively limited despotism of the father is a relief to us. In some part of ourselves we do not really want to be our own bosses; all we want is to be bossed a little more finitely and comprehensibly. And this part of ourselves tells the other part, the part that wants to shake off submission, that really we have already shaken off submission: the boss we have now is a much better boss, a boss we have chosen of our own free will.

The central opportunity for self-deception, then, that lies in the shift from dependence on female authority to dependence on male, patriarchal, authority is seized by both sexes. In the original self-reversing revolution it is daughters as well as sons who revolt, and the revolt is not against a father but against a mother. What makes it possible to replace that deposed sovereign with another and still feel triumphant is that the new sovereign is of a new gender: *If a different, apparently blameless, category of person were not temptingly available as a focus for our most stubborn childhood wish —the wish to be free and at the same time to be taken care of— we would be forced at the beginning, before our spirit was broken, to outgrow that wish and face the ultimate necessity to take care of ourselves.*

As things are, having achieved the shift and found ourselves still unfree, we make the best of our new situation. At the thought of tampering with it too far, we are faced with the specter of reversion to the greater helplessness we have escaped. Patriarchy remains a refuge that we are afraid to dismantle. We feel that the reign of the early mother is waiting for us just outside its walls; and besides, we must balance our dislike of constraint against our fears of freedom. Our stance, in submission to patriarchy, is the stance of tired old revolutionaries: our self-assertion is on the record, so to speak. We have, after all, overthrown the first and worst tyrant, and we are still defending ourselves against the ever-present threat of her return to power. What more can we expect of ourselves?

The sense that our refuge from maternal power is besieged is

constantly reinforced, unfortunately, by the surprising vicissitudes of life outside the nursery. Our hopes for this splendid life
out from under female dominion are bound to be in part disappointed, and this fact acts, paradoxically, not to undermine our
trust in the patriarchal refuge but rather to reinforce our dread of
that from which it shields us. The paradox works as follows: Male
authority carries the breath of the rationally controllable world,
the world that the child —even, in a qualified way, the girl child
— looks forward to being part of when it becomes an adult. But
this world, as we enter it, turns out of course to be far less
controllable, far less rational, than it looked from a distance. We
find in it many of the constraints we met in the nursery.* What
we learn, when we finally manage to escape the enforced obedience of childhood, is that we are still not our own bosses. And we
feel in this shocking lesson an echo of the related lesson that we
learned at the beginning under female auspices: that our powers
to manipulate the environment are limited, and that there exist
other human wills strong enough to prevail over our own. The
echo adds depth to the mother-raised human's fear and resentment of female authority. That we are never, after all, wholly our
own bosses means that the early mother has after all won. We
have not escaped helplessness as well as we thought we would
when we left her; the proof is that we must still submit to uncon-
querable forces: to the indignity of bodily illness, and the inexor-
abilty of bodily aging; to the thwarting of ambition; to unwelcome orders from more powerful adults; to the pressure of social
custom and economic need and the ravages of natural disasters.

* This is partly because people feel at home with those constraints and
reinstate them in a new guise and partly because, for the pre-rational reasons I outlined in Chapter 5, we never feel as grown-up as we expected to
feel when we were children. It is also partly because it would have been
impossible in any case to foresee at all clearly, from the perspective of the
nursery, the setbacks that adult life holds in store: the child has no realistic
basis for supposing that adult power and freedom are anything but glorious
and limitless. The lure of adulthood —the compensation that it promises for
loss of the young prerogative to be silly and shiftless, carefree and playful—
is unbridled self-direction. How is the child to know that this lure exists
only in its own imagination?

Every such proof of our weakness and fragility silently activates a rage that goes far back to our first encounters with the angry pain of defeat. *If these first encounters had not taken place under all-female auspices, if women were not available to bear the whole brunt of the unexamined infantile rage at defeat that permeates adult life, the rage could not so easily remain unexamined; the infantilism could more easily be outgrown.* Under present conditions, what happens is that each setback imprisons us more firmly than ever in the patriarchal trap: inside it, safe under the control of a new boss, we can go on raging at the old one.

On an inarticulate level, then, *both men and women use the unresolved early threat of female dominion to justify keeping the infantilism in themselves alive under male dominion.* Patriarchy provides woman, like man, with a boss for the baby in her at the same time that it affirms her freedom from the boss she had when she was in fact a baby. It provides her —vicariously, through him— with the satisfaction of making the old tyrant knuckle under, bow down, and at the same time lets her enjoy directly a slave's freedom under a new tyrant. (On the other hand, see Box L.) For her, some of the sting is taken out of her capitulation to this new tyrant by the sense that he fears the old one in her, that she is a magic captive, that he handles her gingerly. For him, what takes the sting out, what makes life under the dominion of other males livable, is in part his ownership of her, his access to her resources. This neutralizes his sense of being himself owned and exploited by the social order: He may be a slave, but he is a rich, a slave-owning, slave. He is a free slave, too, free to vent, in his bullying of her, the rage he feels at other men's bullying of him. Feminists have been pointing out for a long time that the subordination of woman helps maintain societal oppression by way of this mechanism.

But there is something more that also helps take the sting out for man, helps blunt the edge of his impulse to resist tyranny: Woman's old power over him is not wholly dead. It is contained, fenced in, but it is still potent enough to help counterbalance the

(Continued on page 196)

Box L

Woman's original power over each life, I have been saying, not only makes man want to keep her down later. It also makes her want to be kept down by him. But the wish to be kept down is never wholehearted: It is no more wholehearted in her case, so far as I can see, than it is in his. Just as he keeps trying, ambivalently, to shake off tyranny within his male world, so she keeps trying, ambivalently, to shake off his tyranny over her.

To live out this impulse toward autonomy that she and man share, however, woman must face difficulties peculiar to her own situation. Since these are utterly invisible to man, and only very dimly understood by woman herself, their effect comes to be perceived as part of her own intrinsic passivity, as evidence of her biologically immutable female self-insufficiency.

I am talking here not about the gross external obstacles —legal, economic, political, etc.— that society puts in the way of female self-determination (although it is true of these, too, that their effect is generally attributed not to its actual source but to some inherent deficiency of their victim), but about complex internal trouble that grows out of female-dominated female childhood. This trouble includes a number of feelings which I have already discussed. (It includes the other side of her ambivalence, the yearning for patriarchal protection that she shares with man. It includes her empathic understanding of, and her fear of, the special retaliative displeasure that female self-assertion arouses in the people she must deal with. It includes the concretely sexual crippling of her sense of personal authority that I pointed out in Chapter 4, her perception of herself as a bluff [Chapter 5], her feeling of "it"ness [Chapter 6], and her bodily self-rejection [Chapter 7].) But it also includes two major emotional handicaps to which I have not yet referred.

The first of these handicaps has to do with a difference between the sexes as to the *kind* of refuge from maternal authority that patriarchy provides. When a man asserts himself against tyranny, when he takes some measure of responsibility for his life into his own hands and becomes to some degree his own boss, his life is still in male hands and his new boss is still a male boss. When a woman does this, her life is moving —moving back— into female hands, and her new boss, like the original one, is a female boss. *Her first fight for some personal autonomy, fought against an authority so total that male authority seemed comfortingly limited by comparison, was in a sense fought against herself.* It was fought against a parent of her own gender, a parent with whom she is apt to have remained passively identified, as a baby, longer and more deeply than a boy baby would, and with whom she is apt to have identified herself actively, as a small child, more fully than a little boy could. Separating the sense of oneself from the old sense of continuity with the mother is a problem for every child; but it is ordinarily a much harder problem for a daughter than for a son.°

In her own hands, then, woman feels to some degree in the hands again of the very authority that she replaced by male authority in order to emerge from infancy. In this respect, the responsibility to maintain one's own life, under one's own auspices, is under prevailing conditions typically more frightening for her than for man. The responsibility frightens man too. But woman, besides being cajoled and pushed from the outside to give in to this fear, is at the same time urged from the inside in the same direction by her recognition that her fight has in it an ingredient that his does not; and her feeling that this is so confirms society's verdict that if anyone is to take on the responsibility for fighting societal tyranny (a responsibility which both fear) he is the one more qualified to do so. To the extent that he does take it on —and as I said before efforts toward self-determination, self-direction, are a minor trend in most male lives too— her sense of this difference between them makes it easy for her to believe that the best thing she can do is stand behind him.

But if a woman manages after all to arrive at some sense of active autonomous self-creation, if she refuses the option of acting as man's assistant and succeeds, against all the odds that I have discussed so far, in organizing her life around projects of her own, she is then

° The son, correspondingly, is apt to feel more continuous with the father than the daughter does. But his problem of separating the self's identity from that of the same-sex parent is less primitive than hers since awareness of and attachment to that second parent becomes salient at a later stage of development. He has, of course, other problems; the full story of what our arrangement does to men will have to be attempted by a man; I can only touch its edges.

faced with a final handicap which is perhaps more insidious than any of the others. Like certain kinds of bodily malnutrition, it typically goes unidentified: The limits that it sets on her creativity are likely to be seen as inherent in her creativity itself. Just as a human body, stunted by semi-starvation, or bloated or bent by some dietary imbalance, looks intrinsically meager or nondescript, intrinsically ignoble and unimpressive, her talent often looks lusterless and narrow (even to herself) alongside the better-fed, more exuberant talent of a comparable man. *What female talent tends to be deprived of, starved for, is the quasi-parental nurturant support that most of us, male and female, still need in adult life from other adults.*

As I said earlier in describing the powers of the first parent, one thing that we need at the beginning from this parent, if we are to come to believe in ourselves as legitimate centers of self-assertion, is help in enduring the inevitable defeats of our own will. We rely on the parent's sympathy with the chagrin that these defeats carry and the parent's determination that they be kept in the perspective of our successes, of our burgeoning competence. We need help, too, in launching this competence: concrete help, and the moral support of knowing that our efforts are interesting, important, to this other, central, person. And if this competence is to be felt as centered in the self, not in the parent, it must include competence to resist the parent. The parent's will must yield to our own on occasion: at the same time it must never abdicate, never go so slack that it cannot foster our enterprises. These are needs that all but a very few of us continue in some measure to feel, as adults, toward the other adults on whom we centrally depend for emotional sustenance. But under present conditions —and this fact in turn helps crucially to maintain our present conditions— it is mainly women who are expected to fulfill these needs, since the original parent is female, and primarily men for whom they are expected to fulfill them.

Men try, of course, to do this kind of thing for each other when they must, and they succeed in varying degrees under varying circumstances; but it is lucky for them that they do not have to do it much, because it is hard for them, by and large, to muster the intimate tenderness that is required; to manage that, a man must identify himself with the opposite-gender parent who provided such tenderness at the outset. In this respect women can do it for each other more easily. But the trouble is that they can do it only with what mutual solidarity they are able to maintain against the forces that pull and push them apart (which include the divisive forces described in this chapter, and in Chapters 4, 6, and 7). Furthermore, they can do it only with what energy they have to spare (and this, like every other factor I discuss here, varies in weight from one social setting to another)° from doing it for men.

Least of all do men do it for women. Women seem to them the ones from whom this kind of help should come, not the ones to whom it should be given. They themselves do not feel ideally qualified to provide it. And besides, women do not seem entitled to it. Female will, under our present arrangements, needs to be curbed, not supported. And female competence, if it is to be available to support the outreaching competence of men and children, must not itself be squandered on the kinds of enterprises for which support is necessary, enterprises that push hard against the entrepreneur's limits, adventures from which the adventurer can return tired and self-absorbed, bruised and hungry.

On balance, then, the emotional energy available to support adult enterprise is distributed between the sexes in a grossly lopsided way. This fact makes an incalculable contribution to the way the world is ruled. Not only is female will feared; female enterprise is malnourished. Women who can withstand all the other obstacles that hinder their exercise of active worldly competence must usually, in addition, manage to be active without the primitive nurturance of their activity, on the level of personality which still embodies the world of early childhood, that is readily available to men.†

° In this connection it seems important to look at ethnographic accounts of what anthropologists call "matrifocal" societies. See footnote, p. 204.

† Contemporary feminists are clearly aware of, and eloquently complaining about, the fact that this is so. What I am adding is that although mother-reared men can do more about this fact than they do now (and had better try their best to do it if we are to muster the creative energy to do what only we can do toward getting ourselves and them out of our present trouble), there is a serious limit to what can be gained by dwelling on what they cannot do: For the reasons to which this book addresses itself, men at this point can no more help being somewhat deficient, by and large, as nurturers than we can help feeling a special, non-rational need to be nurtured by them rather than by each other or by ourselves.

male power to which he has chosen (freely, he can believe) to attach and subordinate himself. A part of him is held back from vassalage to men; he still pays some homage to the old tyrant, who, tamed and corralled, rules him now at his pleasure, with his permission.

Even in the efforts man makes to *overthrow* male tyranny — male tyranny over males, that is— he rests on the vassalage of woman. Reassured that he has the original despot under control, he can play with the notion of emerging from under the wing of the new one. He needed that refuge while he was escaping her power. But now his unilateral dependence on her seems to be behind him; she and he are mutually dependent: he still needs her, but most of the overt power is securely in his hands. He can draw on her vitality, take heart from her obedience, and fight for brotherhood. He can even deny to himself that she is helping him: in Freud's account of brothers banding together against the primal patriarch there is no mention of support from sisters or wives.

But such efforts are inevitably abortive, given our present sexual arrangements. What makes them abortive is not only the inner ambivalence toward the mighty old man that Freud so well describes. What keeps the rebel helpless to surmount that ambivalence is the gender-related instability of his stance in this kind of fight. He is drawing strength from the subservience of woman for a struggle against the tyranny of man; but he can keep woman subservient only with the strength he draws from the sponsorship of the male tyrant. If he wins the struggle, what he at once begins to miss is not only the old man himself, and the intrinsic sweetness of subjugation to him, but also the super-male backing* that the old man provided, which made his control of woman emotionally possible. The ground he stands on as he fights melts under him as his adversary retreats. He is balancing

---

* A man once told me this dream: He was on top of a woman, thrusting, thrusting, with a huge erection. What kept it huge was that another, paternal, man was in turn on top of him, thrusting. Male energy came into him from behind and moved through his body out into the woman.

terrors, dependencies, against each other; the balance keeps tipping, and he keeps slipping back into the patriarchal trap.

This must happen, again and again, until we start outgrowing the original dependency, the original terror of eternal helplessness, instead of trying all our lives to keep it at bay. And we will take on this emotional task only when we no longer have the option, at the beginning, of shirking it by running for refuge from the first tyrant to another of a new gender. When we can not run away from the task we will face it: we will then put tyranny in its place instead of trying to keep woman in hers. The project of brotherhood cannot be achieved until it includes sisters. It is inseparable from the project of sexual liberty.

PART THREE

Sexual Arrangements and Human Malaise

Notes Toward Chapter 9

Male rule of the world, Chapter 8 said, has its emotional roots in female rule of early childhood. Man's private ascendancy in his relations with woman, and his public prerogative to represent the common adult will, serve inexorable needs for mother-raised humans of both sexes. Male rule is, to be sure, wasteful, overburdening as it does the willful-executive resources of man and the empathic-nurturant resources of woman while maiming and stunting the willful-executive resources of woman and the empathic-nurturant resources of man. It is, to be sure, a vehicle of communal self-betrayal, appeasing as it does our impulse to overthrow tyranny while allowing us to go on dodging freedom's challenge. It does, to be sure, constrict and deform us as individuals, and allow us as a species to put off the awareness of communal self-responsibility that could still save us. Nevertheless, *male rule has embodied an essential human effort, an effort to cope with the emotional problems posed by our long infancy.*

It is clear that this effort has been in large part a neurotic one: the societal process over which men have ruled is in itself —that is, in ways other than those discussed in Chapter 8— twisted and driven by life-threatening pathology. Chapters 6 and 7 explored some aspects of this pathology, and some ways in which our gender arrangements are part of it. But psychopathology, to be understood, must be seen as a holding operation, as an emergency strategy for fending off unbearable stress. Like any emergency strategy, it carries its own costs and dangers. Still, there is always a chance that the core of constructiveness in us will prove to have been provided, by this inner policy of desperation, with vital time and experience: time to grow stronger, experience that can put it in more articulate touch with itself. It may be, in other words, that what the holding operation embodied in male rule has made possible is a development in our communal sensibility that could not have been achieved at any earlier point in our cultural evolution. We may now have the beginnings of a usable perspective on the hazards of our long infancy, the beginnings of courage to handle these hazards in freer, more direct and exuberant, ways.

To use that new perspective, to exercise that new courage, is also to take a step toward the center of the scary old question implicit in myths of half-human beasts like the ones after which this book is named: the question of where we fit in the animal kingdom. Facing the actual problems of feeling which patriarchy is an evasive attempt to solve is a step that scares us not only in its own right but also because it brings us to grips with this question. It does so by forcing us to renounce the notion that male rule of the human world —and the pattern of blind coerciveness of which it is part— is a simple expression of our continuity with certain of our non-human relatives, i.e., that this is a pattern built into our animal nature as it is built into theirs and therefore —even if deplorable— inevitable. To face the problems that patriarchy helps us dodge we must grasp patriarchy's humanly psychological crux, which means coming closer to knowing the so far unbearable truth of what we are.

This crux lies in certain features of our infancy, and in the nature of our adult cognition: first, in the baby's helplessness, together with the depth and complexity of its perception of, and response to, its situation; and then in the fact that our memory reaches back so far, and therefore that our later awareness, in which articulate, rational processes play so large a part, is at the same time suffused with the atmosphere of our very early, pre-articulate and pre-rational, experience. It is because of

these specifically human facts —whose overall implications we
have not yet found it in us to embrace— that female authority
(*under prevailing but now mutable early-child-care conditions*)
is endowed with a specifically human force: a force that must be
overthrown and then kept alive in captivity, brought to heel
and then appeased, cajoled; a force that must be ritually
murdered and then revived, ritually exorcised and then
re-invoked, if our communal mental stability —nutty and
precarious as it is— is to be preserved at all.

The male-governed world-making enterprise has had at its
heart, then, our ongoing struggle against our own infantilism,
*our ongoing struggle to carve out, and fence around, a realm for
the exercise of sober self-reliance.* (See Box M.) It is true that
this realm, insofar as we have succeeded in carving it out,
is polluted (in important ways increasingly polluted as the
enterprise goes forward) with bluff, with death-ridden

(Continued on page 205)

Box M

Humans take an odd comfort and pleasure, they seem to draw some
sense of moral justification, from observations of continuity between
their own social arrangements and those of other creatures. And yet
we have sensed for a long time that male dominion is a condition
somehow less simple and fixed in our own life than in the lives of
baboons and gorillas. Indeed the point I made in Chapter 8 —that
this condition is in our case a reaction to, a revolution against, earlier
experience of female dominion— is an insight embodied not only
in the proverb to which Part II's title refers, but in still earlier folklore. I am referring to the widespread presence, under varying cultural
conditions, of myths depicting bygone eras in which matriarchy, not
patriarchy, prevailed, and describing the reversal of power relations
that then took place.

These myths stir lively interest in feminist circles. They stir it,
however, for what I think is a mistaken reason: they are welcomed
as actual historical evidence, hard evidence, that a world free of male
dominion is a feasible, not an unnatural or unheard of, possibility.

But the case for such a possibility does not need to rest on this kind of "evidence." The main significance of these myths, it seems to me, is psychological, not historical: the conclusion that their existence tells us something factual about prehistory seems to me very much open to question,* and this question has more active societal importance for the light that thinking about it sheds on our fantasy life than for the light that its definitive answer might shed on our actual history.

If what I have said in Part II of this book is valid, one is forced to wonder how genuinely matriarchal —i.e., female-ruled— regimes can ever have prevailed in human society. Folk tales describing such a period make excellent sense as a fantasy projection back into our species' past of a central drama in each individual's past. As a possible record of real event, they make (to me at least) very ambiguous sense indeed. It seems improbable not only biotechnologically, but psychologically as well, that the hand that rocked the cradle can ever in fact have predominated in the ruling of the world. I cannot swear, of course, that this state of affairs has never existed. But what I am willing to say with some confidence is that if it had indeed at one time existed it could not have been a state of affairs that should now inspire feminist nostalgia.

Consider the possibilities. Could men have dominated early child care in some past epoch, as women have done in every situation we know of? If they had, and if my thesis in Part II is correct, the ruling of the world would have rested in female hands then for the same reason it rests in male hands now. But why should that have happened? And in any case that unlikely world, if it had existed, would have been in all essentials the same as the one we already know. Alternatively, could men and women have shared early child care at one time on an equal basis? How surprising! And in that improbable case, what emotional basis for matriarchy can be supposed to have resulted? What seems by a huge margin the likeliest supposition is that prehistoric children, like more recent and contemporary ones, lived their early lives under predominantly female auspices. *If matriarchal power had actually prevailed at some early stage of our cultural evolution, then, it would almost certainly have prevailed in a world*

---

* I question it on the grounds of this book's examination of the childhood roots of preference for male authority. But see also the argument offered by anthropologist Bamberger in her essay, "The Myth of Matriarchy."

*of mother-raised humans. And if that had happened, it would be al-
most certain to have happened because the relatively limited and
rational power that fathers° necessarily represent for mother-raised
offspring seemed at that time a power too finitely human to be relied
upon in any central way.*

Such a matriarchy would have needed badly to be outgrown: its
existence would have meant that humanity had not yet achieved the
strength to try —even half-heartedly, as we now try— to understand
that limited, puny human power, the power that we ourselves actually
embody, is the only kind of power on which we can realistically rely.

*In the dubious event, then, that the transition from matriarchy to
patriarchy depicted in myth ever had in historic fact taken place, it
would be apt to have represented, phylogenetically, a positive development, not a negative one.* It would have been for the species —as
it is among us, on balance, for the individual— a development away
from a world stance in which magical passive-omnipotent infant
feelings run rampant, toward another stance (neurotic, but more
promising for the possibility of future growth), in which the need
to keep such feelings within bounds is recognized. It would have
meant not a falling away from some early paradise but a move toward the more confident, more purposeful use of human reason and
will: in short, progress.

° An alternate possibility is that there have been eras in which men for
some reason were not fathers at all, when they lived apart from women
(except for brief sexual encounters) and had no responsibility for, or contact with, the young. Under such conditions the world of women and
juveniles would of course have been ruled by women. But for that world
the term "matriarchy" —with its implied correspondence to patriarchy,
which refers to the dominance of one gender over the other in a social
order based on close interdependence between men and women, with both
taking a strong interest in offspring— would not be appropriate.

Anthropologists describe cultures, which they call matrifocal, in which
men are relatively peripheral to the domestic scene and women carry a
relatively high degree of economic and social authority. It would be interesting to know more about how men are perceived by children under
these conditions. Such cultures —if men do not in some sense really run
them after all— might help us foresee how people will handle the problem of surmounting early parental controls when there is no counterbalancing later-met parental will available to knuckle under to in protest against
the reign of early parental will. (See Tanner's paper in *Woman, Culture, and
Society*.)

The term "progress" rings ugly in our present situation. And I use it in a bitterly qualified spirit, a spirit of the weariest and wariest possible hope. For it is surely clear enough by now that the confidence we rest upon our own reason and will as these have been exercised in our cumulative creation of civilization —in other words, in patriarchally governed enterprise— is a rash, ill-advised confidence. It is clear enough that the vigor that carries this enterprise forward is an obsessive vigor, steered by cruelty and grandiosity, greed and self-delusion.

And yet this driven, neurotic overconfidence of ours does constitute —in the individual life when commitment to the exercise of competence is first undertaken; and in the species' life as this commitment grows deeper, even if it does at the same time grow crazier— a kind of progress: progress toward surmounting that deep yearning for magic superhuman protection which is a carry-over from infancy.

pseudoactivity. It is true, also, that to counterbalance our own boldness in daring, even feebly, to try to grow up, we go on paying heavy, hostile, costly magic homage to the original magic protector: not to woman herself, but to an abstraction of woman as captive goddess of a more archaic realm. Still, the attempt to grow up —however equivocally made— is in each life a step forward.

It may be, in its cumulative societal outcome, a doomed step: we may never get past it. But if we do, it will be because the accelerating material achievements* that are the furniture of this carved-out realm, and the steady growth of communal self-awareness that has taken place within it, have at last put us in a position to make the central integration with which the following chapter is concerned: *integration between our awareness, on the one hand, of the need for reliance on the pooled competence of our own puny human selves, and those misgivings and reluctances, on the other hand, that have so far kept this awareness half-hearted and unsteady.*

* As Marcuse points out, the fact that we have (in principle) outgrown scarcity opens revolutionary new possibilities for the psychological organization of social life.

To achieve that integration is in part a matter of facing what is infantile, cowardly, in our reluctance. But it is also in part a matter of *reconciling the impulse toward competence and self-responsibility with the legitimate opposition that this impulse — because of the pathological form that it has so far largely taken—meets in the human psyche. This is a reconciliation that will be impossible without fundamental revision of our sexual arrangement. And vice versa.* Feminists who accept at face value the worldmaking motive itself want what they simply cannot have. And so, correspondingly, do those male critics of the worldmaking motive who accept at face value the helpful omnipresence of nurturant, subordinate, everyday-life-maintaining woman.

The feature of our sexual arrangement that remains to be discussed is the one that is most tightly and directly part of what is morbid in our collective worldmaking enterprise, in history. It is a feature that has therefore acted, until now, as a potent force for stability, a force that has crucially supported both the arrangement itself and the larger sickness with which history is permeated. But because that sickness itself has now reached so critical a stage that the self-deceptions on which it rests are starting to break down (see Chapter 10), this same feature of our sexual arrangement has now, by the same token, begun to dissolve; and its dissolution will act from now on —within the arrangement and in turn within the larger societal process— as an explosive force for change. What Chapter 9 explores is *the special way in which men and women have collaborated to maintain, unresolved, that central ambivalence toward enterprise and self-creation which lies at the heart of human malaise.*

9

Mama and the
Mad Megamachine

Male rule of the world has two aspects. The first, on which Chapter 8 focused, has to do with privilege: man's privilege to impose his will directly, to exert overt power and authority, to be the official boss. The second, to which I now turn, has to do with responsibility: man's primary responsibility for that cumulative process of worldmaking, of purposeful self-conscious communal self-creation, which most centrally distinguishes us from other animals.

This second aspect of male rule fits so closely with other features of our sexual arrangement, it grows so intimately with them out of female-dominated childhood, that I have already, by implication, said a great deal about its psychological basis in Chapters 4–8. Let me summarize these implications more directly now before going on to the central point that remains to be made.

Bases for Man's Worldmaking Monopoly Implicit in
Chapters 4–8: A Review

One basis for woman's exclusion from history follows self-evidently from the aspect of male rule discussed in Chapter 8. If she is unacceptable as a boss, leader, or teacher in adult life woman must obviously overcome massive opposition if she is to be formally recognized, even in a minor way, as an autonomous source of historic content, as an independent contributor to the pool of memorable event, communicable insight, teachable technique, durable achievement, that history is. But a number of additional, and probably less obvious, bases for her exclusion lie in the facts discussed in the four preceding chapters.

Implicit in Chapter 4 is the way in which man's monopoly of history-making follows from the double sexual standard. As the unpossessed possessor of woman he is freer than she is to come and go —geographically or psychologically— from the place where they are intimate: It is he, not she, who can leave what belongs to him —to go to a war or a laboratory, to spend all night writing or painting— without violating the terms of ownership. Second, since it is he whose sexual impulsivity is legitimate, while she is expected to be receptive and undemanding, it is he, not she, at whose initiative erotic energy can with propriety be withdrawn from love and invested in worldly affairs: She, not he, is the one who must wait when the other turns away and be sexually available when he comes back. Finally, since personal sentiment is less closely tied to sex for him than for her, it is easier for him to uproot himself from their private realm when the public realm pulls at him: He is the one who has more passion to spare for history.

Implicit in Chapter 5 is the way in which the complementary male and female forms of childishness help guarantee this same outcome. Preoccupied with her shaky she-goddess bluff, with trying to embody for him the magic power that the early mother embodied for both of them; sensing that he, by comparison, feels in fuller possession of the more finite powers that he is expected to embody; intuiting that to the tiny child in himself he looks more comfortably like papa than she, to the child in her, could ever look like mama; feeling these things, she is glad enough to see her bluff succeeding, relieved to find herself accepted by him as the one whose blessing is vital, the life-giving witness for whom he performs and whose infinite private female authority he strives to counterbalance with public male achievement. Often this performance of his seems to her comical, childish. But it is important to him, she sees, to believe that what he does would be beyond her powers; and maybe —how can she, without testing herself, be sure?— he is right. In any case, why should she challenge his bluff, since he seems disinclined to challenge hers? She is apt to be concerned not with displaying the human powers that he assumes she lacks, but with continuing to seem in command of the superhuman ones that he assumes she possesses.

Implicit in Chapter 6 —in the "I"ness of mother-raised man and the relative "it"ness of mother-raised woman— is another basis for our common consent that he should make history while she acts as his audience-assistant and captive adversary. History is made by "I"s. They make it with reference to, and in opposition to, the quasi-sentient living stuff from which their "I"ness has carved itself out. Under present conditions, they feel free to help themselves with uncontrolled greed to the richness of this early maternal stuff, as it is embodied both in nature and in women. Indeed, the wild wish to own and control Mother Nature stuff, to manipulate it and make it work for us, so permeates the present history-making impulse that it is staggeringly hard to imagine what that impulse will become if the wish can really be forced up into the light of communal adult awareness —as it can be only when the female monopoly of early child care is broken— and reconciled with our other central wishes. Reconciled, for example, with the wish to survive as a species, and with the wish to enjoy the color, taste, texture, and smell of our short individual lives, the "I"'s stance toward the non-"I" —the stance that sets the direction of the worldmaking thrust— is bound to change beyond what we can now foresee. (Of course, we do not need to know where such change is ultimately apt to take us. All we need to know is that to move, right now, in the direction of that reconciliation is to move, right now, away from universal death.)

Implicit in Chapter 7 is that aspect of the relation between human gender arrangements and human malaise which comes closest to what I want to add here. Woman's status as representative of the flesh disqualifies her, in her own eyes as well as man's, to take part in our communal defiance of the flesh, in our collective counter-assertion to carnality and mortality. The counter-assertion must be made by man: it is he who enacts our rejection of the body's corruptibility, its humbling smelly limiting downward pull, and our renunciation of the body's fleeting, unownable, uncontrollable joys. She exists for all of us, whether we want her to or not, as the statement of these rejected, renounced carnal qualities. It is he, therefore, who must articulate for all of us, because we all want him to, the rebuttal of that statement. This male rebuttal affirms the human impulse toward eternity, immortality, the human yearning toward a truth beyond the flesh. It is civilization, history. But it is a rebuttal whose pathology so colors the way in which this impulse and this yearning have expressed themselves in the world we know that we can only guess what history would be like if the pathology were outgrown.

In sum, woman's exclusion from history is based on something more than sheer force. It is not a simple matter of some massive coup d'état. It is woven into the pattern of complementarity between male and female personality that emerges from female-dominated early childhood. An exclusion like this is necessarily *buttressed* by societal coercion. It could not be maintained without external force since it violates profound impulses in both sexes. But force alone could not maintain it if it were not at the same time supported from within by a powerful web of emotional factors. Among these factors, the central one that remains to be discussed is a particular mechanism of interdependence between men and women without which the brittle communal self-delusions that drive history would crumble. It is this mechanism that has so far permitted us to sustain our commitment — our vital and deadly commitment— to our elaborate, ongoing, cumulative human world, the world which our anatomy and neural endowments adapt us to inhabit, and which now threatens us and our ecosphere with extinction.

The Female Outsider and the Nature of History

Woman stands outside history because man, on balance, wants her outside of it. But she stands there voluntarily as well. She has a number of motives for doing so which are peculiarly her own. And she also has one crucial motive which she shares with man: *Both he and she, for the same neurotic reason, want to preserve the split in our communal sensibility that her status as outsider makes possible.*

Of the motives peculiarly her own, there are two that have been stressed by other writers which must be considered here since they bear upon the crucial one that she shares with him.

Two female motives for abstention from history-making

Socially sanctioned existential cowardice. In de Beauvoir's view, the central bribe to which woman succumbs is the privilege of enjoying man's achievements and triumphs vicariously, honored and treasured by him as arbiter, witness, nurturant servant-goddess, while enjoying immunity from the risks he must take. He too, de Beauvoir points out, would like to have this immunity —all of us fear the freedom and responsibility which in fact we must, as a species, accept— but life does not offer him this option: the option is hers, in return for acting as supportive "other" to him while he makes the human world for both of them. "The disquieting gap," she says, "between the planned works of man and the contingence of nature . . . becomes beneficial when woman" (who represents nature in domesticated form) ". . . too docile to threaten man's works, limits herself to enriching them and to softening their too rugged lines. . . . In woman even frivolity, capriciousness and ignorance are charming virtues because they flourish this side of and beyond the world where man chooses to live but where he does not like to feel himself confined. . . . She is the deep reality hidden under the appearance of things: the Kernel, the Marrow." She is "aware of the original contingency of man himself and of this" (societal, historical) "necessity in which he believes." In counterpoint to "set meanings and tools made for useful purposes, she upholds the mystery of intact things." She is also "a privileged judge" who "speaks from a sense of different values, with an instinctive wisdom of her own. . . . Man seeks her 'intuitions' as he might interrogate the stars." He is "ratified by her." He needs her as a mirror "because the inwardness of the existent" (that is, of the self-aware, purposeful creator of human reality, the history-maker) "is only nothingness and because he must project himself into an object in order to reach himself." So "what he really asks of her is to be, outside of him, all that which he cannot grasp inside himself." Woman's "whole situation destines her" to act as the "concerned spectator" in his life. And she can do and be all this only by remaining "outside the fray." It is through her embodiment of this —to him precious— otherness, as well as through her work as his practical servant, that woman acts to "maintain life while man extends its range through his activities . . ." And in return "she can evade at once both economic risk and the metaphysical risk of a liberty in which ends and aims must be contrived without assistance." This liberty, which it is the person's moral obligation to affirm, is "transcendence." That is, the only "justification for present existence" is "its expansion into an infinitely open future," through "exploits" or "freely chosen projects." The person who succumbs to "the temptation to forgo liberty and become a thing" is "lost, ruined."

There is no hint in this account that what appears to be a "freely chosen project" can in fact be chosen out of neurotic inner compulsion; that the person's "undefined need to transcend himself" can in fact be a need to escape something essential in himself; and that the reason why man wants woman "to be, outside of him, all that which he cannot grasp inside himself" is that if he had to grasp inside himself a certain aspect of what she represents, instead of relying upon her to represent it, the self-evasion

and blind drivenness underlying his "exploits" could not be maintained. His sense that he "cannot" grasp it is based on fear of
outgrowing this drivenness and self-evasion.

The inner "nothingness" of the male "existent" —which de
Beauvoir keenly notes, because she is far too perceptive to miss it,
but which she does not account for— is something more and
other than the legitimate need of human intelligence and will to
exercise themselves, and discover their own nature, through interaction with external objects. This nothingness is the void left
by suppression of the essential part of the self that in a sane
human creature would counterbalance, and be reconciled with,
what she calls transcendence: the part that lives in the present, in
the body, in the steady, stable, living flow between persons and
between each person and the non-human surround.

What I want to add to de Beauvoir's account, then, is that *the
immunity life offers woman is immunity not only from the risks
and exertions of history-making, but also from the history-maker's
legitimate internal misgivings about the value of what he spends
his life doing. The use that both sexes make of this female immunity, their mutual motive in fostering it, is in my view the
morbid core of our sexual arrangement. To uncover it is the main
point of this book.*

Motherhood. The other peculiarly female motive which must
be considered here is one that has been emphasized by Margaret
Mead. Briefly,[1] what Mead says is that woman consents to leave
to man the main responsibility for history —for the formally
recognized spiritual, psychological continuity of the species—
because his self-respect requires it to counterbalance her more
impressive contribution, as childbearer, to the species' physical
continuity. She cherishes his self-respect because —if for no other
reason— his male sexual vigor, which it is in her interest to foster,
depends upon it. Besides, she feels —at least under the technologically primitive conditions with which Mead's survey is mostly
concerned— enough pride and pleasure in the importance of her
own taxing, dangerous, dramatic contribution; he is welcome to

whatever compensatory glory he can muster. Her own need for counter-assertion to the body's mortal limits is met by her greater intimacy with, and responsibility for, the continuous emergence and flowering of fresh, sweet new bodies.*

This account rings clearly true. One recognizes the balance of power that Mead describes; it does contribute to the stability of our traditional arrangements. And yet it seems to me clear as well that it is not the whole story. If contact with babies, with the physical self-renewal of our communal life, were in itself enough to reconcile us to mortality —or, more precisely, to the separateness, vulnerability, and finiteness of each individual person— then men would long ago have discovered the secret and stormed the world's nurseries. Women, moreover, would not take the intense vicarious interest which they do in fact take in the glorious public deeds of men; nor would they ever themselves push, against all the societal and emotional constraints that converge to keep them at home, out into the arena of public achievement, the male arena where "with streaming banners" (as the song says) "noble deeds are done": They would have no reason to dream of doing any such unnecessary and punishable thing.

What Mead does not say is that, *in leaving to man the enactment through compulsive public enterprise of our counter-assertion to carnal mortality, woman makes it possible for him to do what both neurotically need to have done*; and that *in taking upon himself the responsibility to do it, inside an arena fenced around with "Men Only" signs, man makes it possible for woman to express something that both neurotically need to have expressed outside, not inside, this fence: the feeling that there is something trivial and empty, ugly and sad, in what he does.*

---

* The flesh of babies is uncontaminated by self-rejection. This —over and above the biologically essential brute charm that they, like other animal infants, must have for the adults who nurture them— is what makes them so magically attractive to us. Their shit, as it happens, does not begin to stink until just about the time when the human passions of ambition, pride, and shame start to take shape in them.

A motive both sexes share

In agreeing that it is mainly man who should make history, women and men have in common, then, a motive to maintain what is death-denying, life-rejecting, in the process of self-creation that is our species' central distinguishing trait.

Our misgivings about this process —not our cowardly misgivings, our unwillingness to know that we are creating ourselves, but our erotic, life-rooted misgivings— are far too strong to be altogether suppressed. They are strong enough so that if they were not somehow sealed off from the historic process they would disrupt it, overturning the neurotic stance around which it is organized. What male thinkers who do try to make them part of the historic process fail to identify —because their situation (see Box N) makes it impossible for them to arrive at the necessary perspective on our sexual arrangements— is *the actual mechanism by which we manage, as a species, to keep these misgivings sealed off. Keeping them sealed off, so that the malignant stance around which history is organized can be preserved, is a central function of the male-female division of sensibility that demands woman's exclusion from history.*

It is woman who most steadily and matter-of-factly articulates the emotional insight that the realm of enterprise and achievement, the realm of streaming banners where noble deeds are done, is in a crucial way dominated by the spirit —the religion, really— which is organized around what Lewis Mumford calls "the myth of the machine."

(Continued on page 217)

Box N

One reason why it is harder for men than for women to achieve real critical perspective on our gender arrangements is that mother-raised man's self-respect rests too heavily on the belief that he is better than woman and has successfully put her in her proper place; in other words, that he has outgrown her initial power over him: The thought that the arrangement has in some way maimed him too —that it does not represent an unequivocal triumph over her, that it is not wholly to his advantage— is too threatening to be voluntarily entertained.

I have seen on the faces of some men who are on the whole quite likable a certain smile that I confess I find deeply unattractive: a helpless smile of self-congratulation when some female disadvantage is referred to. And I have heard in their voices a tone that (in the context of what women put up with) is equally unattractive: a tone of self-righteous, self-pitying aggrievement when some male disadvantage becomes obvious. This sense of being put upon that many men feel in the face of evidence that the adult balance is not at every point by a safe margin in their favor seems based on the implicit axiom that to make life minimally bearable, to keep their very chins above water, to offset some outrageous burden that they carry, they must at least feel that they are clearly luckier and mightier than women are.

The smile and the tone of voice that convey this attitude become more understandable (though no more charming) when one recognizes that to leave the female-dominated world of early childhood, and to do what is expected of them as adults, men need —in a way women do not— to imagine themselves stronger, less damaged, more in control of circumstance, than they really are.

That women take more initiative than men do in challenging the sexual status quo is not, of course, primarily a matter of their relative freedom to acknowledge themselves maimed. It is true that their situation keeps them in closer conscious touch than men are with a sense of human defectiveness. But what makes this true is not only the fact above, i.e., that they are less pressed than men are to perceive themselves as glorious and triumphant. It is also —indeed, mainly— that they are *more* pressed than men are to perceive themselves as flawed. Box P explores this side of the matter.

The outcome of the pressure on men pointed out here, together with the pressure on women pointed out in Box P (pages 234–38), is an asymmetry so all-pervasive that it goes largely unexamined. Both sexes want something that neither sex has, something that we know —because scattered, sporadic, unhousebroken but deeply significant experience tells us so— is potentially available to both: free use of all those capacities for thought, feeling, and action that men and women have in common. But the partial humanity of women includes awareness of its own incompleteness, while the partial humanity of men can on the whole function as it does only by denying its own incompleteness.

Men manage to acknowledge their emotional need for women without allowing themselves to feel lacking in any important way. They may, on some dim level, recognize mutual defectiveness. But they project this sense that something is wrong mainly onto women, who disappoint legitimate male wishes and at the same time press totally unreasonable female demands. (This male quirk is lampooned by Shaw in *Pygmalion*, and even more broadly in the musical version of that play, *My Fair Lady*: think of Professor Higgins singing "Why can't a woman be like a man?" and —in incredulous exasperation— "Damn! damn! damn! I've grown accustomed to her face!") Women, of course, both need and complain about men too. But they are both more *free* to see, and more stringently *forced* to see, that in fact each sex is flawed.

Mumford's "megamachine." The convergence of his view with Brown's. This spirit, Mumford says in *The Pentagon of Power*, aims "to replace the gifts of nature with those more limited fabrications of man which were drawn from a single aspect of nature: that which could be brought under human domination." It is a spirit that has had in it from the beginning "a touch of defiant pride and demonic frenzy," a spirit that has, as civilization advanced, striven toward "a world of light and space, disinfected of the human presence"; a spirit that, because it set up "the machine as the ultimate model for scientific thought," has now eventuated in a "de-natured" environment "fit only for machines to live in." As Mumford traces it, this "myth of the machine" runs not only through science and technology, but also through social organization: The model of the machine —or, more generally, the worship of what is orderly, predictable, controllable, at the expense of what is alive— also expresses itself in "political absolutism and regimentation." The world this myth has led to, he says, forgets that man is "his own supreme artifact." It is a world which subordinates the *human* (imagination, dream, symbol, religious vision out into the cosmos and inward into the psyche's "heart of darkness") to the *mechanical* (power, speed, remote control; coercive bureaucracy; mass duplication; grandiose gigantism; production for obsolescence —dictated by the machinery of financial profit— and its twin, "indiscriminate and incontinent consumption"). It is life gone cancerous, anti-organic.

Mumford calls this world "the megamachine," the final embodiment of the self-contemptuous human impulse toward worship of dead automatic things and disrespect for what lives. If we continue this form of worship, he says, "man's vital organs will all be cannibalized in order to prolong the megamachine's meaningless existence." But this megamachine, he reminds us, is not self-propelled. There is a man in it: it is driven "above all by a love-rejecting pursuit of power." And this, of course, is the motive to which Norman Brown also points. Indeed, he quotes the Mumford who in *The Culture of Cities* described the last stage of polis (the life cycle of the city) as "Nekropolis," a milieu "rank with forms of negative vitality," a place where both nature and human nature, "violated in this environment, come back in destructive forms . . ."; the Mumford who asked, "Is it any wonder that Dr. Sigmund Freud found a death wish at the seat of human activity?"

Brown's own view of the spirit at large in the male realm, where noble deeds are done, is a reworking not only of Freud's insights, but also of Martin Luther's. In Luther's vision, Brown points out, this busy, restless, enterprising spirit is expressed in "the archetype of the Devil," through which mankind "has said something about the psychological forces, inside man himself, sustaining the economic activity which ultimately flowered into capitalism." "The Devil," Brown goes on to say, "is the lineal descendant of the Trickster . . . in the primitive mythologies. The Trickster is a projection of the psychological forces sustaining the economic activity of primitive peoples; and the evolution of the Trickster, through such intermediary figures as the classical Hermes, into the Christian Devil, parallels the changing forms of

human economic (especially commercial) activity." In Luther's
(and Brown's) vision, money —or, more generally, the accumulation for their own sake of material achievements and worldly
power— is "the work of the Devil." The devil in turn represents
death-in-life, in the form of a preoccupation with excrement —a
preoccupation, that is, with control over "dead matter and inorganic magnitudes"— and a commitment "to non-enjoyment," to
"alienated (compulsive) labor," which generates "an inner need
to produce a surplus," an insatiable wish for "the irrational superfluous."

Money and power involve a compulsive giving and a compulsive taking, in each of which assaultive and expiative impulses are
fused. "Money is condensed wealth; condensed wealth is condensed guilt." The function of this basic guilt is to support our
cowardly renunciation of life's delight, for the "illusion of guilt is
necessary for an animal that cannot enjoy life, in order to or-
ganize a life of non-enjoyment." Further, "time is money" and can
therefore also, like shit, be counted, saved, wasted, manipulated.
In the city, flower of civilized man's realm, this accumulated con-
densation of compulsive human action appears, Brown goes on to
say, in "piles of stone and gold and many other things beside.
Hence a city is itself, like money, crystallized guilt. 'To look at the
plan of a great City,' said Frank Lloyd Wright, 'is to look at
something like the cross-section of a fibrous tumor.' But guilt is
time: 'In the city, time becomes visible,' says Mumford."

*The unacknowledged function of the female outsider. De
Beauvoir's view extended.* If history were not driven by this anti-
organic, time-arresting, shit-manipulating spirit, woman would
insist on taking a direct part in it instead of her present, indirect
part, which —and this is what neither Brown and Mumford on
the one hand, nor Mead and de Beauvoir on the other, has seen—
helps maintain this deadly spirit. She would insist so fiercely that
man could not, out of his own need, exclude her. It is *her* own
need —not only her open and admirable preference to remain
undefiled by that spirit, but also her covert and far less attractive

wish to have man express it for both of them— that makes her willing to be excluded.

At the same time, history is also the realm in which our species' peculiar vitality is played out. (That it is such a realm is the other big fact that Brown —probably because other people know this fact and blindly, forcibly overemphasize it while repressing the considerations he is concerned with— does not acknowledge. This is what makes it necessary to suspend common sense, as he himself suggests the reader should do, to hear what he is saying.) If history were only deadly and not also vital, woman would be wholly content —as she in fact has never been wholly content— in her role as adversary-critic at its periphery.

In making this point, I rest —as anyone who is examining our gender arrangements must— on de Beauvoir's shoulders. She very nearly saw it: What stopped her from seeing it clearly was her tendency to overvalue overt, external expansion of an individual's lifespace as against inner, subjective, growth. This overvaluation goes with her failure to distinguish clearly, within the existentialist concept of "transcendence," between two kinds of human "becoming": the one that repudiates, segregates itself from, "being"; and the other that embraces "being," that includes "being" within itself. This latter involves the integration of action with the development of mental breadth, complexity, and coherence, with the widening and deepening of perception and feeling. These two contrasting forms of "becoming" correspond to what Brown calls aggressive-manipulative, as opposed to erotic, forms of human self-expression.

De Beauvoir recognizes that woman, by virtue of her non-participant's perspective on worldmaking activity, has more leeway than man to see what is arbitrary and false in it, to note the absurd underside of "the imposing structure built by the males." Often, she says, the female "is not fully satisfied with ready-made clichés and forms; . . . she has a sense of misgiving about them which is nearer to authenticity than is the self-important assurance of her husband." The old woman in particular is gifted by her situation with "irony and an often spicy cynicism.

She declines to be fooled by man's mystifications . . ." But to de Beauvoir this female vision is neutral, "sterile": she points neither to the revolutionary, life-liberating potentialities of the vision nor to the conservative, life-imprisoning function it has so far served. "Amused or bitter, the wisdom of the old woman still remains wholly negative; it is in the nature of opposition, indictment, denial . . ." It is limited to "stoical defiance or skeptical irony." What she leaves out is that this opposition, as things now are, is far from irrelevant to the continued existence of what it opposes: it is essential in maintaining what it defies and indicts.

Thus she accepts "what Stendhal asks of women: it is first of all not to permit themselves to be caught in the snares of seriousness; and because of the fact that the things supposed to be of importance are out of their range, women run less risk than men of getting lost in them; they have better chances of preserving that naturalness, that naïveté, that generosity which Stendhal puts above all other merit. What he likes in them is what today we call their authenticity: that is the common trait in all the women he loved or lovingly invented; all are free and true beings." His heroines, she agrees, "are, quite simply, *alive;* they know that the source of true values is not in external things but in human hearts. This gives its charm to the world they live in: they banish ennui by the simple fact of their presence. . . ." She sees their stature: "Thoughtless, childish or profound, gay or grave, daring or secretive, they all reject the heavy sleep in which humanity is mired." Even in the sex act itself, she sees that woman, despite her concrete disadvantage in this act, is in a way closer than man to human wholeness: "The erotic experience is one that most poignantly discloses to human beings the ambiguity of their condition; in it they are aware of themselves as flesh and as spirit, as the other and as subject. This conflict has a more dramatic shape for woman because at first she feels herself to be object and does not at once realize a sure independence in sex enjoyment; she must regain her dignity as transcendent and free subject while assuming her carnal condition — an enterprise fraught with difficulty and danger, and one that often fails. But the very difficulty of her position protects her against the traps into which the male readily falls; he is an easy dupe of the deceptive privileges accorded him by his aggressive role and by the lonely satisfaction of the orgasm; he hesitates to see himself fully as flesh. Woman lives her love in more genuine fashion." And her comparison between the businessman and his wife makes a similar point: "Woman," she says, "gets her teeth more deeply into reality; for when the office worker has drawn up his figures, or translated boxes of sardines into money, he has nothing in his hands but abstractions. The baby fed and in his cradle, clean linen, the roast, constitute more tangible assets; yet just because, in the concrete pursuit of these aims, she feels their contingence —and accordingly her own — it often happens that woman does not identify herself with them, and she still has something left of herself. Man's enterprises are at once projects and evasions: he lets himself be smothered by his career and his 'front'; he often becomes self-important, weighty. Being against man's logic and morality, woman does not fall into these traps." It is for this reason that "her conversation is much less tiresome than her husband's whenever she speaks for herself and not as her lord and master's loyal 'better half.' "

The very limits on woman's life, as de Beauvoir says more clearly than anyone else I have read, get her in a way in closer touch than striving man can be with what life is: "From the depths of her solitude, her isolation, woman gains her sense of the personal bearing of her life. The past, death, the passage of time — of these she has a more intimate experience than does man; she feels deep interest in the adventures of her heart, of her flesh, of her mind, because she knows that this is all she has on earth. And more, from the fact that she is passive, she experiences more passionately, more movingly, the reality in which she is submerged than does the individual absorbed in an ambition or a profession . . ." Even what man sees as her frivolity has depth in it: "She is enchanted by the useless charm of a bouquet of flowers, a cake, a well-set table; she enjoys turning her empty leisure into a bountiful offering. Loving laughter, song, adornments, and knickknacks, she is prepared to accept all that throbs around her:

the spectacle of the street, of the sky; an invitation, an evening out, open new horizons to her. Man often declines to take part in these pleasures; when he comes into the house, the gay voices are silenced, the women of the family assume the bored and proper air he expects of them."

And still it seems clear to de Beauvoir that man's situation "is far preferable; that is to say, he has many more opportunities to exercise his freedom in the world. The inevitable result is that masculine accomplishment is far superior to that of women, who are practically forbidden to *do* anything." Woman's attitude toward herself and the world is ambiguous, she says. "The domain in which she is confined is surrounded by the masculine universe, but it is haunted by obscure forces of which men are themselves the playthings. . . . Society enslaves Nature; but Nature dominates it. The Spirit flames out beyond life; but it ceases to burn when life no longer supports it. Woman is justified by this equivocation in finding more verity in a garden than in a city . . ." But *is* this really more of an "equivocation" than de Beauvoir's implication that there is of course, on the contrary, more verity in a city than in a garden? Woman "endeavors to combine life and transcendence," she remarks, as if this is a self-evidently impossible combination. "She craves a good that is a living Harmony in the midst of which she is placed simply by virtue of being alive. The concept of harmony is one of the keys to the feminine universe; it implies a stationary perfection. . . . In a harmonious world woman thus attains what man will seek through action: she meshes with the world, she is necessary to it, she cooperates in the triumph of the Good. The moments that women regard as revelations are those in which they discover their accord with a static and self-sufficient reality. . . . The joy that lies in the free surge of liberty is reserved for man; that which woman knows is a quiet sense of smiling plenitude."

Woman, she sums up, "cannot be reproached for enjoying a fine afternoon or a cool evening. But it is a delusion to seek the hidden soul of the world here. The Good cannot be considered something that *is* . . ." Why not? one wonders. And by what criterion is it more misguided to "seek the hidden soul of the world" in a "sense of smiling plenitude" than in "the free surge of liberty"?

So despite her insight into the ways in which woman's hold on reality is deeper, despite her (unassimilated) recognition that striving, self-important man tends to lose a kind of direct human aliveness —"authenticity"— which his wife tends to keep, de Beauvoir still takes the male worldmaking enterprise at face value. Freedom for woman still seems to her a simple entering into man's realm. That man's realm must change for this to happen, and what this change must be, is a problem to which she does not address herself. For just as she never questions the need for female-dominated early child care, or grasps its full psychological consequence for the later development of the child, she does not see the interdependence between the deathliness of the male realm and woman's place outside it.

When she considers at the end of the book, then, what men have to gain and to lose by "complete economic and social equality" for women, she discusses their misplaced nostalgia for "feminine charm": This she consigns —along with other lovely remnants of oppression like "the rare lace of slavery days and the crystal-clear voice of the eunuch"— to the "attics of time." But she does not mention the need for men to embrace within their own sensibility the values that they now count on charming women to embody. She sees that real equality between the sexes will both "spare men many troubles" (by which she means the economic and emotional burdens imposed by dependent women) and "deny them many conveniences" (by which she means woman's practical services, the enjoyable luxury of her presence as "at once his like and a passive thing," and "certain forms of the sexual adventure"). But she does not in any way indicate that what men will lose is the dangerous comfort of the "normal" neurosis that now pervades their enterprises, their exploits, their projects; and that what they will gain —if time permits— is the opportunity to be "transcendent" creatures whose "immanence" is not a sterile, dead part of the self but a living one: "existents" whose "becoming" is nourished by, and nourishes, their own fertile "being."

Male-Female Collaboration to Keep History Mad

Freud called woman "the enemy of civilization," and in a sense this is true. But he radically oversimplified. She is the loyal opponent, the indispensable defanged and domesticated critic, of what he himself identified as the essential, and imminently lethal, sickness of civilization. Without her sabotage, civilization as it is could not go on. This sabotage is harmless to what it purports to assault. Indeed it dissipates what could be effectively explosive feeling, discharges potentially subversive emotional energy in frivolous and impotent, homey and comfortable, ways. It farts away internal pressure that would otherwise shatter the social system. She is not civilization's enemy: she is its court jester, without whose jibes the court would collapse.

The jibes come in a steady stream. (When she goes too far, man lets her know; and, like the jester, she backs down, for she is not a true enemy but a house-trained menial, willingly ruled by the power she mocks.) Insistently, they ventilate the intuition (see Box O) that the human process of self-creation is in essential ways destructive; that the rational, controlling planfulness which step by step produced the peculiar environment in which our peculiar bodies step by step evolved (see Chapter 2) is in essential ways irrational, uncontrolled, chaotic; that the talent for enterprise and mastery that is such a basic pride and joy to us —the talent whose use embodies our central effort to overcome our earliest griefs; the talent that exercises our most distinctive organ of pleasure, the higher central nervous system— flourishes in essential ways at the expense of another kind of pride, another kind of joy, to whose loss we can never be reconciled.

As I pointed out in the review of Chapters 4–8 at the beginning of this chapter, the emotional contrasts and complementarities between woman and man, as these grow out of her sameness of gender, and his difference in gender, with the earliest nurturing adult, fit her to embody this intuition, just as they fit him for the historic undertaking to whose pathology the intuition points. But the essential point is that both depend on the pathology, and both want the intuition steadily and harmlessly ventilated. He is capable of the intuition, and articulates it now and then, here and there. She is capable of history-making, and engages in it now and then, here and there. But if he allowed himself more gener-

---

Box O

Woman's resigned, implicitly collusive, ventilation of everybody's intuition that the world men rule is murderously crazy is a central theme in folklore, literature, drama.

Think, for instance, of the proverb that groups woman with wine and song as a necessary counterpoint to battle, a counterpoint that makes it possible for men to draw back from their will to kill just long and far enough so that they can then take it up again with new vigor. Or think of the saying "Men must work and women must weep." Woman's tears over what is lethal in man's work, this saying implies, are part of the world's eternal unalterable way. What makes the way seem eternal, self-maintaining, is that the tears serve not to deter man but to help him go on, for she is doing his weeping for him and he is doing what she weeps about for her.

Another example of this theme —and I choose at random— is Romain Gary's story of beautiful old *Lady L.*, who ironically supports her men in their insane worldly enterprises, and meanwhile secretly treasures the rotting corpse of the one who was most insane, the one whom she loved most and had therefore murdered when they were young in a self-contained and historically harmless explosion of rage against history.

For another instance, recall Moravia's novel *Two Women*, whose heroine moves with sorrowful, derisive, survival-oriented contempt through war-ravaged Italy. The author deeply respects the personal, domestic, erotic values that make her so scornful of men's reasons for fighting. Yet it is an anti-fascist war —World War II— the necessity for which he himself does not question.

Finally, look again at the scene in Altman's wonderful movie *McCabe and Mrs. Miller* in which the heroine, in passive despair at the hero's stupid determination to get himself killed in an uneven duel, wearily and lovingly snaps at him, "Eat your dinner. It's getting cold."

ally to dwell upon the intuition, to give it full status in his pattern of conscious concerns, he could not go on making the kind of history he makes. And if she immersed herself more generally in that kind of history, she would have to bury the intuition.

Not only is this intuition, this body of misgivings and reservations, too well-developed in woman to be pushed under as men push it under. She is also unwilling to bury it. Her unwillingness rests in part on a sense of responsibility, a fear of what the world would be like if the perspective that she embodies were lost to all of us: she knows, and man knows too —hence his enraged alarm at the prospect of her entering history— that the side of life she protects, maintains, and stands up for is the side that keeps the world at least partly sane. Both need to have this side of life affirmed. But her unwillingness rests also on the darker need, which she also shares with man, to keep the world mainly mad. It is this darker need, more than the sunnier one (for the sunnier one could be fulfilled in other ways, and on some level we all know that), which makes him honor her, even while deriding her, in her role as jester, and which underlies much of his angry fear when she starts to withdraw from this role: *the need to go on, as a species, playing out our death-denying impulse through life-denying enterprise, and at the same time* —since otherwise the playing out would become impossible— *to go on airing our truant conviction that this renunciation is unnecessary and this self-mutilation futile, to go on cherishing our truant wish that we could stop marching out to meet death halfway.*

Woman cannot enter history, then, without shattering the collaboration between herself and man that maintains our present way of "coping" with what Freud calls civilization's discontents. What will happen when the split in sensibility that the two sexes now work together to preserve breaks down, melts away? We cannot be sure what will happen. We can be sure only that so long as this split is preserved the mad megamachine of which Mumford writes will inexorably grow and proliferate, destroying and displacing the flawed but still vigorous human life on which it feeds.

This flawed life may yet be capable of outgrowing its birth defects in time to save itself, and the web of life in which it is embedded, from extinction. We cannot know whether such an outgrowing is possible until we have managed to melt the split: *to contain the two sides of our central ambivalence toward what we are —contain them direct, undiluted, undeflected— inside each individual human skin, where they belong.* We cannot know until we have tried living out in full awareness, instead of dream-acting out in lethal charades, the human malaise of which our sexual arrangement is now a part.

10

At the Edge

Nostalgia for the familiar is a feeling that has so far been mobilized primarily in opposition to social change.* Enthusiasm for (indeed, even resignation to) social change has seemed to demand suppression of this feeling. To articulate it, to live it out, while at the same time moving voluntarily toward the unfamiliar, is a painful and strenuous task which has on the whole been dodged. Indeed it has been regarded not as a task at all, not as work requiring strength, but as a maudlin and self-indulgent form of backsliding. In the context of historic activism, people have typically treated open expression of nostalgia for the familiar as a grave offense: at best a dangerous distraction from, at worst an actively malevolent sabotage of, the worldmaking effort. We are just starting to see† how necessary a part of that effort it is.

History that moves as fast as our history in recent centuries has been moving means renunciation, by masses of individuals, of roots that tap the magic layers of personality: roots, for example,

---

* There is a related feeling upon which what this book says has no bearing, a feeling in spirit quite different from the nostalgia discussed here, but in practice not always separable from it and often mobilized along with it: plain unwillingness to give up special privilege; simple reluctance to stop preying on other people. That kind of literal holdout against change is apt to yield, in the short run at least, only to head-on coercion: to material bribes and threats or to externally imposed social pressure. What characterizes the feelings upon which this book bears is that they change as we become in a private way more aware of their underlying nature.

† See, for example, Dubos' *So Human an Animal*, and Blythe's *Akenfield*.

in the mystique of such archetypes as the hand plow, the sailing ship, the spindle; in the light and odor and sound of childhood barns and churches; in the dark fantasy-laden love-hate attachment between aristocrat and menial. And part of what has kept history malignant is that in making it people have mainly disowned or denied, or in any case pushed into limbo, their homesickness for the magic that inhered in these renounced roots. They have buried that side of their feeling, or walled it off, and so made their new arrangements in a way that took no account of what most deeply tied them to the old ones. This has necessarily limited their understanding of what most deeply drove them to break out of the old ones, and as a result new forms of life-impoverishment emerge, new bases for oppression are established.

Faced with its own fearful errors, the worldmaking enterprise is forced now toward self-reflectiveness. And as this happens one point that becomes clear is that the special nostalgia that haunts the atmosphere of worldmaking must be lived out, not pushed away. Living it out does not mean —by definition cannot mean; but this is easier said than felt— sinking back into the familiar. The unavailability of that alternative may be what people find it hardest, in fact, to come to final emotional terms with: So long as homesickness is not felt through, what made staying home out of the question is not fully felt through, either. An intrinsic ingredient of this special nostalgia —its distinctive ingredient— is knowledge of something deadly wrong with the familiar. Living it out means plumbing the feelings of "but" that go with this central, inexorable knowledge; it means knowing them too, and working them into what they have been sealed off from, so that they become part of what shapes our new arrangements.

It is clear enough by now that the prevailing symbiosis between women and men has something deadly wrong with it. Outgrowth of a gender-based division of concrete responsibility for human life whose core —predominantly female care of the young— was once, and is no longer, a biotechnological necessity, this symbiosis now helps maintain, and is in turn maintained by, that obsolete concrete division. Meanwhile it supports a grow-ingly perilous societal posture; it helps lock us, as a species, into a suicidal stance toward the realities on which our collective sur-vival hinges. Within each person, too, something deadly rests on this symbiosis; it maims, stunts, distorts. On both levels, societal and individual, it serves lethal functions. But —the "but" of dis-owned nostalgia— it serves vital ones also. To see clearly what that lethality is —and what it is depends in large part on our failure to see it clearly— is to identify that vitality as well. Let us look at the crux of this psychological symbiosis as it works on the magic layer of sentience, the layer that needs integration into the articulate worldmaking effort.

The Crux of the Arrangement

The rules of personal symbiosis between women and men offer us a silent ready-made language, a tacitly formalized and stylized set of expectations, perceptions, and skills, around which to or-ganize some unexamined and crucial aspects of emotional life.*

It is for this reason that so many people who find the symbiosis oppressive nevertheless feel frightened and bereft at the thought of living without it. That fear and grief have something to teach us: it would be a mistake to rely on self-righteous indignation to

---

* Like any human language or body of life-ways, any product of societally pooled problem-solving effort, these rules act *both* to constrict personality *and* to enable it to function. They necessarily violate individuality, drown out or starve or distort aspects of each person's unique endowment and ex-perience. Yet individuality could not emerge or flower without them. With-out a framework for the interpenetration of subjectivities, without a set of agreed upon, humanly arrived at principles for the organization of our shared life space, we would be fish out of water. A structured social milieu, developed and elaborated in an at least partly intentional way over millennia and passed on with its life-supporting features intact, is as essential to us — see Chapter 2, pages 16–22— as light and air. Still, the constricting and the enabling influences exerted by any given aspect of this milieu vary in their relative weights. As the worldmaking enterprise grows more self-reflective, we see that our task is to feel out what these influences are, how they inter-act, and what is involved in restructuring them so as to minimize constriction and maximize enablement.

carry us through the work of revising these rules, a mistake to try
dismantling them without making a massive effort to come to
terms as we do so with the uses which, at the pre-rational level of
sentience, they have so far served. These uses can be summed up
in two ways.

First, our gender rules provide each sex with its own set, time-
polished pattern of opportunities *to relive and rework*, in interaction with the other sex, *fundamental feelings that first took shape
in the original infant-parent relation.*° This means —since a
highly developed sense of what one's companion must be experiencing is an essential feature of human interaction— that
they also provide each sex with vicarious access to the other's
sex's complementary patterns of opportunity.

Second, these rules furnish us with modes of collaboration
across gender lines (lines that are hardened and thickened, deepened and elaborated, in the service of this purpose) *to maintain
certain basic inner ambivalences*: set, time-polished modes of
collaboration to fend off the necessity for resolution, within each
person, of unresolved attitudes toward central conditions of
humanness itself.

All the matters surveyed in the preceding chapters, and others
that have doubtless occurred to the reader en route, could be
reviewed from these two perspectives. But anyone who wants to
can do that without me. A few instances should suffice to show

---

° How much and in what way these early-born feelings are modified by
later experience depends, obviously, on the individual's special history. Ordinarily —and this is why I referred to them in Chapter 2 as "massive
orienting passions"— they survive more or less intact, more or less unmuted,
throughout life.

This statement, to be sure, like most of what this book says, is wide open
to contradiction: I cannot imagine any way of "proving" it that would begin
to approach scientific respectability as that term can be applied, say (to
choose instances from my own work), to a laboratory study of rote memory
or of weight perception. It is necessarily based in large part on intuition, on
informal experience with people; and it is necessarily addressed to the
reader's own intuitive understanding. It may, unarguably, strike no chord of
"Aha!" there. But of course even a technically flawless experimental report,
resting on the hardest and tightest possible data, may be quibbled with,
plausibly reinterpreted to support an opposed theory, or ignored as trivial, on
grounds that are equally unarguable.

how each of these ways of summing up our gender rules bears on our effort to outgrow the stasis those rules help us maintain.

Before going into these instances I should explain again why I refer to that stasis as a stasis just when it has begun at last to be radically undermined, why I refer to those rules as rules just when the exceptions to them (which have all along been numerous and lively) have begun so vehemently to multiply. My reason is this. The rules under discussion presuppose —rest upon needs created by— female-dominated childhood. Yet they are being challenged now —in an active minority overtly repealed, even— by mother-raised people. In response to developments to which I shall presently turn, the part of each person that has always said "no" to these rules (see Box P) is in many of us saying it much more loudly now. But there remains a part of each person that says "yes" to them; a part upon which they still exert a pull; a part that makes revising them uphill —internally, not just externally, uphill— work: and it is the basis for this "yes" which must now be felt through. Feeling it through may well make that uphill work in some superficial respects harder. But it is a way of making sure that the work turns out to matter: that it moves us to a place authentically different from the place we are at now.

What follows, then, is not a summary of this book's argument. (Indeed, it will not be wholly intelligible to the reader who, sensibly enough, reads last chapters first; to make full sense of it, that reader will have to go back and forth.) It is, rather, an illustrative guide to such a summary. It indicates, with examples, how what has been said above can be reviewed: how the prevailing sexual arrangements can be re-examined, in a spirit of respect for the complexity of our own emotional situation, as part of the process of withdrawing our consent to them.

Complementary Patterns of Re-access to Early Experience

To review just one example from Chapter 4: our double standard of erotic conduct grants man the opportunity to act out directly *the early wish to own a woman* (or more precisely, a

(Continued on page 238)

Box P

It is mainly women who challenge the old gender arrangement. Yet in doing so many of us assert —as I have asserted repeatedly here— that the pressures it imposes on men are at least as mutilating, distorting, and debasing as those it imposes on us. If this is so, what needs accounting for is why the arrangement seems to be so much more sharply intolerable to us than to men.

There are a number of reasons for this difference. An acute one that is emerging only now is the explosive female predicament discussed below. A chronic one is the special female sexual bind discussed in the section "The Upshot" in Chapter 4 (pages 71–75). Another chronic one is the special pressure on men to feel advantaged and undamaged discussed in Box N (pages 215–217). But the main and most massive reason why women challenge the male-female status quo more insistently than men do is the chronic one upon which I touched in Box J (pages 173–174), and which deserves fuller discussion than it got there.

Woman, who introduced us to the human situation and who at the beginning seemed to us responsible for every drawback of that situation, carries for all of us a pre-rational onus of ultimately culpable responsibility forever after. And this incomparable onus —so heavy and so unjust that one must keep it out of focal awareness if one is to stay sane: this literally unspeakable and unthinkable onus— keeps a radical feeling of "No!" strong in every girl and woman whose core of self-affirmation is not wholly crushed by it. The feeling is usually buried, but it is buried alive. It exists as an inarticulate source —the most profound source, I believe— of that refusal to accept the way things are that keeps simmering close to the calmest-looking surfaces of our communal awareness.

When Freud, like other men, asks in bitterness "What do women want?" he is reacting to the depth and the force —the irrepressible yet never clearly mobilized force— of this bitterest human protest of all: *What women want is to stop serving as scapegoats* (their own scapegoats as well as men's and children's scapegoats) *for human resentment of the human condition.* They want this so painfully and so pervasively, and until quite recently it was such a hopeless thing to want, that they have not yet been able to say out loud that they want it.

What hinges on our continued consent to carry this onus is nothing more or less than the pathological equilibrium of our species life itself. This is part of why we still hesitate to mobilize the force that is latent in our diffuse protest, hesitate to withdraw our chronically grudging consent. And it is also part of the uneasiness —tinged, I suspect, with some shadowy, fearful hope— behind Freud's testy question. Men, too, both fear and long for what will happen when women can really say what they want. What will happen is a self-revision of our collective life that has to have been incubating as long as live-bearing mammalian bodies have been animated by human sentience.

The nature of this onus that women carry is sketched out in some detail in Part II (i.e., Chapters 4–8). What needs to be stated here is its moral gist. Woman bears throughout her life, for everyone around her, a certain magic female burden of unilateral parental responsibility. But the unilateral parental power that counterbalances actual, adult-child, parental responsibility is hers only in the nursery. Outside the nursery it is mainly in man's hands: she is subject to it. Yet his view of her is not the early parent's view of the child; it remains in many ways the child's view of the early parent.

In the actual early parent-child relation, the child can do no really unforgivable wrong: The parent may punish the child or not, but in either case owes it helpful understanding. Any grave wrong done by the parent, however, is by definition unforgivable, since the child is both more vulnerable and in less of a position to be understanding: The child is less able to retaliate, or pass punitive judgment, or defend its interests against the adult's transgressions; but by the same token it is not called upon to see the adult's point of view, not responsible to be helpfully nurturant toward the adult's frailties. Forced to accept some hurt from the magic provider (for every parent is necessarily —not to speak of unnecessarily— hurtful), it may feel uncomprehendingly resigned and/or more or less helplessly vengeful (often turning anger inward, or splitting it off); but it does not forgive.°

In relations with man, woman is expected, by and large, to embody this one-sidedly nurturant tolerance of the early parent: she

---

° In our religions, we do not forgive God. (We examine our souls when he inflicts hurt on us to see what we have done wrong, and/or we plow back anger —as Job did— into the masochistic component of grateful love.) But God forgives us.

must understand and forgive his faults; her own are unforgivable.°
At the same time, she is without the early parent's superior practical
power and immunity from retaliation: her transgressions, like the
child's, are punishable; his, like the parent's, are not. (She can punish
him, of course, by withdrawing her love. But this is a painfully two-
edged weapon. His punishments of her, on the other hand —since
he is economically and socially more powerful and independent, and
freer to turn elsewhere both for sex and for the emotional contact
that goes with sex— tend to hurt her much more than they hurt him.)
She thus carries the moral obligations of the parent while suffering
the powerlessness of the child.

Man, conversely, carries parental powers while enjoying the child's
freedom from moral obligation. He has the right, like the child, to
remain unaware of, uninterested in, her point of view even though
nurturant awareness of it is in his case within intellectual reach. This
means that he is encouraged in a kind of moral laziness which stunts
his growth: his capacities for empathic emotional generosity (like
woman's capacities for enterprise) atrophy through disuse. He is
allowed to remain childishly irresponsible for embracing her perspective,† and childishly entitled to her parental nurturance and forgiveness, while enjoying parental power to defend himself, to discipline
her if she offends him, to place practical constraints around her
destructiveness if she tries to hurt him.

No wonder masochism and split-off fury are "truly feminine" traits.
They are the underside of the "truly feminine" woman's monstrously
overdeveloped talent for unreciprocated empathy, an adult talent
that she must exercise in a situation in many ways as vulnerable as
a child's. In this situation man, armed with much of the early parent's
power over the infant, vents against her the infant's boundless rage at
the early parent. It is a situation that calls for masochism: since the
helpless fury it evokes in her would destroy her if she let herself

---

° How this works between women is a more complicated question. They
may be mutually parental, i.e., forgiving; or mutually infantile, i.e., unfor-
giving. One-sided nurturance among them, when it occurs, is a matter of
individual situation and temperament.

† Indeed he is less responsible for embracing anyone's perspective than
she is. He retreats from the safe but relatively callous male fraternity into
her dangerous arms when he feels the need for a certain kind of "understanding."

feel it, splitting some of it off and turning the rest of it inward —joining man against herself, lending her person to the project of getting back at mama— is the best that she can do.

There is another way to look at this most massive, most central, reason why initiative to change our mutually maiming gender arrangements comes mainly from women.

The sketch offered in Chapters 4–8 largely presupposed, for simplicity of exposition, a mother who herself is never actually capricious and withholding, never actually hostile to the child's growing autonomy, never dominated by attitudes toward the flesh that do make her physical presence gross or loathsome. In fact, of course, there is no such mother, because there is no such human being: all of us have some cruel, coercive, destructive, rejecting impulses toward other people; all of us have feelings toward carnality which make our bodies seem, to ourselves and others, disturbingly non-consonant with human spirit. The trouble is that in the mother these negative qualities have their impact where it is most possible for them to do deep damage: on the vulnerable sensibility of the very young child. It is for this reason that certain real faults of women are felt as so much less tolerable than the same real faults in men: in women, these faults in fact inflicted worse wounds, cramped and stunted other people in more crippling ways. The mother's major human frailties are at bottom less humanly acceptable than the father's. His capriciousness, hostility, physical grossness, bossiness, are more bearable, because later encountered, shortcomings; they can be distressing, but they do not put him outside the human pale. Man is of course willful, tough, earthy, masterful. In her, these same shortcomings are those of a monster: a bitch, a slob, a ball-breaking battleax.°

It is obvious that we all have character traits which make us less than perfectly parental. What is not faced head-on- is the fact that under present conditions woman does not share man's right to have such traits without loss of human stature, and man does not share

° As de Beauvoir points out, she is allowed some minor deficiencies: petty malice toward peers, improvidence, physical vanity, are in her deplorable, annoying, but human. Interestingly —and this should be true across cultures, regardless of differences in the specific traits involved— the faults for which women are derided but forgiven are faults that do not directly hurt small children.

woman's obligation to work at mastering them, at shielding others from their consequences. Woman never will have this right, nor man this obligation, until male imperfection begins to impinge on all of us when we are tiny and helpless, so that it becomes as culpable as female imperfection, as close to the original center of human grief. Only then will the harm women do be recognized as the familiar harm we all do to ourselves, not strange harm inflicted by some outside agent. And only then will men really start to take seriously the problem of curbing, taming, their own destructiveness. They may even at that point start taking seriously the biblical swords-into-plowshares injunction; they may start at last to face the task of transmuting the angry feeling inherent in our species' life —the enraged sense of being assaulted by some ultimately blamable outsider— into energy that works toward that life's growth. But *this can happen only when the early core of human rage can no longer vent itself on the mystical figure of the early mother, when we all take on ourselves the blame for the damage we do each other and the responsibility for stopping it.*

being who turns out in retrospect to have been a woman) and enjoy sole access to her erotic resources, while at the same time — —reversing their original situation— he remains free to turn elsewhere at will for what she, now, can get only from him: the primitive contact he once depended on her to provide. Meanwhile the owned woman can enjoy this opportunity vicariously, imagining how he feels, how it is for him to own her and still be free; at the same time she can enjoy through him access to another woman, to a body like the one she herself loved at the beginning.

They are also —here as in many other aspects of our arrangement— *punishing the mother.* She can experience, in her own jealous pain, the pain they are visiting on the fantasy-mother, and at the same time masochistically re-experience — thereby (but in a partial way, which requires endless repetition) mastering— both her infant distress at her first love's inevitable infidelity and the double-edged jealousy of both parents that

came later. And he, on whom the pressure to re-experience these
things also falls (though in somewhat different ways), can do so
vicariously, through sensing how his exercise of his unilateral
freedom must make her feel. Conversely, meanwhile, the satisfaction felt by the punisher and avenger is available first-hand to
him, while to her (whose need to feel it may be equally lively,
though in obvious respects different from his) it is available
second-hand through him.

What makes the strict gender patterning of this set of opportunities feel "natural" to so many of us is, of course, the fact that
mama (or plural mama, "mama" including grandma, sister,
auntie, nanny, and/or whoever) was virtually always and only
female. It is this fact, too, that makes our acting out of such
opportunities stereotyped, repetitive, static. But before turning to
that point let us consider some more examples.

To review, for instance, an early realization, whose consequences are explored in Chapters 6 and 8: *woman's is the first
outside center of awareness and will* that we meet, the first proof,
to the nursling who still in some sense lives on in each of us, that
its own is not the solitary, omnipotent, all-embracing subjectivity.
This realization helps confirm and clarify for the nascent self its
sense of its own existence, and encourages exploration of the
finite powers that it does in fact have. Still, it is a setback. It is
this setback that woman reverses —directly for man, vicariously
through him for herself— when she anticipates his bodily wishes
before he utters them, follows his impulses, unswervingly shares
his point of view.

This early maternal subjectivity seemed both rampant and
alien; it belonged to an ill-defined, boundless external presence,
not a clearly delineated fellow creature. This is why the rules
define strongly marked female individuality as unseemly (why
female caprice, charming so long as it carries a haphazard, mystifying aura, must not appear to issue from a formed, firm center;
why, although "a lady has a right to change her mind," an overtly
strong-minded woman is no lady). It is why woman traditionally

agrees to listen to man's opinions and keep her own to herself, lets him hog the limelight and offers herself as audience, allows herself activity only as it nurtures his projects. In these ways she provides him directly, and herself vicariously, with the opportunity to re-experience the presence of mama's separate subjectivity with its alien, alarming, dissonant aspects deleted and only its supportive aspects in evidence. Now this maternal awareness exists not to serve any purpose of its own, but solely to reflect and verify the child's active existence, to set the stage and supply the needed backing for the child's discovery of what it can do, to offer just the amount of resistance that the child needs to test its own will against, and win.

A difficult truth is for the moment, in fantasy, abolished, a truth which life forces us to face, tangentially at least, from time to time, but which our gender arrangements let us avoid accepting head on and once and for all: that the other to whom we look for nurturance has, like any sentient other, needs and a viewpoint separate from and never wholly subject to our own. Because we have not really assimilated that truth and cannot escape it, either, we must go on pretending, again and again in the same way forever, that it does not exist. It is this necessary game —necessary, that is, under present conditions; necessary for enough of us, in any case, to make the rule enforceable— that our she-listens-charmingly rule allows us to enjoy. (The rule, as the reader familiar with this book's argument realizes, serves other such needs as well; this one is spelled out only as an instance of how it works to serve them.)

Because woman was the first "you," the "you" who could not be wholly corralled at the outset and is for that reason precious later in willing captivity, man is the one for whom this "you" —tamed, controllable, subordinated, its enterprise-encouraging services purged of all threat— can be directly available in the prescribed adult male-female bond. It is there for her only insofar as she provides it for him and enjoys his enjoyment of it. She is seen as merely selfish and odd if she insists on pursuing her own endeavors instead of nourishing his. But she is seen as an outright freak if, not content with self-exile from the (for her vicarious) atmosphere of parentally fed exploit, she goes so far as to look to him for the kind of support (see Box L, pages 192–195) that the rules say he should be receiving unilaterally from her.°

What these rules do say she has a right to enjoy, on the other hand, is another aspect of the baby's part in the now-you-be-mama-and-I'll-be-baby game: he may be able to offer her certain features of *the early parental response to the infant's magic charm;* he may celebrate and confirm her existence as the mother once did his, not yet as a striving center of will, but rather as an alluring, delicious being, movingly needy and mysteriously sentient, whose responsiveness across that mystery is thrilling. She may see in his eyes the delighted recognition of herself as sweet animate flesh, the rapturous contemplation of her sheer living presence, that she once saw in her mother's. He may do this for her more fully than she can do it for him, since what she is more stringently called upon to do for him is serve as nurturer of his purposeful selfhood, shield him from the threats her gender carries, and elicit from him (since he cannot accept it as easily from her) the active initiative on which their relation hinges. What he may surround her with (and thereby, through her, live within himself) is the atmosphere of affirmation that first tells the baby to trust the world, that makes it aware of itself as miraculously attractive, by the sheer fact of its existence, to the powerful being on whom everything depends.

What he may also surround her with is *a sheltering framework of protectiveness and providingness,* a formal, overt framework of a kind which (in view of her gender continuity with the first parent, whose brute power he must feel he has surmounted) he could not comfortably accept from her.† In this way he can act

---

° Virginia Woolf and George Eliot were freaks of this kind. So was Colette in her last marriage. None of them was soothing to contemplate from a position inside the prevailing arrangement.

† It is true, to be sure, that in surrounding her with this framework he acts as he saw his father act toward his mother. But the wish to emulate the

out directly, and she vicariously, the tiny child's fantasy of taking care of mama, a fantasy in which impulses of loving gratitude, and of reparation for the hostile feeling that one is bound to have harbored toward her, merge with the pleasure of a redress in the balance of one's power relation with her. Meanwhile she relives first hand, and he second hand, both the joys and the chagrins of being frail and helpless in the hands of a benevolent despot.

The gender rules offer innumerable channels, of course, through which to replay our reactions to this fact of the mother's *immense unilateral power* during the period when we need feeding, carrying, cleaning, shelter. For example, while man takes over her overt power, as protecting and providing despot, woman as food preparer continues literally to feed him, as body servant goes on grooming him, as housekeeper maintains for him the comforting surround over which he, however, formally presides: again, her old services are made available with the old indignities and risks deleted, indeed to some degree reversed.

Radically incompetent physically in our first encounters with woman, we are all invited to take compensatory pleasure in man's bodily prowess, and expected to be tolerant of his boastfulness about it. We may be reassured in a familiar way by physical strength, energy, and skill in woman, particularly if it is displayed incidentally in the course of helping or nurturing others; but so that we may be in fact reassured, not enraged, the rules demand that she exercise it *very* modestly.

Or consider the right woman had at the outset to bribe and punish the child's body by giving or withholding delight, by soothing or inflicting pain: this is why it is so widely the case that she and man alike are in some sense soothed by the reciprocal power over her body that he has later; why it "fits," emotionally, that the time of lovemaking is mainly set by him, and that he gives her (and she is expected pleasantly to accept from him,

---

father comes later; it is overlaid upon the passions formed in the very early mother-infant interaction, and draws much of its affective depth from this more primitive layer of feeling.

even if she herself would prefer more of it than he gives, or less) as much of it as he sees fit; why both are so apt to enjoy his ability (if he has it) to lift her across thresholds; why they may also enjoy (at least in fantasy) his power to rape her or beat her up, or in any case the fact that he has this power and forbears to use it.

Indeed, even if she outweighs him and could in principle wrestle him down, both may feel comforted by the head-on emotional authority which in fact he wields over her anyway. The emotional authority she wields over him, on the other hand, is typically endurable only if both meanwhile deny its existence: if she does so openly, in earnest, and without his chivalrous permission, the rules are not working.

Similarly, it is because "mother knows best" at the beginning that man must know best later: what woman knows better she must deprecate; she must be in essential respects more ignorant; if not, she must manage in any case, by guile or heroic tact, to find some way of allowing him the position of leader and instructor. When this rule works, both can enjoy, second hand and first hand respectively, the triumph of teaching teacher.

Play of this kind moves along best when the players are equally unaware, or equally aware, that they are playing. Under present conditions, both are apt to be in large part unaware, if the process between them is going strong. The rules we use have too much anxiety, anger, and vengeance behind them to make for easy and cordial conscious playing. Many of them, indeed, are usable *only* insofar as we remain self-ignorant. And because it is an earnest form of play —because it allows us to feel reconnected to life's original center of magic power without full re-immersion in our old unilateral helplessness, and this is a feeling we need— we tend to cherish that self-ignorance. But it is unawareness that forces this male-female process into monotony, that gives it its treadmill character: it can stay urgently necessary, and still become in a way deadly boring.

There is no reason to suppose that our need for games of the

now-you-be-the-baby-and-I'll-be-the-grownup-for-a-change variety will disappear when early parental care is as much male as
female. It is a legitimate need. The emotional repercussions of
our long infancy, and the multilayered nature of our sentience,
will inevitably still color and flavor adult life. But under those
conditions the rigid male-female complementarity of emotional
opportunity offered by sex should disappear. The game should
become more flexible, its make-believe roles more straightforwardly exchangeable and far more open to innovation. The feelings on which it bears should be available to be taken out and
played with, so to speak, in a freer way, and in this unstereotyped
play (unstereotyped not only in adult lovemaking but throughout
the many years of childhood make-believe that precede it) more
genuinely reworked, so that they both modify and are modified
by what we now think of as adult awareness, with consequences
for the deepening of this awareness which we can now only
schematically imagine. The personalities who play this game,
moreover, will have been developing from the outset along far
less constricting gender lines. Whatever gender comes to mean
under those conditions —and I expect that it will remain (though
for partly changed reasons) salient*— its meaning will no longer
be dominated by girls' continuity, and boys' discontinuity, with
the adults who initiate us into the human condition.

   The project of bringing the rational and the pre-rational layers
of sentience into easier mutual reach is central to all the forms of
earnest play we engage in: art, religion, even (though many of
them would surely disagree) the research that psychologists do.
But this project is central in a particular way to the earnestly
playful use we make of an opportunity which sex —that is, adult
lovemaking and the intimate interactions that surround it—
provides: access, incomparably literal sensuous access, to that
vital level of the self which is continuous with infancy. Our

_____

   * As I argued near the end of Chapter 7, the facts of procreative
anatomy, some of which are bound to be more keenly felt when men share
early child care than they can be felt now, make it overwhelmingly likely that
gender will continue to be an intensely meaningful category.

present gender rules offer us this life-essential opportunity in forms that we fear tearing ourselves free of because, whatever else they are, they are forms that we know and that in important ways work. We use them in part to dilute and keep vague our commitment to that broad project; yet while using them we have, in fact, made some headway with it after all;* and if the disease which the project is part of our effort to outgrow does not kill us off first, we will make more. But further headway now is inextricable from headway with the related project of sexual liberty: the project of restructuring those gender rules.

What this restructuring should do, in sum, is loosen and open up the at present rigid and stereotyped modes of male-female interdependence; make genuinely playful reworking of the realms of experience to which sex gives us access more possible; and in that way allow its sister project to flower.

But what keeps the structure of this interdependence intact, what makes this body of rules strong, is something more than the vital opportunity for play that it provides. Let us turn now to the second way in which its uses can be summed up.

The Maintenance of Basic Ambivalences

A neurosis, individual or collective, can be described as a costly strategy for maintaining mutually incompatible feelings, which we lack the strength to reconcile, in a provisionally stable state of equilibrium. And this strategy, in turn, can be seen as a part of a longer-range growth process (a process that is often, but not always, aborted).† Looked at in this way, our male-female compact can be summed up in terms of the wider neurotic equilibrium —the body of unresolved ambivalences— which it helps

---

* Freud, working inside these forms, contributed prodigiously to this headway, for example.

† It can be cut short (a) by "natural" life-span limits which other processes set, and/or (b) by the killing costs and risks of the strategy itself. "We grow too soon old and too late smart" is a folk expression of (a), and "He burned himself out young" of (b).

us, as a species, to sustain; and also in terms of the part which this dangerous provisional equilibrium plays in the still longer range development of our cumulative ongoing self-reflective life.[*]

Features of the strategy. Thus, this compact helps us maintain *our ambivalence toward our own carnal mortality.* Chapter 4 showed how we depend on it to take the sweet, threatening bodily edge off sex feeling and seal off much of its potential emotional depth, and at the same time to provide set channels within which this feeling, tamed and constricted, can flow. Chapter 7 showed how the compact enables us to hold at bay, and at the same time keep nearby, the acute knowledge of fleshly transience, without which aliveness itself cannot be fully felt. We hold this knowledge at bay by rejecting what is hardest to endure in the immediate sense of our own vulnerable animal existence, by demeaning it, splitting it off from our humanity. And we keep this knowledge nearby by embodying that immediate sense, disowned and degraded, in our pre-rational image of woman (an amorphous image which survives largely unmodified under and around and within one's more formed, reasonable later view of her as a person, even when that person is oneself; which both stands apart from that view and infiltrates it unacknowledged, permeating its substance and distorting its shape).

In the same way, our gender symbiosis helps us maintain *our ambivalence about growing up.* As Chapter 5 showed, we use it to keep ourselves childish —and we are ominously unrealistic, ominously powerful, children— while pretending that we are

---

[*] A development that seems all too likely to be aborted soon unless it is drastically speeded up now. The "natural" limits on the time we have for collective psychological growth are beyond our ability to estimate: we have no way of judging where, short of the sun's cooling off (if there), these limits fall. What we can estimate are the consequences of our neurotic strategy itself. Experts arrive, of course, at differing estimates; but the most thoughtful among them seem to agree that the malignant societal and ecological trends which this strategy has set in motion, if they are not already irreversible, may shortly become so. (See, for example, Dubos' *So Human an Animal,* and Heilbroner's *What Is the Human Prospect?*)

adults: use it to divide responsibility, that is, in such a way that members of each sex can feel more or less sure that what most urgently matters in life is in their own hands, and more or less sure at the same time that what seems beyond them and out of their control is probably being taken care of by the other sex. Also, as Chapter 8 showed, this symbiosis allows us to appease our wish for freedom with the patriarchal lie: It lets us dodge our self-responsibility as a species, delegate our common fate over and over again to despotic power (which we try, in the long run always vainly, to see as benevolent and competent). And at the same time it lets us go on venting, through our demand that this power be male, our old anger at the inevitable power of nurturant adult over helpless infant, an anger that we have never outgrown because we are still hooked on the sense of being taken care of that went with it.

Correspondingly, our male-female arrangement helps us maintain *our ambivalence toward the existence of other separately sentient beings*, beings whose sentient separateness imposes upon us burdensome obligations (to recognize differences of viewpoint, reconcile divergencies in interest and impulse, respect rights that may force us to redefine our own rights) yet at the same time supports and confirms and enlarges our own existence. From the infant outset the company of these beings, vital to us for this and other reasons, makes minimally necessary demands upon us which we are reluctant to meet; and eventually (since they of course feel just as we do) it makes exorbitant demands as well, which we could not in any case meet. So it is upon them that both our central passion for the world we are born into and our central rejection of it are mainly focused. Also, as Chapter 6 showed, what this arrangement lets us do is deny each other as fellow creatures (not wholly, of course; but in all the predatory, life-mutilating ways that keep what men call brotherhood a so far radically unrealized project) and still imagine that we are not alone, that nature is somehow our inexhaustible, infinitely exploitable mother. What it lets us in large part renounce, in other words, is the only relief of our human loneliness that is realistically available —each other's actual human company— while at the same time pretending that there is nothing unavoidably, irreducibly lonely in our condition itself.

The ambivalence that is at this point in history hardest to maintain unresolved, however, is *the ambivalence about worldmaking, about human self-creation*, discussed in Chapter 9. We have been using the interdependence between women and men to help us handle a neurotic need which we cannot start outgrowing without at the same time starting to outgrow all those referred to above: our need for more and more control —irresponsible, blindly coercive control— over nature. We have been relying upon the split between male and female sensibility to let us go on acting out our compulsion to dominate and manipulate every object and process that surrounds us, while at the same time articulating our misgivings about that driven need —our knowledge that it despoils our life and our world— in terms that cannot interfere with its enactment.

The strategy as part of a growth process. So our gender arrangements help keep us neurotic. Still, the tense, fragile equilibrium that this communal neurosis provides has served in its turn to keep us rooted enough in our interdependencies, reassured enough of some precarious, tenuous mutual support, so that we could move slowly toward seeing what it is we are afraid of, what emotional threats we are fending off. And meanwhile the mounting cost of the neurosis, its mounting destructiveness, pushes us toward questioning the means we are using to fend these threats off.

A full survey of this process in both its aspects —its growth-facilitating, opportunity-providing aspect, and its growth-forcing aspect— is too much to attempt here. But some instances should suggest its nature.

The feature of our male-female symbiosis discussed in Chapter 5, for example, works not only to keep us childish and at the same time to provide us with equivocal ways of affirming our wish to feel grown up; it also *gives us the opportunity to explore,* insofar as we are able, our reasons for fearing to affirm this wish un-equivocally. Woman, a little girl posturing as goddess mother, and man, a little boy contrapuntally play-acting formidable worldly might, are both in a position to feel out —even as they fend off the need to do anything about it— the gap between realistic adult authority (the authority they themselves would have to exert if they outgrew their charade, stopped bluffing, and started sharing both the care of the young and the making of the world) and the mythic authority (intrinsically opaque and in-scrutable) with which as infants and small children they felt adults were endowed, and which they now collude to imagine still exists somewhere outside themselves.

Or to consider in this same connection (i.e., our ambivalence about growing up) the other aspect of this kind of growth pro-cess: The patriarchal solution of the problem of early maternal authority discussed in Chapter 8 not only embodies, side by side and mutually unreconciled, both our unexamined, unmodified rage against the first parent's power and our unbroken and un-acknowledged addiction to the feeling that someone else is in charge. The inadequacies of this "solution" also *force us into an effort* —so far chronically abortive, but increasingly self-insightful — *to outgrow it.* It is within the framework of male-dominated history —of male-dominated thought about the repeated self-reversal of male-dominated revolutions— that we have started to see how the assimilation of this early rage and the acknowledg-ment and breaking of this early addiction form parts of a single task. So it is true that our gender arrangement has helped us keep unintegrated the two sides of our ambivalence about becoming adults, about embracing the freedom and responsibility and lone-liness of our actual condition. But it is true also that what we have learned about our own potentialities by living in this ar-rangement pulls us, and what we have discovered about its costs pushes us, toward the fended-off integration.

Another example: The feature of our male-female symbiosis discussed in Chapter 4 works not only to keep balanced against each other, unintegrated, the fear and the delight, the contempt and the awe, evoked in us by the perishable sentient flesh and by the living sense of the present moment that the flesh carries. It works also to *force this integration.* Sexuality, because of its resonance with infancy, is the realm in which our sense of the moment can become most radically salient: the realm, as Auden said in his poem "Lullaby," in which it becomes most radically clear that "soul and body have no bounds"; in which lovers' "ordinary swoon" (carnal as the swoon of the sated nursling) carries visions "of supernatural sympathy, universal love and hope."* The double standard of erotic conduct constricts this realm, keeping the threats it holds enough at bay so that we are encouraged to enter it and *given the opportunity,* within neurosis-protecting limits, to enjoy its charms. But there is no reliable way to sustain neurotic stasis while enjoying those charms. They are ineradicably subversive. The rules offer us a tame garden which can prove after all to be a wild place from whose center the double sexual standard, the gender arrangement of which it is part, and all the ordered life-ways that this arrangement supports, are thrown (*pushed, forced*) into shattering perspective.[1]

Similarly, the equilibrium-sustaining features of our gender symbiosis that were discussed in Chapters 7 and 9 work in a network of ways toward the disruption of what they sustain. A major thread in that network is this: Abhorrence for the flesh and passion for it, side by side and mutually unreconciled, can stay tied to the chaotic pre-rational image of woman, and in that way segregated from the organized, purposeful male human world-making effort. This segregation allows us to push into abeyance —into the demeaned realm of the quasi-human early mother— the (necessarily carnal) sense of the moment, and to focus on enterprise, on what can be controlled and manipulated.† But the

---

* *City Without Walls and Other Poems* (New York: Vintage, 1971).

† This is part of why the spirit of enterprise, when it surfaces openly in a woman, tends to be perceived as male: it has to be kept sealed off from the

more sternly we renounce the moment the more we hate enterprise for its inevitable failure to repay that renunciation. Work is
poisoned; we lose even our direct pleasure in it; we start pushing
against the constraints it imposes: we yearn for the moment. But
the living moment is uncontrollable, dangerously intense; in it we
are mortal and defenseless. We handle that yearning by a tacit
agreement: our feeling that the worldmaking enterprise is in
some essential ways lethal is mainly ventilated by woman, on her
own behalf and man's; and he takes the main responsibility, on
his own behalf and hers, for keeping that enterprise going. The
stasis this agreement preserves, however, is increasingly shaky. As
the deadliness of that which she so harmlessly carps at increases
of its own momentum, it becomes less and less possible to keep
her running critique in the peripheral place that is assigned to it.
It is *forced* into focal awareness.

Of all the growth processes at work within the wider neurotic
equilibrium of which our self-disrupting, self-transcending gender
arrangements are part, it is this one that has now reached its
crucial stage. Before trying to say in more detail how this has
happened, let me sketch an overview of that wider equilibrium.

Overview

What the mermaid and minotaur images say in dream language is translating itself into waking prose under the pressure of
historic event, event that has itself been shaped, in turn, by the
process —in part somnambulistic, in part rationally planful— to
which Mumford refers in his recent article, "Reflections," when he
says that humanity dreams itself into existence.

The body of gender arrangements discussed in this book grows
and changes, like any other living thing, out of stresses inherent
both in its inner structure and in the larger structure of which it is
part (and which is itself part, of course, of larger and larger
structures). These stresses —as Marx among others has pointed

---

inchoate image of the early mother that is —for herself as well as for others—
part of a woman's identity.

out— generate the tensions that move it to a new stage of development.

So far the changes in this body of arrangements have been so minor, as compared with the one that seems to be imminent now, that I have felt justified in describing as "the" prevailing male-female symbiosis one whose structure has remained constant in some central respects across recorded time and huge cross-cultural variation. The presence of inner stresses and tensions in this structure, which now seem about to precipitate an unprecedented change in it, has been illustrated in the section just above.

But what must be added here is that these inner stresses can now precipitate the imminent change only because the larger structure in which our central sexual arrangement is embedded — human societal life as a whole— has reached a crucial phase of its own development, a phase brought on both by its own inner stresses and by a concomitant crisis within the still larger structure —the web of life on our planet— in which it in turn is embedded.

What has brought on this crisis is a fact which seemed as remote two hundred years ago as the fact that our sun is cooling off seems to us now. The trouble which has at last come to seem real to us —and the project of sexual liberty is a necessary part of our effort to come to terms with this trouble— is that human societal life has been growing far too fast: too fast for its own internal self-governing capacities, and too fast for the mechanisms that keep intact the web of life of which it is part.

This has happened largely because what is unique about us is the huge part played by our own cognitive processes (i.e., by purpose, memory, foresight) in generating and steering the tensions that move us as a species from one stage to the next; the part, in other words, that our own perception of our collective situation plays in the development of this situation.* And to the

* Asch (who is not widely enough read by bright enough people) provides a penetrating analysis of how this works on a small scale, in face-to-face everyday life. To grasp our overall situation we need to focus (more steadily than we normally do) on how it works, or fails to work, in history.

extent that these cognitive processes are inadequate (to the extent that our pooled perception is too narrow to encompass the actual scope, or too distorted by need and fear to take in the actual shape, of our collective situation), the development of our species life is cancerous, out of control: Not only does it proceed in directions that we ourselves would not on balance choose, while at the same time these directions are inescapably the result of our partially thought-out choices. It also threatens (since cultural evolution is much more rapid than biological evolution) to outdistance the controls* that the non-human biosphere can exert to keep itself and all its interdependent parts going.

For a long time the cancer was undetected: it was growing more slowly than now, and we had achieved far less adequate means of surveying its growth. Now it is growing so fast that we may well be unable to stop it. On the other hand, now that we are clearly aware of it we are at least in a position to try.

This awareness has been growing steadily, along with the disease. If the early myths that still survive meant to their makers anything like what, reading backward, they mean to us now, inklings of it are as old as we are. But it has only recently started to become focal for a large enough number of us to give it a chance to influence what will happen next.

At the core of this emerging awareness is the understanding that we are alone and self-creating, and that nature (i.e., life on earth) is not invulnerable and inexhaustible: that we are in danger of killing "her" as well as ourselves; that nobody is there to stop us; that if we cannot stop ourselves it is a matter of pure chance whether we destroy everything, or only everything human, or only so much of what is human that what is left is too sparse and weak to constitute an immediate threat to any balance that the non-human community of living things manages to regain.

Another part of this broad, and incipiently focal, communal awareness is the understanding that normal psychopathology is in

---

* Dubos makes this point in an unusually clear way.

large part responsible for the danger we and nature are in.* It is responsible because the fear and greed that it stops us from outgrowing have distorted our view of what is happening and delayed (perhaps fatally) our intellectual preparedness to confront our overall situation. Furthermore, it has crippled our love of life so deeply that most of us feel too weak, too numb, for such a confrontation.

But a complementary and equally important part of this shared awareness is our grasp of an additional fact: that our predicament has to do not only with psychopathology, but also with the intrinsic limits of what our pooled sentience could encompass even if it were not distorted and narrowed by normal (i.e., neurotic) fear and greed, or paralyzed by normal (i.e., neurotic) despair. Not realizing the degree to which our situation has to be in our own hands, and not wanting to, we have let the societal process grow so mindlessly complex, so gigantically unwieldy, so unnecessarily and maladaptively overcentralized, that now even when we try to take responsibility for it we cannot: in its present form it is hopelessly *out* of our own hands. (Parts of it, of course, can be manipulated by individuals or groups to their own advantage. But none of us can address ourselves adequately to the whole of it. To do so, even if we could muster universal good faith, would require unworkably massive collaborative efforts: the social aggregates needed for such efforts would be too bulky to govern themseves; their size and structure would be beyond the comprehension of the persons who comprised them.) To make this process governable by human reason, embraceable by human feeling, we will have to reorganize it into much smaller units, units whose dimensions fit our own and which change (internally and in their relations with each other) at a pace that we can handle. This is a radically demanding task.† Whether it is too

---

* Freud, and more recently Brown and Marcuse, have outstandingly contributed to our present grasp of this fact. But as Brown points out, human consciousness has been groping toward it all along.

† For me it is Mumford who has over the past forty-odd years been most lucidly and most passionately making this point.

demanding to be met by our collective mental competence remains to be seen.

This is obviously not the place to attempt a more detailed survey of the considerations that this growing awareness embraces. My reason for trying here to remind the reader of their scope is that the process by which the awareness has started to become focal is the same process that has moved the project of sexual liberty forward into its present acute stage.

The historical developments that have now brought us face to face with our overall predicament have at the same time made our old gender arrangements abruptly untenable for a small but crucial segment of our population. Yet many of the people who feel this untenability in an acute way (mainly young and youngish people for whom this confrontation came just at the stage of life when adult primary-group ties organized around heterosexual attachments are normally formed) feel it without clearly seeing its relevance to that larger predicament. And conversely, many of the people who are focally aware of that predicament (particularly if they are men and no longer youngish: men set in their personal ways, which are apt to rest upon established adult heterosexual primary-group responsibilities and privileges) fail to see that it has anything at all to do with our gender arrangements.

Does it matter, after all, whether people do see the relation between these two crises or not? It matters (apart from the sheer satisfaction of seeing, and of coming to some consensus about what we see) only insofar as our efforts toward social change may possibly still have some real effect on what will happen next. There is no way of being sure whether there is or is not time enough left for such efforts to be at all effective. But if we are going to make them, there is no point in making them blindfold.

It is always advisable, obviously, to try to understand as deeply as possible a piece of nature that one wishes to change. But it is uniquely advisable here, since human life is the one piece of nature whose structure is shaped internally by the way we perceive it, the only one on which our awareness works from the inside rather than from the outside. This means that here our perception of what we want to change is not merely a guide in the effort to change it: the perception and the change are aspects of a single development. A human social (or intrapersonal psychological) system, unlike any other biological system, can strive to become conscious of its own processes of growth and self-maintenance; where these processes conflict, the discovery that this is the case constitutes a change in the nature of the conflict. It is thus the only kind of system in which stagnation, chaos, and self-annihilation —elsewhere in nature a matter of blind chance— can sometimes be consciously averted: the only kind, so far as we know, in which it is possible for living order to be envisioned beforehand and then arrived at voluntarily from within.

Where We Are Now

This review has been pointing to the kinds of forces that should make it psychologically possible now for mother-raised people to break out of the heterosexual stasis that their own needs have supported, and start creating conditions* for the development of new people who will not be possessed by just those needs in just that way.

Some of these forces for change, I have been saying, arise from within the male-female symbiosis itself, others from the larger systems of which it is part. Some are chronic, others acute. What remains to be examined is the specific trend, within the wider crisis to which our old built-in sickness has now brought us, that is in my opinion most immediately precipitating change; the trend that has made our deep-rooted gender arrangement sharply

---

* Psychological conditions, that is: child-rearing conditions. The necessary technological conditions (the practical possibility of making parenthood genuinely optional, the concrete feasibility of adult work flexible enough so that men and women can take equal part in both domestic and public life) are already available. Reorganizing society so as to make humanly beneficial use of them, share their benefits equitably, and meanwhile strike some livable balance with the rest of nature, is a task on which all the central human projects (see Chapter 2, pages 10–13) converge.

unlivable (not just steadily stressful, as it has been for most of us all along) for a germinal minority.

For the people in this minority, the old symbiosis, shattered from within by a profound explosion of feeling, has lost its stabilizing grip. Their problem is not how to break out of the stressful old pattern, but how to shake off its splintered fragments, understand what has happened, and start building new forms; and how, meanwhile, to keep emotional life intact in a fearfully unstructured private milieu. Living at the growing edge of our species' sense of its own situation, they are bearing the brunt of a breakdown in the central mechanism of male-female interdependence that was discussed in Chapter 9: the mechanism by which women and men collaborate to keep our misgivings about the worldmaking enterprise at bay. That breakdown has been precipitated by a massive upwelling of these misgivings: too insistent now to be kept at bay, they have begun to invade the formal worldmaking enterprise itself. And the historical development which happens to have made the breakdown abrupt for this germinal minority is also bringing it about, less directly but no less surely, for the rest of us.

The contemporary American* feminist crisis-within-a-crisis (it is thought of as feminist, but what I am about to say is that men

* I have no personal experience of the local flavor, or immediate psycho-historical background, of this crisis as it has developed in other countries. Neither do I feel competent to try to say how it has expressed itself here outside relatively educated white-middle-class circles. (The "elitism" of which middle-class feminism —like other streams of middle-class insurgency— is accurately accused cannot be surmounted by denying the limitations of one's own perspective. Everyone's perspective is limited. Necessary coordination begins with that recognition.)

All I can say for sure is that the wider crisis of consciousness within which the feminist crisis under discussion here took shape —the overall crisis in our communal awareness of our species predicament examined in the preceding section— *cannot* have national or class boundaries: some shared vision of that predicament must be arrived at, some agreed-upon understanding which crosses such boundaries. Otherwise what may possibly be true anyway is true without doubt: that our interest in understanding the predicament is a purely intellectual-emotional interest with no significance beyond itself, no possible influence on our chances of survival.

played an important part in its emergence) took active political form in the late sixties. It started to peak at just about the time when the predominantly young insurgent movement that came to be known as the "new left" was losing its first self-confidence, beginning to sense the real scope and complexity of the task it had undertaken. I want to point here to some features of the background against which this crisis of consciousness took place. What makes it seem necessary to do this is that the people in whom it took place were for special reasons less aware of the felt quality of the recent past than has typically been true for the psychological heirs of world-conscious elders, and this affected the nature of the crisis itself. The large events of the period before these people were born, events that shaped the atmosphere in which they spent their childhood, were so shocking, so stupefying, that these elders conveyed their impact far less clearly than their own elders, for example, had been able to convey to them the spirit of what happened in this century's first quarter.

The Post-Hiroshima Years

No phenomenon of the past thirty years can be looked at clearly except in the light of a possibility which it may be beyond human strength to look at really clearly, but which on some level permeates the self-consciousness of all but the most narrowly limited lives: the possibility, which exploded into public awareness at Hiroshima, that we are the last generation. The Americans who were young adults on Hiroshima day have been largely inarticulate about the ways in which this explosion —and the light it shed on the period that led up to it— determined for them the quality of the years that followed. And it is during those years, steeped in what remained centrally unspoken, that the young adults of the new left —including the passionate, determined new feminists who were forged in the new left— were growing up. Among the mute spiritual progenitors of those young adults are people who were radicals before and during World War II, and who then spent all or most of the period between the war's end and the late fifties or early sixties in a state of moral shock: that is, in the condition of anaesthesia and blurred comprehension that follows catastrophe. In this condition, they withdrew from history —more or less totally, more or less gradually, more or less blindly— into intensely personalistic, inward-turning, magically thing-and-place-oriented life. Not all radicals,* of course, reacted in this way. I cannot guess at the size or shape of the group who did so. But it is a group with which the young left (out of which the new feminism sprang) was in important ways continuous;† and it is this continuity, inarticulate because what it referred to felt too dreadful to articulate, that needs spelling out now.

What made so many radicals withdraw from emotional involvement in history during those years was not political persecution. (McCarthyism, it seems to me, was an assault on a largely paralyzed and comatose prey.) The important reason was a slowly, deeply, fatefully altered view of the societal process.

First, the people in whom this was happening were assimilating in retrospect some implications of the Nazi episode, including its incubation and its counterclimax. They —we— were doing this in the way that massively mutilated or centrally bereaved humans gradually assimilate the meaning of their loss: circuitously, groggily. What we were working to grasp emotionally was the awe-

---

* By "radicals" I mean optimistic believers in the immediate possibility of restructuring society, by direct political action, around principles of human solidarity and equality, of cooperation and an end to exploitation: believers, that is, in the possibility of profound life-affirmative social change arrived at by planful and relatively rapid means. By this definition one must be a radical now, I think, to envision human survival in anything like practical terms. (The only other conceivable terms would involve the kind of world government by centralized autocracy that Heilbroner despairingly suggests as a possible means-ends compromise. But this is a pipe-dream suggestion: if there were such a thing as centralized autocracy intelligent enough and devoted enough to the common good to make this a feasible means, we would not be in the trouble we are in now. So there is no need to argue about whether or not life under such an autocracy would be worth living.)

† The young new left was continuous also with the beatniks, with those in the old left who did not withdraw from history, and with other streams of sensibility. But the continuity under discussion here is the one that bears most deeply, in my opinion, on contemporary feminism.

some depth and breadth of the groundswell of human pathology and life-hatred which had erupted under Hitler's and other fascist regimes, an eruption against which massive majestic human courage and love had been marshaled, but to which the climactic answer had proved, after all, to be a statement of the most ultimate insanity: the doom-prophetic Hiroshima explosion. At the same time, a twenty-odd year chain of Soviet events, culminating in those following Stalin's death, had been making it clear (at varying rates for individuals of varying temperaments and political perspectives) that those who had been oriented to socialism as a major solution of human problems could not look to the U.S.S.R. for moral leadership.

It was this background that made Hiroshima —immediately for some of us and gradually in retrospect for others— so paralyzing an event: The forces of unreason, of murder and suicide, came to seem overwhelmingly powerful. What made them overwhelming was not just the scale on which they occurred; it was that they now seemed clearly to spring from human social life itself, not just to exist out there in the bad guys.* The impulse to build large-scale societal structures which would contain and eventually greatly reduce these nightmare forces was stalemated by massive evidence that large-scale societal structures *per se* —not just those in capitalist countries— were the habitat in which they managed most hideously to thrive.

When I refer to magically place-and-thing-oriented, personalistic life, I am speaking not of the simple greed, the herd-minded preoccupation with material prosperity, that characterize mainstream American life. I am speaking of a particular group of people, in historic despair so deep that few of us could recognize it clearly as despair, for whom a few beloved things and places

---

* When I first read Norman Brown's *Life Against Death* I recognized in it the core of what we were working to understand after the war. This core insight of his seemed —still seems— to me immeasurably more salient than the omissions and distortions with which I quarrel in Chapters 7 and 9 (just as Freud's contribution to our understanding of most of the matters discussed in this book seems to me immeasurably more salient than his ingenuous, predictable patriarchal bias).

came to be quasi-sacred embodiments of erotic connectedness to life and a few beloved individuals quasi-symbolic centers of connectedness to humanity.* In these people, whose adolescence and youth had spanned the mid-thirties to mid-forties, capacities for connectedness —which in the preceding period had embraced historic considerations and a temporally and spatially extended human scene— were now focused on a world recreated in miniature. Capacities for devotion were kept alive in the service of some spiritual equivalent of the ancients' household gods. The realm of public achievement lost its aura of worldmaking, death-transcending enterprise. It became a matter of simple breadwinning, an arena for what was consciously identified as mere gamesmanship, or (for the very few who were able to immerse themselves in the kind of creative work which is an end in itself) a private-religious mode of personal intercourse with the immediate environment. Vitality drained itself out of broad societal concerns, and plowed itself instead into the blind endeavor to find some minimal basis for a sense of meaning in a life suddenly† bereft of the kind of clear wide outlook into society's future which many had naïvely anticipated enjoying once Hitler *et al.* were defeated.

The direction implicitly established, then, was toward social-emotional decentralization, toward the creation of smaller social units in which day-by-day personal life took on much of the magically self-transcending significance that future-oriented public effort had carried before. (Most people of course have all along lived in small units —that is, on a level more local than the

---

* Doris Lessing's deceptively matter-of-fact account of Martha Quest's postwar London years in *The Four-Gated City* captures, on the stately level of a great work of art, the atmosphere in which people like this lived. So does her account, in *The Golden Notebook*, of the interplay between anguished awareness of public event and the transfigured moral intensity of private life in a former left activist during these same years.

† "Suddenly" in a retrospective sense, that is. Looking back, Hiroshima seems a sharp cut-off point. But for most people this bereavement, like others, was at that moment subjectively blurred by the pain-cushioning shock mechanism.

one on which modern history is made— because of ignorance
and/or of emotional incapacity or disinclination to embrace a
larger human scene.* But I am speaking here of historically
passionate livers, who withdrew their passion from the large
human scene and sought to invest it in something less night-
marish, more coherent and mentally manageable.)

The New Insurgents

Starting in the early sixties, there pushed its way up out of
childhood a crop of young Americans with neither first-hand nor
normally vivid second-hand experience of the events that had
knocked cold these spiritual elders' feeling for history. We had
been too numbed and stupefied to tell our children, or even say at
all clearly to each other, what numbed and stupefied us. What we
communicated were some of the value emphases that were our
quasi solutions to the problem of emotional survival. (I call them
that because, once aware of the wide world, one cannot wholly
forget about it. And of course it was obvious —but we did not
talk about it much: the young had to think it out later for themselves— that the economic and political machinery minimally
necessary to sustain a material technology high enough to support
anything like the earth's present population cannot be maintained
by people whose erotic investment is mainly on the family-cave
or small-band or village level of social organization.) What we
did not communicate was the infernal vision of society that had
driven us to produce these quasi solutions.

In these young adults, vigorous, passionate, sanguine social
conscience, coupled with a strong impulse of cultural-expressive
innovativeness, suddenly flowered.† The sanguine vigor of this

---

* The larger reality to which most people have been oriented is the reality
with which formal religion is traditionally concerned. But that question —
and the question of how the contemporary upswing of fresh interest in religion is related to the historic trend under discussion— must be taken up
elsewhere.

† The flowering seemed, of course, more abrupt than it was. It followed,
for example, the late fifties' reactivation of the long struggle against American

flowering was brief: the special ignorance that was part of it contributed both to the sanguineness and to the brevity; so did the unsolved gender problem at its heart, the problem whose clarification is my main concern here. Still, the themes it articulated survive, stated, in contemporary awareness. They are essential themes, essential to our chances of survival. It remains to be seen what the vigor that brought them forth will do with them now.

The burst of fresh consciousness that was articulated in this brief flowering, and with which communal sensibility must go on trying to come to terms, embodied two mutually contradictory streams of feeling. The first was a rebirth of broad historic concern. The second was an explosively accelerated public reformulation of the personalistic, here-and-now-oriented trend that had begun after Hiroshima. The "counterculture" or "youth culture" version of this trend, as it announced itself during the period that ended just about when "women's lib" emerged, included a principled distrust of highly centralized and planful enterprise (to "do your own thing," to "play it by ear," became an ideological tenet rather than a matter of personal caprice). It also included emphasis on face-to-face interaction ("confrontation," "dialogue," "encounter" became political terms). Most important, perhaps, it involved devaluation of the rational-intellectual, precise-technical, formal, public, and long-term, in favor of the affective-intui-

---

racism; it echoed some features of the earlier "beatnik" counterassertion to the cultural mainstream; and it took on momentum as the Vietnam war issue sharpened.

The emergence of this new movement upset not only conservatives, for obvious reasons, but also some of the middle-aged leftists who had remained political and kept prodding public conscience throughout the "quiet" fifties, and who were put off by certain features of the youngsters' style. It also upset the dormant middle-aged radicals of whom I have been speaking: the ambiguities, revulsions, and despairs which had numbed them, and of which these newcomers were ignorant, now stirred into life; they were angry to be forced to think about the things they knew, and, unreasonably, angry that the newcomers neither knew nor really wanted to know these things. On the whole, however, the old left was probably more respectful of the new left than vice versa.

tive, aesthetic-sensuous, informal, mysterious, private, and short-term (hair, "pot," incense, blurred syntax; aversion to science, mathematics, and indeed any form of abstract, cumulative, or cerebrally strenuous discipline; and so on).

These specific turns of phrase, symbolic practices, modes of negative assertion, became over a very few years steadily less flamboyant, less chic: the thrust behind them was for the time being stymied. But unless civilization itself drastically regresses, the direction of growth in our communal sensibility that they expressed is irreversible.

The two streams of feeling embodied in this burst of consciousness were and remain largely unreconciled except in certain general principles: that expressive, aesthetic, humanistic values must shape the new world; that eroticism must permeate history, not be encapsulated in genital sex; that first-hand, emotionally vivid experience, not theory-dominated policy which violates such experience, must shape social action.

Nobody knows, of course, how such principles can be implemented, given (a) the nature of normal human psychopathology and (b) the centralized economic-political structures on which our high technology seems to depend. Indeed, even to approach such knowledge —to diagnose that pathology, or to start finding out how much centralization is really necessary and which benefits of high technology we are willing to relinquish for the sake of smaller-scale, more humanly flexible societal forms— is dauntingly difficult. This difficulty was part of the vision that paralyzed us. It was part also, of course, of what stymied the new left and flattened the exuberance of the young counterculture. But to survey the many forces which converged to do that is not my task here. What I want to discuss is how in its first popular upsurge the impulse that shaped these general principles pushed feminism —pushed the project of sexual liberty, the project of reorganizing our gender arrangements— into a crucial, sharply demanding new stage of its development.

The Emergent Gender Crisis

In the late forties and the fifties, the central shift in sensibility that I described above (the mute turning of certain world-conscious people's sense of history inward onto the personal here and now) had put unrecognized and unusual responsibility in the hands of women. The private domestic realm, which it had always been their obligation to maintain while history itself —the purposeful development of human reality— was made elsewhere, had now become the realm in which the sense of purposefully developing human reality, such as it was, was centrally located. Numbed, these women and men had returned after the war to their traditional paths, hearthkeepers and providers. Female energy had drawn back from the strenuous public task of redefining these paths because energy itself, regardless of gender, was drawing back from all profound long-range public tasks into the endeavor to find some immediate new core of meaning.*

Clamoring to join the grey-flannel rat race, pounding at the gates of the white-collar salt mines (it was in terms like this that work away from home was characterized in those days) was not, under these conditions, an enterprise that would be apt to fire women's imagination. The public arena inspired in both sexes feelings of revulsion, kept low-keyed both by moral-historic grogginess and by enjoyment (after the austerities of depression and war) of the domestic amenities the breadwinner could wrest from it. The harassed, humanly muffled fathers of the boys who would later bloom for a few years as proudly raggedy, fiercely unco-optable new leftists were not heroes who went with streaming banners where noble deeds were done: they dutifully trotted off to an ugly place, in which success itself was in some sense morally disgraceful,† and trotted back with the wherewithal to

* The domestic mystique that Friedan described in her account of that period surely drew some of its energy from this source as well as from those she attributed it to: her horde of priestess housewives and acolyte husbands included some indeterminate number of the people described here as among the new left's major precursors.

† *The Man in the Gray Flannel Suit* was a novel of those days that ex-

keep the hearth fires where life really burned stoked. As amateur gardeners and carpenters, as backyard barbecue chefs, they were warm and expansive, their erotic work-energies engaged; as buttoned-up attaché-case-carrying commuters, they were pitifully reduced embodiments of traditional worldmaking maleness. And meanwhile the mothers of the girls who would become new left women (and shortly thereafter infuriated feminists) were secure specialists in the arts of the private domain, the domain in which men were assistants who performed essential but non-historic functions and participated vicariously or tangentially in the (implicit) historic undertaking —the undertaking to keep a sense of human significance alive— over which women (implicitly) presided.

In the youth revolution of the sixties, the values that this silent undertaking had nurtured became suddenly and exuberantly outspoken: a bold effort was launched to incorporate them into the formal societal process, to make them explicitly historic. And since what had been a hearth-centered undertaking had metamorphosed into a public one that merged with overt political action, it was men who now laid claim to it. As the male assumption that this was a male right became really clear to young women in this movement, and as they started to see what this assumption meant for the atmosphere of the movement and their own place in it,* an enormous rage took shape in them.

In part, this rage was continuous with the moral indignation that underlies any lively thrust toward social change: What arose was an impulse to resume the feminist task where it had been left off, just as the ideal of socialism was taken up again in this reawakening to history. But the depth of the rage, the special —I

---

pressed this feeling, for example. The musical play *How to Succeed in Business Without Really Trying* was a wry sixties review of it. And Joseph Heller's recent, harrowing *Something Happened* (following after a long silence his retrospective *Catch-22* statement of the special world-sickness born in the war against fascism) depicts postwar male middle-class working life with particular abhorrence.

* See, for example, Marge Piercy's essay "The Grand Coolie Dam."

would guess unprecedented— ferocity with which it possessed them, had other causes.

The principal cause, I think, was this: What had now become a popular public credo included a set of themes for whose private enactment women —and in a special way women in the fifties— had always been the primary responsible agents. In a show organized around these themes and run by men, women were in a pivotal sense disinherited. Things that women have always informally and deeply known, and been heavily relied upon (see Chapter 9) to affirm on an everyday, folk-knowledge level —for example, that personal truth, one's own intuitive grasp of what is going on, is ignored at one's own grave risk; that large-scale politics are pompous and farcical; that science and logic are a limited and overrated part of our array of techniques for exploring reality; that face-to-face relations are in a basic sense the point of life; that flowers, gossip, the smell of food, the smiling of babies, embody and symbolize central human values*— men now seized from their hands and made into a big and characteristically overblown deal, a newly discovered historic tool too significant for women to wield except as men's assistants.

The new left men, on the other hand, had no real emotional choice but to attempt this coup. If they had not attempted it, it is they who would have felt demoted, demoted from lordship not just to equality but to assistantship. This male assistant role was tolerable in the fifties to people by whom the material things obtainable through men's labor in the "salt mines" had not yet been spurned. But in the culture of voluntary poverty that the new left evolved, men as providers were unemployed, on strike, economically powerless: their authority had to be affirmed in other ways.

* These are things, of course, that have been steadily affirmed all along by a few men as well; but these have been maverick men, and the tradition of intellectual, religious, and artistic statement in which they have spoken their affirmation stands outside the practical male mainstream. It is in a day-by-day common-sense way that women —ordinary women, intimately interacting with ordinary practical-mainstream men— know them better.

So what happened has to be seen as part of a wider surge of revulsion against contemporary civilization, a revulsion that took new, acute form in a new generation which had grown up in a world silently and intangibly permeated with the possibility that civilization may not, after all, extend into the indefinite future, and for whom a kind of bone-marrow detachment from the past became possible. *What this mood of revulsion and detachment did at its first peak was force the beginning of a redefinition, by young men themselves, of the traditional male role.*

In the milieu from which the new feminism springs, men tended (mainly tacitly) to reject many aspects of traditional masculine responsibility and to usurp many aspects of traditional feminine authority. At the same time, they remained understandably unwilling to relinquish traditional male privilege. This left women stripped of old forms of support, respect, and protection, and of old outlets for self-assertion, but still as disparaged, subordinated, and exploited as ever. Male leadership of historic endeavor necessarily became less tolerable as that endeavor came to embrace what had always been female areas of expertise. It was one thing for women busy with their own traditional responsibilities to enjoy vicarious participation in public effort at which they themselves had no trained competence and in relation to which their own ventilation of counter-considerations formed one side of a vital balance. It is quite another thing to expect them to take part as menial assistants in a public effort for certain features of which they themselves are by tradition and training clearly better qualified than those they assist, and in relation to which they have no autonomous, unique counterbalancing role to play.

The Refusal of a Hurdle

So the rekindling of feminist awareness toward the end of the new left years follows from a shift of sensibility in certain world-conscious people during the period after World War II, a shift toward the personal, artisan-aesthetic, intuitive; and from the flowering of this shifted sensibility in another generation during the sixties in a form that attempted to reintegrate it into the overt historical process from which it had pulled itself back. This attempt was for the moment abortive (in part, as I said earlier, because of ignorance of the experience of history that had led to this pulling back; in part because of the unrecognized gender problem under discussion here; and of course for other reasons as well). But it was an immensely significant attempt: it galvanized our awareness of communal self-creative possibility; it forced core issues into irrevocable focus. That it had its center within a small sector of our population does not gainsay this significance. Broad societal change is necessarily initiated by minorities, and necessarily proceeds by fits and starts. Hurdles are approached and refused, then returned to and jumped in later tries.

In its first phase, before the sixties, this development of sensibility was carried into practical active expression largely by women, since its core feature was a transmutation of the meaning of private everyday life, since it placed low value on the creative human worth of the formal worldmaking effort, and since it evolved in a groping, unorganized, implicit way. When it flowered into explicit public form men took it over.

The program these men set themselves involved incorporating into their own relation to societal reality vital features of what had always been the female side of the collaboratively maintained ambivalence toward worldmaking discussed in Chapter 9.* That was in itself the beginning of a momentous positive step. *But this program did not involve working, or living, with women whose relation to societal reality would incorporate vital features of the male side of that ambivalence.*

What these men continued to want from women was maternal applause, menial services, and body contact. What they largely withdrew from women was the personal commitment that men in the traditional symbiotic arrangement have been able to offer them, the commitment one offers a deeply, centrally needed person. What they could not accept in women was the primitive

* Hair, daffodils, and incense confronted bayonets and gas masks at the Pentagon. The slogan "In a society dominated by death, any affirmation of life is a political statement" was printed on the purple-and-cerise office wall where an SDS leader in the college I teach at typed part-time for a living.

impulse toward initiative, the straightforward self-reliant pleasure in making dramatic things happen, which is the healthy core of the human response to the loss of infant omnipotence: what they could not accept in women was that which —stripped of its compulsive, life-hostile components* and freed from the constraints of the neurotic patriarchal mechanism for handling infant rage at adult power†— could enable the sexes to share overt formal responsibility for the human self-creative enterprise.‡

This young male program moved partway, then, toward resolving the ambivalence that poisons enterprise —the ambivalence that our male-female split in sensibility has so far kept unresolved — and stopped where the emotional going got rough. It started moving in this direction out of a profound upswell of loathing — the fresh loathing of new people— for the necrotic world that poisoned enterprise has created. Where it stopped, and how, is the principal reason for the female rage that grew out of it.

The feminist struggle itself, as I said above, would have been renewed at this point in any case. Women have a long tradition of trying to be part of formal history (instead of continuing to act as safety valves for everyone's suppressed loathing of the form it has taken — i.e., for the negative side of the ambivalence at its heart). They mainly stopped trying while the overt overall insurgent spirit from which that effort is inseparable was mainly dormant. When this spirit revived, so did their struggle.

* See Chapter 7.
† See Chapter 8.
‡ Men could assume sweetly open, uncertain postures, carry flowers, adorn their bodies in what their society at large regarded as outrageously feminine style, and still be masculine. But women who dominated meetings by sheer lung-power, or demanded that others type their leaflets and make them coffee, would have been unsexing themselves. A roomful of male students of mine during that period, decorative and gentle-looking, charmingly tentative in their style of speech, full of aphorisms of the "Kids are beautiful" and "Where you are is where it's at" and "Like, you know, like, I had this feeling" genre, laughed explosively at the following riddle: "Why won't [name some plain-spoken, forthright female head of state, or congressperson, or controversial author] wear a miniskirt? Because she's afraid her balls will show!"

But the special rage in young contemporary feminism has to do with men's failure (loss of nerve? inability? unwillingness?) to carry through the overt integrative effort they at last began: the integrative effort which in its own sudden and surprising way started to come forward to fuse with what women have tried to do in every foray into history they have attempted; the male effort which started to make bilateral a societal initiative women have till now carried unilaterally (so unilaterally that the project of sexual liberty is thought of as a female project).

In this abortive effort men at last emerged (not just disembodied literary presences like Marcuse and Brown, who provided some philosophic orientation for this effort, but flesh-and-blood young men: men who organized rallies, sit-ins, marches on Washington; who seized university buildings, raided military-draft headquarters, and rebelled at great personal sacrifice against and within the military itself; men who expressed this development in male sensibility not only in the rhetoric that accompanied those overt political actions but also in their speech styles and clothing, in the psychedelic music and drug states that they tried to combine with politics, and particularly in a simple symbolic gesture whose depth of meaning can be measured by the rabid reaction it evoked in mainstream America: their growth of masses of hair) who affirmed in public terms what women had been affirming privately all along: that the realm of poisoned enterprise, as it can be seen at its logical conclusion in advanced industrial society, is inhuman and farcical, mindlessly destructive, heartlessly ugly.

But what these men could not see, any more than their older male mentors could see it, was what they had to see if they were to maintain any deep personal or political connections with women: To start outgrowing the collaboration between the sexes that has made the development of this poisoned realm possible means to undertake another kind of collaboration. If women are no longer needed as outsider court jesters, they cannot be kept on as maternal menials either, or as quasi-sentient magically controllable representatives of quasi-sentient Mother Nature. If the counter-considerations they have so far ventilated in private everyday ways are now to be contained within the formal historic process, then they themselves must be contained in it as well, not only because they want to be, but also because experience has given them more intimate knowledge of these counter-considerations just as it has given men more intimate knowledge of formal worldmaking.

To put this differently: What each sex knows best has been distorted by a neurotically motivated sealing off from what the other knows best. And this means that to melt what even ordinary men have started in their way to recognize as a killing split —the split between male and female sensibility— males and females, if they are to interact humanly at all, must necessarily join as unequivocally equal collaborators. This is a necessity that mother-raised men find it painfully hard to accept, and that mother-raised women find it intolerably bruising to urge upon them.

(The alternative is radical separatism. This alternative, it seems to me, is on a large scale and in the long run wildly impractical. But there are feminists who argue that for women who reject the sexual status quo it is at the moment the only feasible course. Those willing to put it into practice are, and even on the left seem apt to remain, a tiny outgroup; but this tiny outgroup can make valuable contributions to our pooled sense of what is possible. And even if what they propose is not put into significant practice, the issues it raises are instructive. What is also instructive is to consider the provocation in response to which they have proposed it.

Separate, women could in principle set out to learn from scratch —undeflected by the opportunities to evade this task that men's presence has so far offered— what intact self-creative humanness is. ["From scratch" means, of course, children born and raised under separatist conditions. How this can be managed —I wish they would stop talking about cloning— is not clear. And the question of boy children remains to be confronted.] This means learning what it is to be intelligently, imaginatively enterprising while riding fully alive on the ephemeral carnal moment;

what it is to be purposefully, actively engrossed in societal event [a stream of event that flows from long, long before one was born toward long, long —we must still hope— after one will die] while embedded fully alive in the demanding, lazy, pleasure-loving, inexorably aging flesh.

To be convinced of the need to undertake this long adventure on a separatist basis, from scratch, is to be very angry indeed. [It is an adventure, after all, that men must undertake too. And in the development of our awareness of that necessity men have on the whole been as active as women.] To have been ready to undertake it in collaboration with men, on the other hand, is to have been given to understand, much more often than not, either [a] that they had no idea what you were talking about, but in any case it seemed irrelevant, or [b] that they could do the important part of it without you, but loved to have you around helping, minding the kids, cleaning up the shit, listening, and looking pleasant.

This response in new left men was part, I think, of the ordinary human moral laziness that made them falter in the face of other challenges too. But to face the narrow unintelligence of such a response, its complacent ungenerosity, is to give way to ordinary human rage: murderous rage, which one tries to handle, if one is not a murderer, by withdrawing from those who evoke it.)

The Rift

The failure of the men in those circles, then, to carry through what they had started not only led to an historic cul-de-sac; it also opened a fateful personal rift between the sexes. It insulted and disinherited, in personally intolerable ways, the women who could have worked with them as peers. What these men wanted from women in combination with what they did not want, what they could not provide in combination with what they needed, not only deprived the new left of its most vigorous female participants (thus contributing importantly to its demoralization). It also made it virtually impossible for stable primary-group ties —

[handwritten marginal note: to the question on page 24. the way the answer or...]

which in adults tend to be organized around sexual attachments — to develop between these women and these men. And to live without such ties is for most people devitalizing, dismal. How this personal difficulty makes the men feel, and how they try to handle it, someone else will have to say. But for the women it has been acutely —and enragingly— painful. (A number have moved toward sinking their main personal roots in households or close communities that are composed solely of women, or of women and their children. But the peripheral catch-as-catch-can heterosexuality that a commitment like this implies is not for everybody. Neither is celibacy. And the lesbian alternative, to be viable, must be a matter of felt erotic preference, not of default or of political principle.) What has developed in this influential minority, then, is a situation whose emotional edge women cannot blur for themselves as readily as men perhaps can: the old heterosexual arrangement has become in an intimate way —a way that has to do with a person's sense of history but that throws the person privately off balance too, a way that hurts the felt inner core of individual vitality— unworkable.

Not only is this intimate hurt felt more keenly by women than it seems (at least on the surface) to be felt by men.* The wider historical impasse of which it is part puts a different kind of personal pressure on women. That the worldmaking enterprise, traditionally a masculine responsibility, is now in unprecedented trouble —that it is more and more clearly pervaded by madness — is a fact that hits men harder: it assaults their sense of human maleness. What hits women harder, what assaults their sense of human femaleness, is the way this unprecedented trouble undermines our private modes of connectedness to the past and future.

We cannot imagine now under what conditions, if any, the children women make in their bodies, feed from their breasts, and feel traditionally responsible for rearing can survive and pro-

---

* A number of general reasons for some difference in this direction are touched upon in Chapter 4. But I cannot judge how the men whom the breakdown affects really feel about it: women's reactions to it have been more articulate.

duce more children. In women who permit themselves to think about this fact, attitudes toward babymaking vary from (a) tenuous hope, through (b) the feeling that one has children purely for reasons of immediate short-range pleasure, to (c) the conviction that no socially responsible woman would consider having babies (there are already too many, those already born are all too likely to come to a ghastly end, there are urgent societal tasks from which motherhood unpardonably drains one's energy, etc., etc.).

It is not only in the forward direction, moreover, that women's traditional responsibility for maintaining private emotional continuity across time —their role as living link between grandparents and grandchildren; the ceremonial work they do at births, weddings, and funerals to nurture the intimate ties that link the old and the young, the unborn and the dead— is disrupted. It is disrupted in the backward direction too. Increasingly, people are forced to feel out ways of living in a world that their elders cannot begin to conceive of. And the cutting off of psychological ties with parents that this involves is more diminishing for women than for men: it undermines the female sense of human importance that has till now derived from the task of maintaining the intimate bridge between the generations, a bridge on which formal worldmaking, and humanness itself, ultimately rests.

What the historic impasse we have reached has done, in other words, is discredit the essential humanizing functions of stable longstanding generation-spanning primary groups, functions that are by tradition women's concern. This may account for the virulent, reckless, reactive quality of much new feminist rhetoric against the biological family, against permanent personal commitments of adults to children ("children's liberation"), indeed against bodily childbearing itself (at just this moment in history, ironically, when the oppressive features of that aspect of our biology have become obsolete, and its pleasures optimally accessible to those who choose them). Shorn of its humanizing significance, the sheer biological continuity of the species becomes an unacceptable burden; the livebearing, lactating mammalian heritage becomes monstrous. Some women come to feel like jumping out of their very bodies, out of their inconvenient female skins.

Cut off from the main existing form of adult primary-group support (the heterosexual family); cut off even from her parents and her possible children by the historical mess that overt male leadership has gotten us into; then cut out of history itself because her special, traditionally compartmentalized, contribution to the historic process is preempted by man, who sees that this contribution is overdue for integration but is not ready to work with her as a simple equal: how can a woman feel? What can her stance be toward the creature who from her point of view (since she has had no opportunity to feel responsible for it) created this mess, this murderous predicament, and who even now stands blocking her off from the right to make a human contribution to its solution? It seems possible that now, for the first time in history, women in substantial numbers hate, fear, and loathe men as profoundly as men have all along hated, feared, and loathed women.

To return, now, to this book's central point. Just what the particular women and the particular men whose situation is discussed above will do next is of course not clear; what specific form the project of sexual liberty will take next, and which people will be most active in carrying it forward, cannot be predicted. But the meaning of the minority development traced here derives from the wider historical development of which it is part; its significance is that it points to a general direction that our future (if any) will take. What *can* be predicted, I think, is this general direction.

In Sum

In sum, the irrevocable thing that has happened —happened to everybody, though not everybody senses it clearly— is this: *The male-female collaboration to keep history mad that was discussed in Chapter 9 has become impossible to sustain* in the light of the change in our overall perspective summarized above in "Overview" — broadly speaking, our changed perspective on "progress," on the sources of what we have always thought of as "evil," and on the nature of what we are responsible for.

Without that central feature of our symbiotic gender arrangement — central (a) because it bears on the ultimate meaning of our life, the ultimate character of our place in the order of things, and (b) because it is the coordinating matrix for all the other features, the kingpin that has held them together, the fulcrum around which the tensions they generate have been balanced— *the rest of the arrangement crumbles.* So although we (most of us) hate to let it go, we (all of us) have really lost it already. And my effort here has really been an effort to see what it is that we are so sad about: on the one hand what there is in the dying old arrangement that we all have to outgrow or die ourselves; and on the other hand what there is in it that we all legitimately need, that we cannot and should not try to do without, and that we must therefore find other ways of getting.

Notes

Chapter 1. Terms and Aims

1. For an elegant modern reference to the relation between this kind of myth-image and this kind of insight, see Leonard Baskin's cover illustration for the 1958 Anchor paperback edition of Freud's *Civilization and Its Discontents*.

Chapter 2. The Human Project of Sexual Liberty

1. It makes a certain kind of easy sense to assume that she has evolved "inborn" temperamental qualities that fit her for these tasks and disqualify her for others. Scholarly sexual conservatives lean heavily on this assumption in their interpretation of laboratory and other findings that might otherwise seem more ambiguous than they make them out to be.

As has been pointed out many times before, this assumption is self-sustaining: so long as social practice continues to be based upon it, it cannot be tested. Under present circumstances, for example, how are we to gauge the functional depth, or the range of possible outcomes under other developmental conditions, of differences in behavior that can be observed between male and female neonates? Labels like "male aggressiveness" or "female social sensitivity," applied to quantitative measures of such variables as gross motor activity or episodes of eye contact, presuppose —and have the social effect of helping to encourage— later growth patterns that are by no means inevitable. What we can be sure of is that any average gender differences in "temperament" that are observable *after* the neonatal period have been subject to heavy environmental shaping.

Even under present circumstances, moreover (in spite of all the life pressures, in other words, that now work to force male and female personal development into differing channels), variations among individuals are so much stronger than average differences between boys and girls, or women and men, that there is a huge overlap between the sexes in those traits which in children and adults can (a bit more legitimately than in new babies) be assigned labels like "aggressiveness" and "social sensitivity." It is an overlap that makes gender-based social boxes, like racial ones, not only cruel and wasteful in individual terms but also, in societal terms, stultifying.

Beyond this, it must be said that if the behavioral sex differences that we can see in newborn humans *did* in fact amount to what the conservatives say they amount to (if they *were* in fact predictive indices of something that could reasonably be called biologically sex-linked temperamental traits), we would be well advised to look at them as atavisms, as maladaptive differences that ought to be "bred out," genetically, by the natural selection process that social change will induce. Thus "male" belligerence and "female" empathy, which are said to have fitted the sexes so far for history-making and child-rearing respectively, are rapidly reversing their social meanings. (See Maccoby's *Psychology of Sex Differences* for a balanced scholarly survey of these questions, and Toback's "Some Evolutionary Aspects of Human Gender" for a lucid theoretical discussion of them.) Empathy is more useful for history-making now than belligerence is. People of both sexes who had this "female" trait would enjoy a survival advantage in the future both for this reason and because it would help qualify them as childbearers.

In any case, what we must *not* do is justify our present male-female symbiosis on the basis that tampering with it could possibly mean tampering with important, biologically inflexible, behavioral predispositions. Even if this (at present untestable) possibility were as strong as the conservatives would like us to think it is, it would hardly matter, since to *refrain* from such tampering is to court a far clearer and more immediate danger: our sexual arrangements are part of the more general societal stance that is right now threatening to destroy us. Our ability to see that this is so —our tendency, in other words, to use our brains and think about our overall situation— is surely an essential, unambiguous aspect of our biological endowment. Is there any doubt that it is more essential, and less ambiguous, than some hypothetically built-in tendency for women to be sweet and men to be brave?

2. Indeed (see Chapter 9) one part of the massive male alarm at the thought of formal female participation in history stems from an unacknowledged fact: men, usually without overt awareness of their debt, depend on the special perspective that women (like other low-status outsiders) bring to formal history.

3. While the hunter-gatherer controversy among prehistorians does not change the largest outlines of the "fundamental arrangement" sketched by Washburn, or the bearing of these large outlines on the main point of my argument here, it does have relevance for the matters discussed in Box B. What is illuminating about the presence of fashioned stone tools alongside hominid fossils is not the existence of these tools themselves, but the level of mental activity they imply, activity whose other products would have to have rotted along with the flesh of their makers. The implements devised by gatherers could well have involved the same level of imaginative, pooled creativity as those needed for hunting, but the materials they were made of

are far more perishable. So archaeological artifact finds can lead to an overemphasis on the importance of (male) hunting activity in the prehistoric cultural developments that helped shape our bodies.

It would have been true in any case for our ancestors (as it is for herbivorous contemporary primates) that defense of the group's territory against competitors, and of the group itself against predators, had to be primarily a male responsibility, since bearing and suckling young had to be a female one. And the latter is a steadier responsibility, an unremitting drain on individual energy that leaves the one who carries it less free to become engrossed in sustained, sporadically exhausting, unpredictably and extravagantly demanding enterprises of other kinds. Certain important worldmaking tasks must, therefore, have fallen mainly to our male ancestors.

Still, food gathering and the associated technology would have been more feasible work for females than wide-ranging, long-term hunting forays. To the extent, then, that such inventions as storage containers and digging sticks and techniques for drying, winnowing, or pounding of grains were economically more central than Washburn's account suggests, and spears and spearmaking tools and skills of detecting, stalking, or exhausting one's quarry less central, the female contribution to the beginnings of human culture is apt to have been more substantial.

Chapter 3. The Rocking of the Cradle

1. Not every culture, the ethnographers tell us, clamps down on erotic body contact as ours does between the earliest years and puberty: in some groups it goes on throughout childhood. These interim years are doubtless the ones in which the urge toward such contact is for biological reasons easiest to suppress, and it would be valuable to know more about the actual quality that the contact has when it does permissibly go on during this relatively un-urgent period. Since these are years during which the child is taking vital steps toward competent, responsible membership in society, one also wonders what special effects the clamping down that is done during these years in our culture (even if it *is* more painlessly achieveable at this stage than earlier and later) may have on the eventual social docility of adults. See Chapter 4, pages 73–75.

Chapter 4. Higamous-Hogamous

1. The extent to which the sexually loved man himself represents for a woman the early mother, around whom passion and possessiveness are focused, varies enormously from case to case and depends upon a large number of emotional factors. (People, obviously, differ; my account is by necessity schematic and simplified.)

Another important variable is the strength of the woman's own sense of continuity with the early mother. If negative feeling toward her in infancy and just afterward was too strong, for instance, to permit the kind of identification with her that would make the woman feel herself now as a

Notes

center of the primitive maternal richness, a rival would be less tolerable. Also, such a woman's homoerotic feeling could be as sternly buried as a man's —for different reasons— more typically is, and her jealousy might therefore take on the special subterraneously fed rage that a man's sometimes does.

2. Males in some other primate species also show a tendency toward the formation of strong all-male groups. This observation can tempt the observer to conclude (see, for example, Tiger's *Men in Groups*) that the segregation of women, their exclusion from public enterprise, the need of men to find sanctuary from them in each other's company, are somehow "built into" our gene composition; that these are tendencies handed down from our ancestors and for practical purposes permanent, since they are outgrowable (if at all) only through processes of physical evolution too slow and gradual to make any difference for contemporary life.

Yielding to this intellectual temptation means overlooking the distinctively human psychological content of the human male impulse toward what ethologists call "bonding"; it means cherishing one's ignorance of the ways in which this impulse is shaped by tensions peculiar to the now mutable structure of family life in our own species — a species whose *continuity* with its animal relatives is savagely misinterpretable when looked at outside the framework of its *discontinuity* with these relatives.

(Yielding to this temptation also means, by the way, side-stepping the interesting question of just how *non*-human forms of male "bonding" actually develop. Like all conclusions based on the concept of instinct —or on some more recent, equally opaque, new version of that concept— this one crushes, under the weight of a big impenetrable abstraction, the scientist's healthy impulse to ask questions about how, in detail, a particular form of behavior comes into being under the particular conditions in which it is observed.)

3. Alternatively, he could transfer some of the *bad* feelings toward the father. But if he did this more than slightly, it could preclude the formation of any positive tie to his same-sex parent and handicap him as a member of the wider male community. The older, more life-essential tie to the mother can withstand more strain and remain in some important sense intact.

Notes Toward Chapter 5

1. Or even for baboons or gorillas: I have chosen a more extreme contrast only for simplicity of exposition. Study of the mental capacities and social interactions of these cousins of ours is fascinating, and could perhaps cast light on the possibility that some of the emotional functions of our male-female arrangement already existed in our intelligent, culture-making hominid ancestors. But none of our living primate relatives have started to create for themselves the kind of cumulatively pooled culture (including language) that makes our own interactions so intricate and our education of our young such a massive, extended, complex process. This means that — no matter how much brighter than cats or rats they may be— almost nothing of what I am saying about the tensions in our life as parents, the role of

foresight and memory in it, or its mutability, can apply to them significantly more closely than it applies to cats and rats: their brightness, and their similarity to us in other ways, would just complicate the comparison and disract us from the main point.

Chapter 5. "Children! Every One of Them!"

1. The present analysis is in no way meant to discount other reasons for adult childishness. The most general one of all is our simple unwillingness to give up the protected, infinitely promising situation of childhood to take on adult responsibilities and limitations. Furthermore, childhood fantasies of grown-up power and freedom are durable, and compared with them actual adult life, seen from the inside, inevitably feels puny, ambiguous, uncertain. This difficulty is probably nowhere absent, but it varies with cultural content and with the rate of cultural change. In stabler and technologically simpler societies than ours, people feel in a sense more adult (even though less arrogantly powerful over nature) because they have more fully mastered the skills needed to meet all tasks that seem to fall within human scope. For us, much that seems to require human coping, much that it is obviously up to us to handle, is too novel and/or too massive and complex for the ablest adult to master.

There are also some additional sources of adult childishness specifically inherent in our sexual arrangements whose importance is clear. For example, it is surely true that a mother's infantile worldly subordination to her husband, and a father's infantile self-importance with his wife, witnessed by their son and daughter, help form these children's conceptions of appropriate adult behavior (see Sampson's *Psychology of Power*). What I wish to point to is a less self-evident set of very early emotional factors, which would operate even if we could sweep away all other differences between mothers and fathers —a wholly impossible feat, of course— while leaving intact the female monopoly of child care.

2. Schachtel's account of the functional split between pre-verbal and language-influenced cognitive processes, in "On Memory and Early Childhood Amnesia," is relevant for much of what is discussed in Chapters 3–8 of this book. His point is that everyday life is to a maladaptive degree drained of the richness of the former as we develop the latter. My analysis is concerned with an area of life that *is* actively permeated and enriched by the former but in a maladaptive (because inadequately integrated) way. Both discussions bear on the project of reconciling the rational with the pre-rational layers of our sentience.

Notes Toward Chapter 7

1. Many people, of course, react to this conception by rejecting it point-blank: the impulse toward belief in individual immortality is strong. The present discussion assumes that this belief is based not on fact but on need: the need to blunt death's sting is only one of its many roots. But the reader does not have to agree with this assumption to go along with my argument. It is

clear in any case that abstract faith in *spiritual* immortality —at least as such faith is held by ordinary people in our own culture— does not dispel the trouble we have in accepting the eerily solid and inscrutable fact of concrete *physical* death. If it could, it would, and the problems explored in this discussion would not exist.

2. Many streams of religious thought offer metaphors that attempt to soften this aspect of death's pain by pointing to a paradoxical consideration: While death, which separates us from the world, does carry the meaning of separation from the mother, it also carries the opposite meaning. In death the self, which was forced to define itself as a distinct entity when its oneness with the original mother was broken, melts down again: it is relieved of the terror of its isolation and the burden of its will. This melting can be thought of as a reunion with the old, lost, true mother, who has never been adequately replaced by that foster mother, the world.

All that is needed to achieve the comfort of this thought is the conviction that the self somehow survives the body's death (how it does this is of course a mystery, but after all the abrupt nonexistence of a self is mysterious too) and is taken back to the bosom of some original and ultimate parent. (Why so many religions characterize this Parent as a father rather than a mother is another question. The reply that has sometimes been offered — that men have the power to grab any glory they want, and are especially apt to want a glory that makes up for their inability to give birth— is surely only part of the answer: see, for example, the section on patriarchal despotism in Chapter 8.)

Chapter 7. The Dirty Goddess

1. By "us" I do not mean all of us, and by "evade" I do not mean wholly evade. We all make *some* effort to handle this task, and we all have *some* success at it. It would be logically possible, even under present conditions, to achieve this kind of integration completely. In principle, for example, one could even now go back and revise the image of the early mother so totally that no trace of a split remained. Many of us make impressive progress toward such ends, and many others want to. (If this stopped being so, psychoanalysts, clergymen, and other specialists in the cure of sick souls would suffer mass unemployment on the one hand; and on the other hand all criticism of and struggle against societal evil, except the most narrowly self-interested, would come to a halt.)

Still, most of us leave a major part of the task of reconciliation undone. Enough of us leave enough of it undone so that the overall trend of civilized life is on balance in the lethal direction that Brown (whom I summarized and quoted above and will again below) indicates. It is to this balance that my discussion of the contribution of our sexual arrangements refers. The direction is not monolithic, or I would not be writing all this and you would not be reading it. So long as it is not monolithic, we can hope it is reversible. But to reverse it decisively, we would surely have to take away the support that it gets from the present female-male symbiosis. This is of course not —

to repeat— a sufficient condition for such a reversal: we may fail anyway. But it is a necessary one.

2. See, for example, Robert White's article "The Concept of Competence." Asch's *Social Psychology*, in a more massive way, pushes against Freudianism on the one hand and behaviorism on the other to restore human societal activity —civilization— to its proper place as an expression of our biologically given mental capacities. On the other hand, neither Asch's book nor White's paper acknowledges the force of those darker emotional uses of civilized activity to which Freud pointed.

Notes Toward Chapter 8

1. In 1919, for instance, of the masses of Americans who saw woman's right to vote as a logical extension of the universal suffrage principle, many doubtless saw the double sexual standard either as God-given or as a private matter inappropriate for political discussion. Similarly, there are today masses of Americans who see equal pay for equal work as a wholly reasonable social demand, but find girls with plain hair and no makeup unattractive and/or unnecessarily defiant of the mores ("They hurt their cause!"); who think lady mayors, lady physicists and telephone-line repairwomen are fine, but don't believe they can really mind —and/or wish they wouldn't— make such a fuss about— being whistled at on the street; who understand why a wife might want to keep her own name and her own bank account, but react with much sharper irritation to a woman who is a poor listener and insists on dominating conversations than to a man with the same bad habit. This kind of personal conservatism can be as unreflectively self-righteous as the ideological conservatism of down-the-line sexual fundamentalists. Alternatively, it can have the self-forgiving tone that political dissidents often adopt toward atavisms in their own private style: "I guess I *am* a product of my upbringing. But honestly, don't you think we have more urgent social problems to struggle with than this one?"

Chapter 8. The Ruling of the World

1. To some varying degree the bossy male, since he proves to be so powerful once we are out of the nursery, eventually takes on for most of us —especially for women, who learn early that they are destined to remain forever subject to this power of his— certain maternal meanings. Flexible beings that we are, we do on occasion turn to him for a kind of response that on some level of our mother-raised psyches is labeled female. To the extent that this happens, the primitive feeling-swing originally referred to the first parent comes to be referred to him too. But it is referred to him only in a limited way, a way deeply modulated by our sense of his maleness.

Chapter 9. Mama and the Mad Megamachine

1. "Briefly" because Mead's survey is mainly intended, as I read it, to show the existence of wide intercultural variations, alongside certain basic

intercultural constants, in our gender arrangements: the observation of hers that in my view needs extension here is not essential to the shape of her overall argument. De Beauvoir's account needs more detailed discussion since the point examined here is central to it.

Chapter 10. At the Edge

1. Against this possibility, one societal countermechanism that operates to protect the status quo is the emergence of conventionally sanctioned sexual license. Marcuse describes this countermechanism, in *One Dimensional Man*, as "repressive de-sublimation," a phrase that strikes me as misleading. But his account of how it works to degrade the revolutionary potential of body-erotic experience is a splendid one. Exploration of the possible wilderness is made so permissible, so convenient, that its depths, crisscrossed with marked paths, are soon littered with beer cans, polluted with the smell of exhaust fumes and the sound of radio commercials.

Bibliography

ASCH, SOLOMON E. *Social Psychology.* New York, 1952.

AUDEN, W. H. "Lullaby" in *City Without Walls and Other Poems.* New York, 1971.

BAMBERGER, JOAN. "The Myth of Matriarchy: Why Men Rule in Primitive Society" in *Woman, Culture, and Society,* M. Rosaldo and L. Lamphere, eds. Stanford, California, 1974.

BEAUVOIR, SIMONE DE. *The Second Sex.* Paris, 1949. Quoted from the H. M. Parshley translation.

BLYTHE, RONALD. *Akenfield: Portrait of an English Village.* London, 1969.

BROWN, NORMAN O. *Life Against Death:* The Psychoanalytical Meaning of History. Middletown, Connecticut, 1959.

CHILDE, V. GORDON. *Man Makes Himself.* London, 1936.

COLERIDGE, SAMUEL TAYLOR. "The Rime of the Ancient Mariner." London, 1798.

COLETTE. *The Vagabond.* Paris, 1929. Quoted from the Enid McLeod translation.

DOSTOYEVSKI, FYODOR. *The Brothers Karamazov.* Russia, 1881. Quoted from the Constance Garnett translation.

DUBOS, RENÉ. *So Human an Animal.* New York, 1968.

ELIOT, GEORGE. *Middlemarch.* London, 1872.

———. *Mill on the Floss.* London, 1860.

FIRESTONE, SHULAMITH. *The Dialectic of Sex.* New York, 1970.

FISKE, DONALD W. and MADDI, SALVATORE R., eds. *Functions of Varied Experience.* Homewood, Illinois, 1961.

FREUD, SIGMUND. *Civilization and Its Discontents.* Vienna, 1930. Quoted from the James Strachey translation.

————. *The Future of an Illusion.* Vienna, 1927. Quoted from the W. D. Robson-Scott translation.

FRIEDAN, BETTY. *The Feminine Mystique.* New York, 1963.

FROMM, ERICH. *Man for Himself:* An Inquiry into the Psychology of Ethics. New York, 1947.

GARY, ROMAINE. *Lady L.* New York, 1959.

GREER, GERMAINE. *The Female Eunuch.* London, 1970.

HAYS, H. R. *The Dangerous Sex:* The Myth of Feminine Evil. New York, 1964.

HEBB, D. O. and THOMPSON, W. R. "The Social Significance of Animal Studies" in *Handbook of Social Psychology,* G. Lindzey, ed. Reading, Massachusetts, 1954.

HEILBRONER, ROBERT. *An Inquiry into the Human Prospect.* New York, 1974.

HELLER, JOSEPH. *Catch-22.* New York, 1961.

————. *Something Happened.* New York, 1974.

JANEWAY, ELIZABETH. *Man's World, Woman's Place.* New York, 1971.

KAWABATA, YASUNARI. *Snow Country.* Japan, 1947.

KLEIN, MELANIE. *Envy and Gratitude.* London, 1957.

LESSING, DORIS. *The Four Gated City.* London, 1969.

————. *The Golden Notebook.* London, 1962.

MACCOBY, ELEANOR E. and JACKLIN, CAROL N. *Psychology of Sex Differences.* Stanford, California, 1974.

MARCUSE, HERBERT. *Eros and Civilization.* Boston, 1955.

————. *One Dimensional Man.* Boston, 1964.

MEAD, MARGARET. *Male and Female.* New York, 1949.

MILLET, KATE. *Sexual Politics.* New York, 1969.

MITCHELL, JULIET. *Woman's Estate.* New York, 1972.

MORAVIA, ALBERTO. *Two Women.* Milan, 1957.

MORGAN, ROBIN, ed. *Sisterhood Is Powerful:* An Anthology of Writings from the Women's Liberation Movement. New York, 1970.

————. "Know Your Enemy" in *Sisterhood Is Powerful:* An Anthology of Writings from the Women's Liberation Movement. R. Morgan, ed. New York, 1970.

MUMFORD, LEWIS. *Culture of Cities.* New York, 1938.

————. *The Pentagon of Power.* New York, 1970.

————. "Reflections" in *The New Yorker,* 1975.

PIERCY, MARGE. "The Grand Coolie Dam" in *Sisterhood Is Powerful: An Anthology of Writings from the Women's Liberation Movement.* R. Morgan, ed. New York, 1970.

RÉAGE, PAULINE. *The Story of O.* Paris, 1954.

ROSALDO, MICHELLE ZIMBALIST and LAMPHERE, LOUISE, eds. *Woman, Culture, and Society.* Stanford, California, 1974.

ROSENBLATT, JAY. "Nonhormonal Basis of Maternal Behavior in the Rat" in *Science*, June, 1967.

SAMPSON, VICTOR. *Psychology of Power.* New York, 1968.

SCHELL, JONATHAN. *The Village of Ben Suc.* New York, 1967.

SCHACHTEL, ERNST. "On Memory and Early Childhood Amnesia" reprinted in his *Metamorphosis: On the Development of Affect, Perception, Attention and Memory.* New York, 1959.

STENDHAL. *The Charterhouse of Parma.* Paris, 1839.

———. *The Red and the Black.* Paris, 1830.

TANNER, NANCY. "Matrifocality in Indonesia and Africa and Among Black Americans" in *Woman, Culture, and Society*, M. Rosaldo and L. Lamphere, eds. Stanford, California, 1974.

TIGER, LIONEL. *Men in Groups.* New York, 1969.

TOBACK, ETHEL. "Some Evolutionary Aspects of Human Gender" in *Journal of Orthopsychiatry*, 1971.

TOLSTOY, LEO. *War and Peace.* Russia, 1869.

WASHBURN, SHERWOOD. "Tools and Human Evolution" in *Scientific American*, 1960.

WHITE, ROBERT. "The Concept of Competence" in *Functions of Varied Experience*, D. Fiske and S. Maddi, eds. Homewood, Illinois, 1961.

WOLF, MARGERY. "Chinese Women: Old Skills in a New Context" in *Woman, Culture, and Society*, M. Rosaldo and L. Lamphere, eds. Stanford, California, 1974.

WOOLF, VIRGINIA. *Orlando: A Biography.* London, 1928.